# *The Christ Letter*

# *The Christ Letter*

A Christological Approach to Preaching
& Practicing Ephesians

DOUGLAS D. WEBSTER

CASCADE *Books* • Eugene, Oregon

THE CHRIST LETTER
A Christological Approach to Preaching & Practicing Ephesians

Copyright © 2012 Douglas D. Webster. All rights reserved. Except for brief quotations in critical publications or reviews, no part of this book may be reproduced in any manner without prior written permission from the publisher. Write: Permissions, Wipf and Stock Publishers, 199 W. 8th Ave., Suite 3, Eugene, OR 97401.

Cascade Books
An Imprint of Wipf and Stock Publishers
199 W. 8th Ave., Suite 3
Eugene, OR 97401

www.wipfandstock.com

ISBN 13: 978-1-62032-243-7

*Cataloguing-in-Publication data:*

Webster, Douglas D.

    The Christ letter : a christological approach to preaching & practicing Ephesians / Douglas D. Webster.

    xvi + 206 pp. ; 23 cm. Includes bibliographical references.

    ISBN 13: 978-1-62032-243-7

    1. Bible. N.T. Ephesians—Commentaries. I. Title.

BS2695.3 .W36 2012

Manufactured in the U.S.A.

To the household of faith in Christ
at Central Presbyterian Church in Manhattan, New York

# Contents

*Preface* | ix
*Introduction: The Preaching Paradox* | xi

1. The Explicit Christ | 1
2. The Power of Christ | 14
3. The Life of Christ | 27
4. The Peace of Christ | 47
5. The Mission of Christ | 64
6. The Glory of Christ | 78
7. The Body of Christ | 88
8. The Ethic of Christ | 104
9. The Example of Christ | 116
10. The Wisdom of Christ | 131
11. The Relational Christ | 141
12. The Care of Christ | 153
13. The Slaves of Christ | 166
14. The Strength of Christ | 178
15. The Spirit of Christ | 191

*Bibliography* | 203

# *Preface*

*The Christ Letter* is a conversation partner for pastors and students of the Bible who want to wrestle with the meaning of the text for Christian living today. This commentary offers lines of thought, illustrations, and applications that carry the gospel message into the present situation. It is only after working through Ephesians with multiple congregations and in different cultures that I saw how Paul's Christological methodology shaped everything he said. The chapter titles came last, not first, in this process of learning how to preach Paul's letter. If they strike you as a bit contrived, I hope you will come to agree that they are expressive of the apostle's spiritual direction. My audience is the serious disciple who seeks to explore the impact of Ephesians on the contemporary body of Christ.

I imagine that people who pick up this book will have on their desk one or two excellent commentaries that explore the intricacies of the biblical text. These works weigh the scholarly debate on controversial passages and offer a solid understanding of Paul's letter. My companions along the way have included Markus Barth, Lynn Cohick, Harold Hoehner, Andrew Lincoln, Klyne Snodgrass, John Stott, and Frank Thielman. This book is indebted to their work.

The body of Christ has shaped this pastoral commentary. Scholars and congregations have weighed in giving form and substance to this work. I have had the opportunity to preach through Ephesians in churches in San Diego, California; Bhar Dar, Ethiopia; Bloomington, Indiana; and in Manhattan, New York. Each time this happens the conversation between pastor and congregation deepens and the work of New Testament scholars gets played out in the real world of congregational life.

My hope is that this work will be a catalyst for your study of Ephesians. Seminary students often resist reading pastoral commentaries, because they want to do their own independent work. With little hesitation they espouse the detailed exegesis of a scholarly commentary, but they may question the appropriateness of following another pastor's exposition. They want to come up with the shape of the sermon, its illustrations and applications on their own. Such an independent effort may be a form of self-reliance that gets in the way of good preaching. We need all the help we can get bringing the biblical text into the twenty-first century. I encourage my students to read and interact with good sermons, not so they can become lazy plagiarists, but so they can prayerfully think more deeply about how the text speaks to us today.

Along with many other preachers, I believe that when the Word of God is proclaimed, the Holy Spirit does something very special in the midst of the body of Christ. Don't let my "typing" get in the way of your powerful preaching. My prose is that of a working pastor who writes sermons that are better delivered without notes. You will find nothing eloquent here. Nothing to intimidate. I am not appealing to your pride when I say that in the Spirit on the Lord's Day you can do better work in that preaching moment than what I have done here. The transforming work of the Spirit of Christ uses what little we have for the Father's glory.

# Introduction

## *The Preaching Paradox*

How should we speak of Christ? We are aware that in the presence of excessive Christian rhetoric it is difficult to speak of Christ convincingly to one another. The innocuous nature of so much sermonizing leaves us sensitive to the implicit phoniness of Jesus talk. A certain type of explicitness is linked to hypocrisy in the minds of many confessing Christians who consider themselves refugees from mindless religious cliché. The purpose of this book is to rediscover the true character of the apostle's explicit Christ.

The Book of Ephesians serves both the message and the method of the gospel. Paul's Christ Letter not only preaches the gospel, but it critiques its preachers. The apostle offers a powerful and concise description of the holistic impact of the message of Christ as well as a penetrating and incisive critique of the methods we use to communicate the gospel. This epistle makes a forceful statement on two fronts: on style and substance, on form and function, and on meaning and motive. It is not only what Paul said but how he said it that is important. We believe that the Spirit's inspiration extends to the *way* Paul said *what* he said.

In Ephesians, Paul captures the essence of spiritual theology, the interplay between emotion and ethics, doctrine and doxology, thinking and feeling, deep worship and practical living, but you wouldn't know it from our typical sermons. Paul sets the beat, but we have trouble catching the rhythm. We are out of step with his doxological dance. Our hearing and timing are off, and the number one problem may be the run-of-the-mill sermon. Paradoxically, the very means we use to convey Paul's message has distorted the message.

(1:1–2) *"Paul, an apostle of Christ Jesus by the will of God, to God's holy people in Ephesus, the faithful in Christ Jesus: Grace and peace to you from God our Father and the Lord Jesus Christ."*

To set apart Paul's opening praise from what preachers are in the habit of doing requires some deconstruction. We begin with Paul's greeting. In as few words as possible, he introduces himself, extends greetings in the name of the Lord and gets into his message. Modern Western sermons tend to be different in this regard. Sermonizers feel compelled to generate human interest and felt-need compatibility. Like a standup comic or a motivational speaker, the preacher is under the gun to establish some common ground. Preachers begin with the notion that they must ingratiate themselves to their audience.

Paul's introduction waves off the superfluous and offers the only ground he has for communicating the Word of God. He is an apostle of Christ Jesus by the will of God. Like an ambassador, the message he is authorized to deliver is not about him and it is not tied to his personality or his ability to regale his audience with interesting anecdotes. If this seems impersonal to some, so be it. Preachers are often the main feature in their sermons, but this was not true of the apostle, who stood behind his message and under the Word. For Paul, it was enough to say to the congregation, "Grace and peace to you from God our Father and the Lord Jesus Christ." We are pastors called to preach the Word by the will of God. We stand before a congregation to preach on the basis of divine authority, not by virtue of an interesting life or cleverness.

Sermonizing can distance us from the very text we intend to preach. We interrupt the natural flow of thought from salutation to message with methods alien to the biblical tradition. Four common sermonizing approaches that interfere with moving from introduction to text are bland religious rhetoric, homiletical form, textual flattery, and catering to felt needs.

We have become so accustomed to the bland recital of religious rhetoric that our minds shift into neutral the moment we hear it. Simple words, such as *grace* and *peace, praise* and *blessing,* have lost their potency. They are sanctuary words that dress up familiar religious speech. Code words for innocuous and boring Jesus talk. Some preachers remind me of flight attendants repeating the safety instructions before a flight. They seem to think that by repeating explicit truths they have done their job. They abide by the mantra I'm going to tell you what I'm going to tell you, then I'm going to tell you, and then I'm going to tell you what I told you.

They are seemingly oblivious to their congregation's blank stares and glazed looks as they plow through their bland sermon. This type of explicitness reminds me of the husband who proudly displays the bumper sticker "I ♥ my wife."

A second approach is to reduce the text to its "proper homiletical form." This takes Paul's symphony of praise and recasts the so-called raw data into timeless theological propositions. This is done by abstracting ideas from the text to get to a general principle of timeless theological truth. Exegetes distill the meaning of the text down to a condensed form and put it into a rhetorically effective statement. A sermon on Ephesians 1:3–14 might reduce the passage to three headings, such as, *The Righteousness of the Father*, *The Redemption of the Son*, and *The Recognition of the Spirit*. Or, *The Plan of the Father*, *The Provision of the Son*, and *The Promise of the Spirit*. These exegetically derived headings are true, but somewhat misleading. Why bother with the passion of Paul's poetic prose, if our task is to basically reduce it down to three nouns? The sermonizer then clothes the homiletical skeleton with amusing anecdotes, grammatical pointers, clever insights, and personal opinions. This type of explicitness attempts to satisfy our spiritual hunger with a recipe or a menu rather than sitting down to enjoy a full-course meal.

A third sermonizing approach is to flatter the text. The preacher praises the genius of Paul, "the greatest of all New Testament writers," and compliments the beauty of the apostle's inspiring words, as "the most beautiful description of the gospel ever given." The sermonizer exudes admiration, saying such things as, "I simply stand in awe of this holy Scripture and marvel at its splendor and exquisite form." This inflationary rhetoric is given without expounding the meaning of the text and drawing out its truth. The claim that there is more here than meets the eye is advertised, but not enlarged upon. The preacher's overt efforts at magnification become the substance of the sermon, and divert attention away from the text itself. The congregation is supposed to be impressed that the preacher is impressed. By congratulating the text, the sermonizer assumes a kind of power over the text which belongs to a judge or evaluator, not to its humble interpreter. This greeting card explicitness is for those who are at a loss as to what to say, because they have not embraced the meaning of the text.

A fourth sermonizing approach is to over-indulge the listener by catering to felt needs. Instead of flattering the text, the emotional self is flattered and receives the lion's share of the attention. The orientation of the sermon turns on how the preacher wants the hearer to feel. The meaning of the sermon rides on whether or not the listener is moved emotionally. More often than not, it is the power of the preacher's stories and anecdotes that move the listener and not the truth of the biblical text. And then, it is often not the substance of the story that determines the impact but how dramatically or humorously the preacher tells the story. Yet this shift of responsibility from text to felt-need sermon is hardly noticed because everything is cloaked in the Scriptures. This people-pleasing explicitness turns the self into the main text.

## Outburst of Praise

How do we avoid these hermeneutical pitfalls? What helps us unlock the text and get to its true meaning? I paid Jack Keith a pastoral visit shortly after he became too weak to attend worship services. Leaning back in his leather recliner, his legs propped up to help circulation, he asked his wife Anne to read from what he said was his favorite text in Scripture, the first chapter of Ephesians. Sitting in the Keiths' living room, we worshiped the Lord. "For where two or three come together in my name, there I am with them" (Matt 18:20). Jack loved the apostle's outburst of praise. He found comfort here. There was nothing in the chapter that addressed his particular suffering directly, only Paul's pure, refreshing, pulsating praise.

Ephesians begins with truth set to music, a benediction of blessing, a symphony of orchestrated praise. Meaning is expressed in a melody of joy and rhythms of grace. The wonders of salvation rehearsed and celebrated in one long sentence, "presenting one cascading description of God's work in Christ after another."[1]

Jack was my hermeneutical key. From his recliner in a small apartment in an extended care facility, he triggered for me the fourfold hermeneutical motion described by literary critic George Steiner. The "act of elicitation and the appropriative transfer of meaning" involves trust, effort, embodiment, and humility.[2] By an initial act of *trust* we allow ourselves to be invested in the text. We believe that there is something truly in the text that is worth exploring and understanding. This exploratory investment of belief leads to the hard work of mining the passage for truth. This *effort* is crucial to our understanding. "The translator invades, extracts, and brings

---

1. Snodgrass, *Ephesians*, 45.
2. Steiner, *After Babel*, 312.

## The Preaching Paradox

home."³ The third step is to own the material, to bring the meaning into ourselves and to become infected by it. In sacramental terms, this *embodiment* leads us to incarnate the truth. The fourth step is to remain *humble* before the text, to respect its mystery, and to reject domesticating the text for the sake of our egos.

These four terms help describe what it means to engage the biblical text. Fidelity to Ephesians chapter one is not merely technical nor exegetical, no matter how precise and exhaustive the work on the text may be. The one-thousand-page commentary on Ephesians may miss the mark. Jack's weakness is his strength. His feebleness is critical to his faithfulness. If a dying man entrusts himself to the truth proclaimed in this text, how dare I skim over it and move on.

Jack's trust comes with the testimony that there is something profoundly meaningful in the text. His life is lived in the light of the text. All true biblical interpretation is deeply personal and resists abstracting the text from everyday living. We cannot divorce the text from daily life. Jack refused to abstract ideas; he embraced the truth. Through diligent attention over time he has saturated his soul with the Word of God. He has ingested, internalized, and embodied its meaning.

The text is no longer strange and it cannot be boring, because it is transformative. But just because the text is no longer foreign to him, does not mean that he is overly familiar with the text. Steiner's fourth hermeneutical motion is important. Humility is critical. Jack's humility before the text, which is based on his understanding of the text, resists the temptation to control the text. Without this humility, the interpreter is tempted to flatter his or her interpretation and magnify the process of elicitation. Steiner warns, "The over-determination of the interpretative act is inherently inflationary."⁴ Honestly, this old saint did more for me getting into Ephesians one than all the commentaries. As helpful and as necessary as the commentaries are, Jack's explicit Christ made the difference for me. His example said without words, "Pay attention. This is vital. The stakes are high. We're not playing games."

---

3. Ibid., 314.
4. Ibid., 316.

# 1

# *The Explicit Christ*

> *"Praise be to the God and Father of our Lord Jesus Christ,*
> *who has blessed us in the heavenly realms*
> *with every spiritual blessing in Christ."*
>
> EPHESIANS 1:3

Paul's starting point offers invaluable spiritual direction. His explicit praise provides implicit pastoral care. How would it be if we began each day in the spirit of this praise? What if instead of complaining about life, we began, "Praise be to the God and Father of our Lord Jesus Christ . . ."? What if instead of blaming we blessed, instead of feeling dejected, we worshiped our Redeemer? From prison, Paul began by singing the doxology, lifting his voice in praise so that others would join in.

The apostle Paul used syntax and synonyms, repetition and rhythm, relative clauses and participial constructions to build his praise to a crescendo. He used prepositional phrases to knit this doxology together that ought to inspire our own recital of praise. Critics have called this single sentence, the longest in the New Testament, a "monstrous conglomeration," but other biblical scholars have seen it for what it is, a "marvelous spiral" of praise without rival in Greek literature.[1] If we skip over this text too quickly we miss something important. We want to pay attention until our souls resonate with the apostle's uninhibited praise.

---

1. Lincoln, *Ephesians*, 11.

# The Christ Letter

(1:3–14) *"Praise be to the God and Father of our Lord Jesus Christ, who has blessed us in the heavenly realms with every spiritual blessing in Christ. For he chose us in him before the creation of the world to be holy and blameless in his sight. In love he predestined us for adoption to sonship through Jesus Christ, in accordance with his pleasure and will—to the praise of his glorious grace, which he has freely given us in the One he loves.*

*In him we have redemption through his blood, the forgiveness of sin, in accordance with the riches of God's grace that he lavished on us. With all wisdom and understanding, he made known to us the mystery of his will according to his good pleasure, which he purposed in Christ, to be put into effect when the times reach their fulfillment—to bring unity to all things in heaven and on earth under Christ.*

*In him we were chosen, having been predestined according to the plan of him who works everything in conformity with the purpose of his will, in order that we, who were the first to put our hope in Christ, might be for the praise of his glory. And you also were included in Christ when you heard the message of truth, the gospel of your salvation. When you believed, you were marked in him with a seal, the promised Holy Spirit, who is a deposit guaranteeing our inheritance until the redemption of those who are God's possession—*
*to the praise of his glory."*

## Beginning Right

*Eulogy* is the key word and Paul used this familiar word in an unfamiliar way—to kick start his blast of praise. If he were a symphony conductor, this would be his overture. What it is not is a rhetorical flourish, a flowery introduction to be read perfunctorily to get to the good stuff. On the contrary, it is Paul's statement of faith. Our English word "eulogy" is derived from the Greek word εὐλογέω, which means to speak well of someone, to commend the character and services of a person. We associate the word with praise for one who has recently died, but Paul linked the word to everything praiseworthy of God. To eulogize was to bless God and be blessed by God. Everything good and right and true in our lives is wrapped up in praise to the triune God. Verse three reads, "*Blessed* is the God who *blessed* us with every spiritual *blessing*." Our own eulogy is embedded in God's eulogy.

The language Paul uses to eulogize God is exuberant and exalted. His horizon is as broad and as wide-angled as it could be. His scope is cosmic. His praying imagination is stretched to the limit. When he wrote this eulogy, he was thinking on a grand scale—the grandest! He was focused on the trinitarian pattern in creation and redemption—God the Father, Son and Holy Spirit at work creating, saving, and binding everything together by God's grace and for his glory. The picture Paul paints with poetry uses the cosmos as its canvas. There is nothing small or individualistic about this description. All of this high-minded praise and truth on a grand scale is in contrast to how we have been trained to think. Paul is caught up into something grander and more real than himself. We have to pause right here and realize how unusual Paul's perspective is. His embrace of these invisible realities is not common today.

In his novel *Saturday*, Ian McEwan captures the general ethos of the modern worldview through the eyes of Theo, an eighteen-year-old. Theo belongs to a "sincerely godless generation." "No one in his bright, plate-glass, forward-looking school ever asked him to pray, or sing an impenetrable cheery hymn. There's no entity [like a loving, redeeming God] for him to doubt. His initiation, in front of the TV, before the dissolving towers [World Trade Center towers], was intense but he had adapted quickly."[2] Theo has his own unique philosophy for coping with life, but it is really not a philosophy as much as an aphorism—a maxim. It's only a saying, not even a sentence, but it reduces everything down to a manageable size. Theo's advice is this: "the bigger you think, the crappier it looks." He explains, "When we go on about big things, the political situation, global warming, world poverty, it all looks really terrible, with nothing better, nothing to look forward to. But when I think small, closer in—you know, a girl I've just met . . . or snowboarding next month, then it looks great. So this is going to be my motto—think small."[3]

These two concepts side-by-side sum up two very different worldviews. *Think small* is Theo's strategy for self-preservation; *think big* is Paul's strategy for praising God. Theo and Paul are both dealing with the meaning of life. Theo's coping strategy is fairly typical of Western affluent people who have little to live for apart from the immediate moment. Paul's eulogy for salvation was written from prison, where he was incarcerated for the

2. McEwan, *Saturday*, 32.
3. Ibid., 35.

sake of the gospel. Theo limits his imagination out of fear, so as not to be overwhelmed by human tragedy. Paul explores the heights and depths of God's love, for the sake of the glory of God.

I cannot imagine the apostle Paul resonating with *Life's Little Instruction Book*, at least not as a go-to source for living. Jackson Brown's five hundred and eleven random one-liners may be a neat idea. Sage advice is always in and it never hurts to be reminded to "Compliment three people every day," or "Watch a sunrise at least once a year," or "Remember other people's birthdays." You are definitely not going to go wrong if you "over tip breakfast waitresses," and give people "a firm handshake." But, and this is important, the notion of reducing life to little proverbs to live by is silly. Life is way too complicated for one-line maxims. The person who follows Brown's advice may be very nice and Brown may very well be a Christian (rule number 115 says, "Give yourself a year and read the Bible cover to cover"), but why reduce life to little rules to live by when we are invited into relationship with the God of all creation, who loved us and gave himself for us?[4]

Most of us struggle with the largeness of Paul's God-centered, Christ-focused, Spirit-empowered worldview—and that's a good thing! We are so easily tempted to reduce everything down to the small world of self-realization and self-discovery. Give us comfort, convenience and entertainment and we are happy campers. May it not be so!

Are we more like Theo or more like Paul? Coping with stress, realizing one's dreams, finding happiness, are thought by some to be the modern equivalent to salvation. The pressure in our culture is to narrow our vision down to the things we can control or to focus on the things that can distract us from the truly important realities of life. A four-dollar Starbucks drink is nice, but not a taste of heaven.

The net effect of a self-focused, distracted life, causes us to think too small. Theologian David Wells writes: "The self is a canvas too narrow, too cramped, to contain the largeness of Christian truth."[5] Paul begins big and if we need to struggle to catch up, so be it. If we are honest, the language of Ephesians one, no matter how modern the translation, is increasingly foreign to Christians, let alone those who don't know Christ. Paul's theology of praise flies over the heads of many believers. His prose may not connect nearly as well as when he challenges believers to put on the full armor of God or love their wives as Christ loved the church.

4. Brown, *Life's Little Instruction Book*.
5. Wells, *No Place For Truth*, 183.

*The Explicit Christ*

We have to be careful here. We could read Paul's benediction and conclude that Christians have a failure to communicate. What if people are confused by Paul's terminology? Ideas like *redemption* and *atonement* strike the modern person as old and archaic. Words like *chosen* and *predestined*, concepts like *grace* and *glory*, allegedly have no meaning for the average North American. That may be right, but the reason these words have no meaning is because the truth conveyed by these words has gone *unexplained*. The faith that seeks understanding requires explanation. This is the very language that the followers of Christ need to use and become articulate in. The solution is not found in eliminating the vocabulary, but in discovering the truth. The meaning is real and the language is necessary.

Imagine a student walking into a physics class and interrupting the professor's lecture by saying, "Wait a minute. You can't expect me to understand what you are talking about. Every other word is like a foreign language to me." The student may know the lyrics to hundreds of songs on his iPod and follow the NFL religiously, but the student is offended that his physics prof is using words and terms that he has never heard before. How would the professor respond? Would she apologize? Would she stop the lecture and console the student? Or would the professor say, "That's not my problem. Keep writing the stuff down. It'll be on the exam."

No one learns physics by being born in the West and no one learns the truth of the gospel by growing up in North America. Grasping the truth of the gospel is a reach for most people, and perhaps especially for North Americans. "It's going to take a lot of time and effort," writes William Willimon. "There'll be stuff you won't get at first hearing. We've got people in their eighties that still come out shocked on a Sunday morning. This is the way of the Cross, and it's a narrow way. It's not for everybody, but it just happens to be true. No matter how hard you try to make it so, the gospel of Jesus Christ will never be user-friendly—which is why we call it 'conversion.' Part of being a Christian means to take up a new language."[6] The gospel is accessible but it is not neatly packaged for the consumer.

Paul's use of theological language in chapter one assumes that his hearers have some understanding of what it means to be chosen, predestined, loved, adopted, redeemed, forgiven, and sealed. But his overture of praise is only the beginning. He will spend the rest of the letter describing the meaning and impact of these truths for the followers of Christ. Worship is informed by the power of the gospel before Paul has had an

---

6. Willimon, "Working on Our Grammar," 30–31.

opportunity to explain salvation, missions, and Jesus' kingdom ethic. This is true in our worship as well. We lead with the richness of the gospel and then let the household of faith catch up as we proclaim Christ. To excuse shallow worship on grounds that believers or seekers don't understand these profound truths has no basis in the apostle's thinking or practice.

## Benediction with a Beat

By design, Paul's doxology draws believers out of themselves and into thanksgiving and praise. Regardless of our circumstances this benediction reassures, inspires, and emboldens. From prison, Paul invited believers out of their natural bent, out of their self-focused worlds and their chronic compulsion to complain, into the large world of God's salvation. His symphony of praise builds to a crescendo, highlighting the work of God the Father, Son, and Spirit. Blessed with all blessings by the Father. Chosen in Christ. Sealed by the Spirit.

Sensitive to God's timing, Paul sets the rhythm of praise, by remembering the past—"before the creation of the world," rejoicing in the present—"when the times reach their fulfillment," and anticipating the future—"until the redemption of those who are God's possession." His benediction roots "every spiritual blessing," including adoption, redemption, and hope *in Christ*.[7] Every believer is included in this praise, those who were the first to put their hope in Christ and those who have since heard the word of truth.

All theology leads to doxology. This is doctrine set to music. Paul's outburst of praise was not meant to be dissected and analyzed under a microscope, but heard as a cascading flow of praise. Speech, as in music, has a certain cadence, a rhythmic flow of thought, a movement with a beat. I am reminded of rock music's aggressive four-beat line in Paul's constant repetition of "in Christ." If there is a base line, it is the "in Christ" theme which is repeated over eleven times. And as with rock music there is a kind of corporate or tribal personality to this praise. It is neither flowery nor romantic. This is not soul-searching music as much as it is soul-defining music.

---

7. New Testament scholar Gordon Fee emphasizes that "every spiritual blessing in Christ" refers specifically to "the manifold ways that God has chosen to bless his people by means of his Holy Spirit. Thus the emphasis lies not with the 'character' of the 'blessings' themselves, but with their divine origins within what the later church came to call the 'blessed Trinity,' blessings which have been lavished upon God's people through the Holy Spirit." Fee, "On Getting the Spirit Back Into Spirituality," 40–41.

In the tradition of country and western music, this doxology is a working-man's song, with simple three-chord progressions transposed into simple theological patterns: Father, Son, and Holy Spirit; blessed, chosen, and predestined; and, before time, in time, and future time.

The spiraling conversation between doctrine and praise has a jazz like quality. The somersaults of prepositions, in both Greek and English (*to, of, in, with, before, for, through, into, according to*), serve to knit everything together. There is something more creative and dynamic going on here than a three-stanza hymn. The prepositions provide the swing beat. "With the help of prepositions the origin and order of God's decision, the means and mode of carrying it out, and the goal and effect of its fulfillment are at one and the same time distinguished from one another and kept together."[8] If Paul were saying this benediction rather than writing it, it could come out spontaneously a thousand different ways, but the same basic truths would always make the message what it is—truth you can dance to. Along with the exuberance and exalted nature of the language, there is an experimental quality to this free-flowing praise. There is nothing stodgy and cumbersome about it. The syntax and syncopation can hardly keep up with Paul's passion. The apostle's praise has movement and momentum.

Like a great symphony the entire composition has a unity and singularity commensurate with its depth and breadth. There are no extraneous attachments, every measure adds and builds in a pattern of themes that illuminates and expresses the eulogy. All the truths play as one voice, one instrument, one message. "The totality of God's gracious manifestation is extolled in the blessing," serving to introduce the whole message of the Ephesian letter.[9]

Harmony is achieved through variations on a theme, such as the fourfold repetition of God's purpose: "in accordance with his pleasure and will," "in accordance with the riches of God's grace," "according to his good pleasure," and "according to the plan of him who works out everything in conformity with the purpose of his will."

Blessing God is based on being blessed, chosen, predestined, adopted, redeemed, marked, and sealed by God. Everything contributes to the underlying theme, "Praise be to God," which is repeated in a threefold refrain of praise, "to the praise of his glorious grace," "for the praise of his glory," and "to the praise of his glory." The longer we live in this praise, the

---

8. Barth, *Ephesians*, 100.
9. Ibid., 78.

more we become aware of how careful Paul was to craft this worship with beauty and depth. What Oswald Chambers said is true, "When we are indwelt by the Holy Spirit, we never talk in cold logic, we talk in passionate inspiration."[10]

## All Things Hold Together

The Artist/Composer of creation and redemption are one and the same. The history of nature and the history of redemption are reflections and revelations of the same God. Each reinforces the wonder, awe, beauty, and truth of the other. Chosen in Christ "before the creation of the world to be holy and blameless in his sight" unites the physical and material creation with the spiritual and historical reality—all of which is designed by God. This is not a rhetorical flourish, but a statement of fact. The God and Father of our Lord Jesus Christ, who authored DNA and ordained redemption, has purposed "to bring unity to all things in heaven and on earth under Christ." Everything in nature and redemption is moving forward according to plan—"the plan of him who works out everything in conformity with the purpose of his will." Albert Einstein asserted that "without belief in the inner harmony of the world there could be no science."[11] The apostle Paul goes further and asserts that the God and Father of our Lord Jesus Christ has not only created an inner harmony but an ultimate convergence.

We have a decision to make about life. Are we the holy possession of God in Christ, personally chosen by God, predestined for communion with God, adopted into the community of God's people, recipients of God's grace, redeemed by his personal sacrifice on our behalf, and signed, sealed, and delivered by the promised Holy Spirit? Or are we the accidental product of an impersonal universe, subject to blind chance and random forces, existing in a sphere of energy devoid of promise, plan, purpose, and fulfillment?

Plenty of people say they believe in God but do they believe in the God and Father of our Lord Jesus? And are they marked in Christ with the promised Holy Spirit? Do they believe in the God who is eulogized by the apostle Paul? Most people seem to be living in a no-man's land, halfway between a real relationship with God in Christ and surviving on a steady diet of self-help material and built-in distractions. They can't bring

---

10. Chambers, *So Send I You*, 21.
11. Dubay, *The Evidential Power of Beauty*, 40.

themselves to say there is no God but they can't bring themselves to accept the God who seeks to bless them.

## Transformation

The blessing of God in Christ is seen and embodied in the transformed lives of individuals such as Norman Musewe. Norman is a gentle, dignified man, with a quiet, unassuming confidence. He has an easy laugh and relaxed manner. Norman inspires respect. He is the kind of mature adult that I picture children enjoying being around, which is good, because Norman is a pediatric cardiologist. I simply assumed, based on his prayers and wise counsel, that Norman had been a follower of the Lord Jesus all of his adult life. Then I heard his story. The oldest of seven children, Norman was born in what was then Rhodesia and is now Zimbabwe. When he was very young, he was sent to the rural home of his grandmother, where he almost died of malnutrition. He remembers little of the Anglican church they attended, but the shaman who lived next door and who was known for casting spells and wrecking havoc in the community left a vivid impression of evil on Norman.

When he was six or seven his parents took him to hear an evangelist who came to town. He still remembers the people singing, "There is power, power, wonder-working power, in the blood of the Lamb." But whatever Christian influence he experienced growing up was eliminated in high school and at university. A good student, with a gifted intellect, Norman attracted the attention of girls. He became well-schooled in sexual promiscuity and drinking. "I remember my university days with the most sorrow," says Norman. "I met up with young men and women who themselves were as ready to corrupt me as I was ready to corrupt them. Together we spent ourselves in parties."

Norman excelled as a medical student, causing him, as he says, "to become puffed up and full of myself." At the end of six years of training he was number one in his class, which earned him a scholarship to study medicine in England. He continued to drink heavily. He was in and out of one disastrous sexual relationship after another. He remembers being scarred deeply over what he was doing to other people. Back home in Rhodesia as an intern he continued to take "full advantage of the nurses." Then, in 1978, he fled Rhodesia. His choice was either escape and exile or being conscripted into the Rhodesian army to fight his fellow Africans. The government designated deserters as terrorists, who could be shot on sight. He ran to Botswana and from there he fled to Scotland. Depression, anxiety, and hopelessness invaded his life. He spent days in deep regret, dwelling on the events of his past life, reviewing the innumerable ways he had hurt other people. He could not get suicide out of his mind. If it had not been for a professor who gave him a job when he was without food and a doctor who put her own reputation on the line to secure a position for him, Norman may not have survived.

Then, in 1979, he met Endra, who was nursing at the same hospital where he was a resident. He was immediately attracted to her but his strong sense of shame over his numerous unhealthy sexual relationships made relating difficult. He vowed he would treat her differently and in 1981 they were married. One year later they had twin boys, moved to Canada, and Norman specialized in pediatric cardiology at the Hospital for Sick Children in Toronto. In spite of his success, depression continued to dog him. Now a father of four, Norman felt guilty for his past sins, guilty for drinking so much, guilty for overworking, and guilty for letting Endra down. His feelings of worthlessness deepened over the years to the point of overwhelming him. At the breaking point, he resigned from Sick Children's. He still marvels that through it all Endra stayed with him. He found work in a local medical practice but by then his drinking was out of control.

With Norman in a perpetual drunken stupor, he and his family went on vacation at Endra's insistence in March 1992. Norman remembers being alone in the hotel room. Endra had just taken the children swimming. He was withdrawing from alcohol and becoming delirious when he sensed the intensity of a demonic attack unlike anything he had ever experienced before. His head was filled with accusing voices. He was trembling in fear. Everything felt so unreal and out of perspective. It was as if his life was coming to an end and he remembers crying out, "Jesus, if you don't help me, I have had enough." In that very instant something happened. The relentless circular thoughts of accusation and guilt ceased. He didn't know exactly what happened, but he remembers Endra saying he must be feeling better because he was responding to her and the children better. Several more months of turmoil followed, but then on one spring day, he felt as if a heavy load was lifted from him. He had an indescribable sense of freedom and a palpable awareness that everything had changed for him. He couldn't explain it. He had an aversion to alcohol, a love for Christian music, and an awareness that he had to relearn how to live life.

Norman was unaware of any direct Christian influence that would account for this transformation. No one was sharing the gospel with him. No one was urging him to turn to God. In retrospect, he sees his conversion as the direct intervention of God. Some time later he learned that his sister in Zimbabwe had become a Christian and was earnestly praying for his conversion. But at the time, there was no immediate witness. Shortly after his salvation, he and his family were led to a church not far away from their home and to an amazing pastor, Ebenezer Sikakane, under whose care Norman, Endra, and their children were nurtured and discipled. Pastor Sikakane began with Ephesians, carefully taking Norman through the truths of his new-found relationship with the Lord Jesus. Norman recalls, "I remember especially the sweetness of knowing that the Scripture was speaking of me and to me." Norman says, "Ephesians 1:13 continues to mean so much to me: 'And you also were included in Christ when you heard the word of truth, the gospel of your salvation.'"

## Ephesian Explicitness

We are accustomed to the benediction coming at the end, not at the beginning, but in Paul's epistle, blessing God and extolling the blessings of God leads the way. Doxology frames doctrine and ethics. Everything flows from worship. Devotion motivates discipleship. Wonder and praise are front and center. This is not a text to dissect into pieces, nor is it fuel for theological debates. The jaded have no time for meditating on such truths, but faithful, humble believers revel in its truth, beauty, and goodness. If Paul's opening outburst of praise leaves us cold and indifferent, we have a problem. But I believe that problem can be approached in three practical ways: through prayer, meditation, and memorization. Pray through Ephesians 1:3–14. Copy it out and begin to meditate on it. See if you can get into the rhythms of grace that the apostle Paul felt as he was inspired to write out this powerful testimony to the work of God. Commit the passage to memory. You may have to live with the text for awhile, before it sinks in, but it will be worth it.

Paul's explicit Christ offers an implicit ratio of relationship to significance that deserves our meditation. Paul addressed his Spirit-inspired theology to "the saints *in Ephesus,* the faithful *in Christ Jesus.*" We were meant to remember that this book of the Bible is a letter addressed to Christians living in a particular time and place. True spirituality is always rooted in a particular time and place. We also believe that the message given to them is meant for all of us who follow Christ. The phrase *in Ephesus* is followed by ten references to being *in Christ*. The ratio is ten to one. Meditate on the impact of being ten times more impressed with being in Christ than living in, let's say, Memphis or Manhattan. The point is not that we should in any way disassociate ourselves from the place where we live and work, but that we should be ten times more impressed with the reality of Christ in our lives than bemoaning our living and working situation. Whatever your *in Ephesus* experience is, whether you are working on Wall Street or singing on Broadway; whether you live from paycheck to paycheck or have a mansion in Muskoka, your *in Christ* reality is ten times more important for shaping your identity and significance.

James Houston reminds us that "as Christians we are never more our true selves than when we are most 'in' Christ Jesus. There our personal uniqueness is caught up in the reality of God's love for us" and "the more assuredly we are in Christ, the more decisively we will do what the truth calls us to do." Paul's eulogizing praise affirms and challenges. The more this blessing defines us, the deeper we will be, and the less "indecisive, compromising and shallow we will be."[12]

According to New Testament scholar Andrew Lincoln, the Book of Ephesians serves a vital purpose in building believers up and helping them to end strong. He writes,

> When Christians become discouraged, feel weak and insignificant, succumb to an individualistic piety, or lose their sense of identity and purpose, Ephesians can provide the necessary reminder of the important part they have to play in God's cosmic plan, of the fact that the quality of their life together in the Church has everything to do with the Church's carrying out its task in the world, and of the power that has been made available in Christ to move them on toward the fulfillment of such a calling.[13]

In the fourth century, Pastor John Chrysostom commended the apostle's benediction to his congregation, saying,

> Honored as we are with so great a blessing, so high a privilege, so great loving-kindness, let us not shame our Benefactor, let us not render in vain so great grace . . . I entreat you and appeal to you, that all these things turn not to our judgment, nor to our condemnation, but to our enjoyment of those good things,

---

12. Houston, *Joyful Exiles*, 18.
13. Lincoln, *Ephesians*, xcvi.

which may God grant we may all attain, in Christ Jesus, our Lord, with whom to the Father, together with the Holy Spirit, be glory, strength, power, and authority.[14]

This pastoral voice from antiquity makes sense for us today.

---

14. Chrysostom, *Homilies on Ephesians*, 55.

# 2

# The Power of Christ

> *"I pray that the eyes of your heart may be enlightened
> in order that you may know the hope to which he has called you,
> the riches of his glorious inheritance in his people,
> and his incomparably great power for us who believe."*
>
> Ephesians 1:18–19

The blessing of God extolled and elaborated on in the opening symphony of praise forms the basis for Paul's eucharistic prayer. The first sentence of Paul's Christ letter is all praise (1:3–14); the second sentence is all prayer (1:15–23). Having *blessed* God for *blessing* us in Christ with all spiritual *blessings*, Paul earnestly prays for believers to understand the fullness of their blessing in Christ. Eucharist, εὐχαριστέω, is the Greek word for giving thanks and characterizes the nature of his prayer. Paul's introductory phrase, *"For this reason,"* includes all that he has said in his benediction and sets the ground rules for his eucharistic prayer. Paul underscores the motive and the means that makes Paul's prayer possible.

After receiving this opening benediction it would be hard to make the case that we want to communicate with God more than God wants to communicate with us. The intensity of God's passion for us—we have been blessed, chosen, predestined, adopted, redeemed, and sealed in Christ—so far exceeds our passion for God that we dare not imply that God is distant, remote and uncaring.

## The Power of Christ

Praise and prayer, eulogy and eucharist, benediction and thanksgiving, ought to be bound together in the believer's life. Real worship unites doxology and devotion, deepens our understanding of God's salvation, and builds confidence in the Lord. The main thrust of Paul's prayer is that "the faithful in Christ Jesus" might know God better, that they would know the hope of their calling, the riches of their glorious inheritance, and experience God's incomparably great power. Prayer and power are dynamically related in Paul's Christ-centered spiritual direction.

Paul wrote about Christ's power from prison to the saints in Ephesus, who felt depressed and in need of encouragement. Persecution, discrimination, and a lack of social status in the eyes of the world contributed to a sense of insignificance and powerlessness. Paul's prayer on their behalf undoubtedly addressed a strong felt need, but he did it in a way that redefined the meaning of power. What Paul meant by power and what we often mean by power are two different things. The power that grasps how wide and long and high and deep is the love of Christ is different from the power that grasps for more control, more wealth, more glory, and more authority. God's power at work within us is different from the egotistical power at work within us. To be strong in the Lord and in his mighty power is different from having a strong personality, great name recognition, and political clout. Mutual submission in Christ and walking in the way of love is incompatible with throwing our weight around, building a reputation, and being a big talker and name-dropper.

(1:15–23) *"For this reason, ever since I heard about your faith in the Lord Jesus and your love for all his people, I have not stopped giving thanks for you, remembering you in my prayers. I keep asking that the God of our Lord Jesus Christ, the glorious Father, may give you the Spirit of wisdom and revelation, so that you may know him better. I pray that the eyes of your heart may be enlightened in order that you may know the hope to which he has called you, the riches of his glorious inheritance in his people, and his incomparably great power for us who believe. That power is the same as the mighty strength he exerted when he raised Christ from the dead and seated him at his right hand in the heavenly realms, far above all rule and authority, power and dominion, and every name that can be invoked, not only in the present age but also in the one to come. And God placed all things under his feet and appointed him to be head over everything for the church, which is his body, the fullness of him who fills everything in every way."*

## Authentic Spirituality

Paul's letter to the saints in Ephesus begins with a picture of true spirituality and worship that we ought not *mimic ignorantly* nor *criticize cynically*. We face two dangers here: the twin dangers of shallow piety and cynical skepticism. When praise is reduced to pious enthusiasm and prayer inflated into performance, the meaning of true worship is lost and even mocked. Likewise, when praise and prayer are ignored altogether, the believer becomes cold and indifferent to the blessings of God. There is an interaction between these two false spiritualities that requires attention. Each tends to justify itself in the light of the other.

Insincere spirituality provokes some Christians to live like practical pagans without praise and prayer. They are turned off by the emptiness and dishonesty of what some pretentious believers call "worship." Church and church schools can become a hotbed for a religious piety that is empty and platitudinous. As Jesus pointed out the danger of sacrilege can go up as well as down. The impact of sanctimonious Pharisaical prayers is as bad as echoing a pagan mantra. There is nothing like obsequious piety to drive others to distraction and cynicism. Pretentious spirituality is as grave a danger as blasphemy and profanity. However, the solution to insincere spirituality is not found in finding fault with every form of worship and praise. We face two dangers: we can be *hypocritical* on the one hand and *hyper-critical* on the other. Both extremes miss the mark of true spirituality. Resisting false spirituality is no excuse for cynically dismissing praise and prayer, no matter how justified we think we may be. The challenge of true piety cuts both ways.

In John's letters to the seven churches in the Book of Revelation, worship was the number one issue singled out for the church in Ephesus. The saints were hard working, persevering, discerning, and enduring, but they had lost their first love. God in the abstract, with all the accompanying administration, information, good works, and programing, is an easy preoccupation compared to the real work of engaging heart and mind in meaningful worship to the triune God. In the Spirit, Paul seems well aware of this dynamic as he writes to believers not only in the first century but to us today. The emptiness and the indifference of so much modern Christianity threatens to drive us away from God, but in the Spirit we can choose to explore the depth of God's Word, to dwell on the meaning of God's grace and to cultivate a passion for Christ. Paul's praise and prayer are powerful antidotes to pseudo-spirituality and cynical spirituality.

## Teach Us to Pray

We learn from Paul's example to pray for others. This does not exclude prayer for ourselves, but it does teach us the importance of focusing on the needs of others. Paul says here that he "heard about" their faith in the Lord Jesus and their love for all his people, implying that he did not know them personally. Nevertheless, he says, "*I have not stopped giving thanks for you, remembering you in my prayers.*" Paul's sensitivity to the body of Christ and his communion with the emerging church throughout Asia Minor meant that he earnestly prayed for believers he may never have met.

When a disciple of Jesus came to him, saying, "Lord, teach us to pray," Jesus responded by giving an even shorter version of the Lord's Prayer than the one in the Sermon on the Mount. In the Gospel of Luke, Jesus' model prayer was a little over thirty words, followed by two quick illustrations: a man asks his friend for a loaf of bread at midnight and a son asks his father for a fish. In both cases, there is nothing more natural than for a friend or a father to meet the request. The bottom line is clear: "Ask and it will be given to you; seek and you will find; knock and the door will be opened to you. For everyone who asks receives; those who seek find; and to those who knock, the door will be opened." Jesus concluded, "If you then, though you are evil, know how to give good gifts to your children, how much more will your Father in heaven give the Holy Spirit to those who ask him!" (Luke 11:1–13).

The promise of receiving the Holy Spirit may surprise us, because we are in the habit of asking for other things (good health, favorable circumstances, safety, comfort, and peace). We pray about our circumstances and our problems and our illnesses, yet Jesus told us to pray for the Holy Spirit. Instead of asking for the best gift possible—the Holy Spirit—we ask for something else, like personal success and material security. Not so with Paul. He prayed that believers would have the Spirit of wisdom and revelation.

If we amplify Paul's prayer request in the light of his opening benediction, it reads,

> I keep asking that the God of our Lord Jesus Christ, the glorious Father, *who has blessed us in the heavenly realms with every spiritual blessing in Christ, who chose us in him before the creation of the world to be holy and blameless in his sight, who in love predestined us for adoption to sonship through Jesus Christ,* may give you the Spirit of wisdom and revelation, so that you may know him better.

The *earnestness* of Paul's prayer is evident in his gratitude ("I have not stopped giving thanks") and in his persistence ("I keep asking"). The *power* of his prayer is rooted in his trinitarian God-centeredness ("the God of our Lord Jesus Christ, the glorious Father, may give you the Spirit of wisdom and revelation"). The *wisdom* of his prayer is found in the nature of his request. He prayed for the Spirit of wisdom and revelation, "so that you may know him better."

## The Eyes of Your Heart

Before Paul finished delivering his prayer on behalf of the saints he used a number of body metaphors: *eyes, heart, hands, feet,* and *head*. Besides helping to convey abstract truth in a graphic and concrete way, the metaphors reinforce the incarnation of God's truth in ordinary life. Spirituality enters into the physical and historical reality on a personal and cosmic scale. We were not meant to literalize or visualize these metaphors. We can't paint the eyes of the heart or visualize the risen Christ seated on the right hand of the Father with all things under his feet. But we can understand what these metaphors signify.

Seeing with *the eyes of your heart* signifies knowing God in the depth of your inner being—in the real you. This knowing is deeply personal, very different from indoctrination, and beyond mere information about God. "The result is that the 'inner eyes,' the instruments of sight and understanding for the inner being, will receive light by which to see. In other words, the apostle prays that the lights will go on inside people so that they know God and understand the benefit of the gospel."[1] Paul reiterated the same idea in the third chapter when he said, "I pray that out of his glorious riches he may strengthen you with power through his Spirit in your inner being, so that Christ may dwell in your hearts through faith" (Eph 3:16–17).

The way that Paul intercedes on behalf of the saints is the way that we want to intercede on behalf of our children, our friends, our spouse, our loved ones, even our enemies. This is the loving way to pray for one another. Everything lights up when the eyes of our hearts are open wide. There is more to this enlightenment than a glib profession that Jesus saves. This kind of *seeing* encompasses the fullness of heart and mind. The *eyes of the heart* suggest the knowing look of awareness and assurance. You can read a lot in a person's eyes.

1. Snodgrass, *Ephesians*, 73.

## A Three-fold Enlightenment

Paul prayed that the saints would be enlightened in three ways: that they would know the *hope* to which God had called them, the *riches* of God's glorious inheritance in his people, and God's incomparably great *power* for all who believe. Each reality is worthy of careful scrutiny and reflection, but Paul meant for us to grasp the impact of this deeply personal and relationally shared enlightenment as a single empowering truth.

We have to be careful, because these three simple words, *hope*, *riches*, and *power*, can trigger in the modern imagination something very different from what the apostle Paul intended. Detached from their biblical meaning, *hope*, *riches*, and *power*, can be misinterpreted to mean middle class values: optimism, wealth, and success. A *Time* magazine cover story asked, "Does God want you to be rich?" The article suggested that a growing number of evangelical Christians believe that God wants to bless them with material prosperity. But this was hardly what Jesus had in mind when he said, "I have come that [you] may have life, and have it to the full" (John 10:10). He was not teaching prosperity or preaching a health and wealth gospel. In fact, just the opposite. He was contrasting his self-sacrificing path to the cross with the thief who had come to steal and with the hired hand who had come to exploit. If anything Jesus discussed the dangers of riches and warned us not to neglect the poor. Jesus said, "I am the good shepherd. The good shepherd lays down his life for the sheep" (John 10:11). Whatever meaning Paul intended by hope, riches, and power, we know it was and is tied to the crucified and risen Christ.

*The hope of our calling* sums up the meaning of being chosen, predestined, adopted, and redeemed by God in Christ. Hope today is squarely based on what God has done in the past to bring us to himself. We were meant to look to the future in the light of the past. Given what the Lord has done, how can we not but be hopeful for the future: "He who did not spare his own Son, but gave him up for us all—how will he not also, along with him, graciously give us all things?" (Rom 8:32).

God's call in our lives opens up the content of the gospel to us. We have been "called to belong to Jesus," "called to be his holy people" (Rom 1:6, 7), "called to be free" (Gal 5:13), and called to be one body. The call of God is not limited to a special class of Christians, but extends to all believers. We are all called to one hope, one Lord, one faith, one baptism (Eph 4:1–5). We have all been called to suffer for Christ (1 Pet 2:21) and we have all been called to peace (Col 3:15). The fullness of God's call was undoubtedly in Paul's mind when he said, "I press on toward the goal to win the prize for which God has called me heavenward in Christ Jesus" (Phil 3:14).

All believers are called. If we grasp this aspect of the Spirit's enlightenment, our identity in Christ will be secured. We will be impressed with a personal agenda that fills our lives with purpose and worth. We will have found what we are looking for. To be called is to be blessed, chosen, predestined, redeemed, saved by grace, and rooted and established in love. It is all this and more. As I said earlier, the thrust of Paul's praise and prayer is soul defining, not soul searching. There is a place for both, but Paul dwells on that which gives assurance and confidence.

*The inheritance in his people* is best understood relationally rather than materially. The riches referred to here are not possessions but people—the people of God, both Jews and Gentiles, the one new humanity in Christ. Paul liked this concept of riches and repeated it three other times: "the riches of God's grace that he lavished on us" (1:7); "the incomparable riches of his grace" (2:7); and "his glorious riches" (3:16). The believer's wealth is found in people, in community, and in the fellowship of the saints. This new reality recalls Jesus' promise that anyone who has left houses or brothers or sisters or father or mother or children or fields for his sake will receive a hundred times as much and will inherit eternal life (Matt 19:29). The glory of God's inheritance points forward to the worshiping congregation described in the Book of Revelation as a great multitude that no one could count, from every nation, tribe, people and language (Rev 7:9). We are "no longer foreigners and strangers, but fellow citizens with God's people and also members of his household, built on the foundation of the apostles and prophets, with Christ Jesus himself as the chief cornerstone" (Eph 2:19–20).

## Real Power

*The incomparable greatness of God's power* refers to the power that informs, motivates, comforts, and strengthens us in Christ. This is the same power that God exerted when he raised Christ from the dead and seated him at his right hand in the heavenly realms. As Paul said to the church at Philippi,

> I want to know Christ—yes, to know the power of his resurrection and participation in his sufferings, becoming like him in his

death, and so, somehow, attaining to the resurrection from the dead." (Phil 3:10–11)

In an effort to convey something of the greatness of God's power, Paul "attempts to exhaust the resources of the Greek language by piling up four synonyms for power."[2] Paul characterizes the greatness of God's power in four ways: δύναμις, from which we get *dynamic* and *dynamite*, refers to the power of God to accomplish his will; ἐνέργεια, from which we get *energy*, speaks of God's inherent strength and power; κράτος signifies the power of God to overcome all opposition; and ἰσχύς refers to the execution of God's authority and power.[3]

Clearly, Paul wants believers to be impressed with the power of God, but what he does linguistically pales in comparison to what he does theologically. The real thrust of Paul's message on power centers on Christ. Whatever power we were meant to appropriate depends exclusively on the risen and exalted Christ, whose position is "far above all rule and authority, power and dominion, and every name that can be invoked." The power we seek is not found in large numbers or social activism or biblical education or persuasive rhetoric or deep emotion or creative approaches. The power is found in Christ who fills the church with power.

The description of Christ's supremacy extends over every conceivable power, whether it be human or demonic, institutional or emotional, political or spiritual. Jesus is Lord over the principalities and powers and the rulers of darkness. Christ has the last word over every ideology and technology, over every philosophy and religion. Neither science nor spiritual forces can win over the power of Christ. Paul stacks up five different types of power, referred to as *rule, authority, power, dominion,* and *title*. All of which are ultimately under Christ's rule. Paul may have intended to focus on spiritual forces but it is hard to imagine him not applying the superior power of Christ to every sphere of life. The risen Christ is "in charge of running the universe, everything from galaxies to governments, no name and no power [is] exempt from his rule" (Ephesians 1:21, *The Message*). This is the power of eternal salvation and social reconciliation. Can there be any greater power?

Two biblical texts relate especially well to Paul's emphasis here. In Romans 8, Paul comes at this same truth from another angle, by emphasizing that nothing shall separate us from the love of Christ, not trouble or hardship or persecution or famine or nakedness or danger or sword. "For I

2. Lincoln, *Ephesians*, 60.
3. Ibid.; Barth, *Ephesians*, 152, n. 89.

am convinced," Paul wrote, "that neither death nor life, neither angels nor demons, neither the present nor the future, nor any powers, neither height nor depth, nor anything else in all creation, will be able to separate us from the love of God that is in Christ Jesus our Lord" (Rom 8:35, 38–39). The second passage is in Hebrews: "In putting everything under him, God left nothing that is not subject to him. Yet at present we do not see everything subject to him. But we do see Jesus, who was made lower than the angels for a little while, now crowned with glory and honor because he suffered death, so that by the grace of God he might taste death for everyone" (Heb 2:8–9).

How shall we understand the meaning of power? We are aware of conflicting notions of power in the Christian community. So-called power evangelists promote positive thinking and preach a gospel of health and wealth. Latin American liberationists in the name of Jesus call the poor and powerless to subversive political power. Some Christian conservatives leverage political power in the public square, and individual Christians sometimes wield power because of their success and status. We are socialized to handle life competitively and taught to equate success with power. The only game many people know is how to envy power, aspire for power, and acquire power.

The essence of Christ's power is made manifest through pain, persecution, and suffering. The power we seek is, after all, the power that raised Christ from the dead. The power of the resurrection is always connected with the fellowship of Christ's suffering. It is important to realize that this is not a theoretical point but a practical one. Paul never would have said so much about power and prayed so earnestly for power, if there had been no need for power. The spiritual counsel contained in Ephesians was directed to believers who felt intimidated by their insignificance, ridiculed by the surrounding society, under attack by spiritual forces and pressured by syncretistic religions. The venue for showcasing this power is always suffering. This is what accounts for Paul's juxtaposition of freedom and confidence before God and suffering for the sake of Christ and the church (3:12–13). The catalyst for Christ's power is the cross. We have seen this over and over again in our churches. The testimony of God's power is most evident among those marked by the cross, not by success.

We struggle with the practical implications of Christ's power. The church needs Christians who have strong biblical convictions, believers who are not afraid to assert the truth wholeheartedly, passionately. The power of Christ has nothing to do with being push-over nice and pathetically naive, but neither is the power of the cross compatible with egocentric power. We resist the public relations' pressure of mutual self-praise and prayerfully submit to the way of the cross.

A churchman with considerable power chose as his sermon text the well known *kenosis* passage that challenges believers to cultivate the mind of Christ, "who made himself nothing . . . by becoming obedient to death—even death on a cross!" (Phil 2:3–11). But before he began to preach what many later complimented as a powerful and eloquent sermon on the humility of Christ, he spent five minutes praising three men in the audience. He declared that these men were the most powerful and significant Christian leaders in the state. He was honored to be their friend and humbled to preach before them. He predicted that one of them would soon be recognized as one of the top five theologians in North America. Before a thousand people he extolled their virtues and at the end, he had them stand, and led the audience in applause. The whole episode could not have been more ironic. The power of vainglory juxtaposed with the power of him who "made himself nothing, by taking the very nature of a servant, being made in human likeness. And being found in appearance as a human being, he humbled himself by becoming obedient to death—even death on a cross!" After the applause died down we turned to the text, but the stronger message had already been delivered.

We need wisdom on grasping the true meaning of power. The kind of wisdom acquired through prayer and diligent study of God's Word. The power of Christ does not insulate us from the forces of evil or protect us from germs or overrule the laws of nature. This supernatural power is not magical or superstitious. We are not isolated from diseases or broken relationships or saved from accidents or protected from traumas. The powerful presence of Christ in our lives does not make us immune to living in a fallen and broken world. When bad things happen we may be tempted to spiritualize our difficulties and wonder why God's power did not prevent them. The spiritually naive are ready to conclude that the believer has done something wrong. Some years ago when I was a young pastor in the Midwest, I fell and broke my arm at a church ice-skating party. If that wasn't bad enough, some in the congregation felt there must be some spiritual meaning to my fall. Unfortunately, they turned to Proverbs 16:18, "pride comes before a fall," to explain my broken arm. Christ's power does not save us from the laws of nature or the trauma of an accident, but empowers our witness in the midst of life's struggles.

### The Christ Letter

The thrust of Paul's stress on power was not intended to coddle believers but to embolden them. He offered no excuse for weakness. His purpose was to persuade believers of the tragedy of living apart from Christ. Unashamedly he sought to convince the saints of the certainty of God's revelation in Christ and the goodness of their new life in Christ. He admonished them (and us) to live lives worthy of our calling, empowered by the gifts of the Spirit, and incorporated into the body of Christ. Paul showed little sympathy for Christians who wanted to express their feelings of low self-esteem or complain about their identity crisis. I'm not sure Christians even did that back then, but if they did, I doubt if Paul encouraged that kind of self-expression. Paul was a firm believer in the need to learn a whole new way of living, behaving, and relating. He was convinced that in Christ, everything changed, from how we relate as families to how we work for our employers.

Christi Napier knows firsthand the power of Christ. She lives in Arizona with her husband Doug and their two teenage children. In 2007 scar tissue mysteriously began to grow across her trachea and around her vocal cords. One night Christi woke up gasping for breath. Doug rushed her to the hospital, where doctors put her on a ventilator and then performed a tracheotomy. Four years later, doctors had still not figured out why the scar tissue continued to grow. After forty surgeries, Christi has stopped counting.

At one point, when she was at the end of her own capacity to endure, Christi cried out to the Lord, "I just need this to end." She sensed an immediate response. The Lord said to her, "You don't need this to end. You just need me." Christi explains, "A wonderful wave of freedom broke over me. I realized that I didn't need to panic. I didn't need to feel desperate. I didn't need the circumstances to change to feel the peace and rest of the Lord. All I needed was the Lord." In spite of poor health, difficult breathing, and constant surgeries, Christi speaks of being "happy, prosperous, joyful, and peaceful." Christi's circumstances are unique to her, but she is working out her salvation in daily obedience through the effective and powerful work of the Spirit within her.

Paul's picture of strength—the full armor of God—comes at the end, but everything in Ephesians is moving in that direction from the beginning. Against all the worldly powers that seek to manipulate and control, Paul calls believers not to powerlessness, but to God's power. He wants them to be strong and end strong. The power of God is the power that creates, redeems, transforms, heals, unifies, strengthens, feeds, serves, resurrects, makes whole, and communicates the gospel.[4] What the Lord said to Paul makes sense for us as well, "My grace is sufficient for you, for my power is made perfect in weakness" (1 Cor 12:9).

The essence of Christ's power is made manifest in and through the church, the body of Christ. Paul's prayer for Spirit-led enlightenment and empowerment focuses on the church rather than the individual believer. We might be surprised to learn that the supremacy of Christ over all things creates a special identity and purpose for the church. Jesus is not only Lord of the universe but the head of the church and his presence fills not only the cosmos, but the church!

Knowing what we know of the church this would seem to be a demotion for Christ, but on the contrary it fits the pattern established in the Incarnation of God. Paul explained the fullness of God in Christ to the believers at Colossae this way: "For God was pleased to have all his fullness dwell in him and through him to reconcile to himself all things, whether things on earth or things in heaven by making peace through his blood shed on the cross" (Col 1:19). Now Paul extends this "fullness" to the church, the body of Christ in the world. God "placed all things under his feet and appointed him to be head over everything *for the church*, which is his body, the fullness of him who fills everything in every way."

We might think that the cosmos is a far greater priority than the church, but just the opposite is true. Jesus is the Lord of the universe for the sake of the church. Pastor and Bible translator Eugene Peterson describes it this way: "At the center of all this, Christ rules the church. The church, you see, is not peripheral to the world; the world is peripheral to the church. The church is Christ's body, in which he speaks and acts, by which he fills everything with his presence" (Eph 1:22–23, *The Message*). God's plan is for the world to grasp Christ's cosmic supremacy through God's new society the church. From a humanistic point of view, the "plan of him who works out everything in conformity with the purpose of his will" (1:11) may appear obscure and hidden, but to Paul, the mystery of Christ and the manifold wisdom of God, "which for ages past was kept hidden in God," is now being made known through the church "to the rulers and authorities in the heavenly realms" (3:9–11).

This high view of the church and its impact in the world echoes Jesus' authoritative pronouncement in the Sermon on the Mount, when he declared to his disciples, "You are the salt of the earth,"

---

4. Forbes, *Religion of Power*, 139–40.

## The Christ Letter

and "You are the light of the world" (Matt 5:13, 14). That is to say, beatitude-based believers possess God's kingdom, experience God's comfort, and will inherit God's earth. They have been blessed with God's righteousness and they are defined by God's mercy and vision. What more could God give them? They have it all, and for that reason they are salt and light. "'You folks *are*, not 'You folks *ought* to be,' the most significant people on the planet."[5]

Ephesians begins with benediction followed by jubilation. Paul is filled with joy over the meaning of the gospel and the magnitude of Christ's work. He expects a thoughtful church to own its identity, embrace God's mission, and manifest the power of Christ. He leads us in authentic praise and prayer. This is how we should worship the Lord and this is how we should pray for one another. So, Paul prays boldly, "I keep asking that the God of our Lord Jesus Christ, the glorious Father, may give you the Spirit of wisdom and revelation, so that you may know him better" (1:17). Amen. And this is how we pray for one another.

---

5. Bruner, *The Churchbook: Matthew vol. 1*, 188.

# 3

# *The Life of Christ*

> *"But because of his great love for us, God, who is rich in mercy, made us alive with Christ even when we were dead in transgressions—it is by grace you have been saved."*
>
> Ephesians 2:4

Hell is an expletive or a joke, but not a reality that most Westerners fear. Some time ago we passed from despair to apathy. We embraced our own do it yourself survival mode. We became content to live in the moment, trying to make it "one day at a time." We no longer fear the judgment of God. We fear dying, yet people have grown accustomed to the notion that death ends all. Sitcoms, like *The Office*, mock the prospect that there is anything more to life. In one episode, Pam punched Michael for dating her mother, causing Michael to fantasize about his life,

> As Pam's big, strong arm hit my face,
> I saw my whole life flash before my eyes, and guess what?
> I have four kids and I have a hover car and a hover house.
> And my wife is a runner and it shows. And Jim and Pam are my best friends.
> And our kids play together. And I'm happy. And I'm rich.
> And I never die.
> It doesn't sound like much, but it's enough for me.

We have gone from nihilistic despair to cynical indifference. Our critical coping skill is to remain seriously unserious. Life is best reviewed on

Comedy Central. We embrace all forms of escape with a passion so we don't have to think about the realities discussed by the apostle Paul. Even Christians struggle to keep up with Paul's preaching. To enter the most real world of heaven and hell, sin and judgment, grace and salvation is shocking. The Bible says we are already dead in our sins and the culture says death ends all.

(2:1–10) *"As for you, you were dead in your transgressions and sins, in which you used to live when you followed the ways of this world and of the ruler of the kingdom of the air, the spirit who is now at work in those who are disobedient. All of us also lived among them at one time, gratifying the cravings of our sinful nature and following its desires and thoughts. Like the rest, we were by nature deserving wrath.*

*But because of his great love for us, God, who is rich in mercy, made us alive with Christ even when we were dead in transgressions—it is by grace you have been saved. And God raised us up with Christ and seated us with him in the heavenly realms in Christ Jesus, in order that in the coming ages he might show the incomparable riches of his grace, expressed in his kindness to us in Christ Jesus. For it is by grace you have been saved, through faith—and this is not from yourselves, it is the gift of God—not by works, so that no one can boast. For we are God's workmanship, created in Christ Jesus to do our good works, which God prepared in advance for us to do."*

## The Human Experience

In ten short verses, Paul describes the depth and height of the human experience. He contrasts dying in sin and living by grace; he compares the ruler of the kingdom of the air to the God who is rich in mercy; he contrasts the cravings of sinful nature with the good works, "which God prepared in advance for us to do." He compares the wrath of God with the love of God, the ways of the world with the ways of God, the bondage to sin and death with "the incomparable riches of God's grace." In a little over two hundred words, Paul lays out the depravity of the human condition and the life-giving mercy of God's saving grace.

What follows does nothing less than overcome the most irreconcilable gulf ever imagined by humankind. The chasm between the sinful self and the holy God is greater than any distance known to the astronomer or experienced by the explorer.

Sin's power separates parent and child and alienates husband and wife. We know how bondage to addictions, perversions, and passions can separate us from our true selves, opening up a seemingly unbridgeable chasm in our souls. We feel the pain of this irreconcilable separation within ourselves and with others, but that chasm is nothing compared to the gulf between the risen and exalted Christ and ourselves dead in our transgressions and sins.

We forget this. We think that our big problems are fear, insecurity, loneliness, frustration, and anxiety, but these are only symptoms of a far deeper problem. We need to trace the roots of despair back to their source. Any illusion that a convenient marriage of sentimental piety and self-help will free our souls is sadly mistaken. The power of sin has us in its grip and no amount of money, success, weight-loss, adventure, sex, plastic surgery, or power frees us from bondage. There is no workout routine or a cool set of friends that saves the soul. The big lie today is that we find ourselves by living for ourselves.

"Are evangelicals today undermining the gospel by forgetting the nature of evil?" asks historian Nathan Hatch.

> Is it possible that we are witnessing the development of what once would have been a contradiction in terms—a romantic or sentimental gospel? Promoting evangelism or bolstering self-esteem may seem far easier if you represent man's plight as a mere fly in the ointment rather than a poisoned well. Yet glib sentimentalism may distort the essence of our faith.
>
> Why does the gospel seem dull, insipid, even trivial today? We have removed the drama from salvation by underplaying the plight of humankind and overbilling the potential of persons to achieve their own self-fulfillment . . .[1]

## Dead In Our Sins

Garrison Keillor's nostalgic tales of Lake Wobegon impress me as the way most Americans would like to be "spiritual." The thrust of his message is that we have to learn to laugh at ourselves and not take ourselves too seriously. His popular radio show, *Prairie Home Companion*, is an entertaining blend of Americana: a mix of country-western, gospel, jazz, comical

1. Hatch, "Purging the Poisoned Well Within," 15–16.

vignettes and childhood remembrances. Keillor combines an easy, almost affectionate familiarity with church culture and a dismissive attitude toward the Christian faith. He refers to his fictional Lutheran minister, Pastor Ingqvist, preaching an Advent sermon as if he actually half believed the Christmas story. The audience laughs at his mild dig at Christian gullibility. The thinly concealed supposition is, "Does anybody really believe this anymore?"

Keillor's gospel of human interest stories resonates with what many people feel they need. His reassuring tone and playful teasing offers humorous glimpses into human nature. His radio show is what many would like worship to become: warm and friendly, entertaining and non-threatening. Keillor's stories may be about nasty, cantankerous people, but he always tells them in a nonjudgmental, endearing sort of way. His anecdotes provide an emotional catharsis, encouraging tolerance and acceptance. Life is about coping. Think small. Learn to laugh, especially at yourself. Human nature can be fascinating and frustrating, but it is not sinful. There is nothing in Keillor's world as serious as the bondage to sin and death. He is all parable and no proclamation. There is no sin or salvation, only personalities, pleasing or otherwise. Sentimentality substitutes for redemption and nostalgia replaces worship. But there is something nihilistic about a philosophy of life that says the best you can do is to learn to laugh at yourself.

C. S. Lewis wrote,

> Niceness—wholesome, integrated personality—is an excellent thing. We must try by every medical, educational, economic, and political means in our power to produce a world where as many people as possible grow up "nice"; just as we must try to produce a world where we all have plenty to eat. But we must not suppose that even if we succeeded in making everyone nice we should have saved their souls. A world of nice people, content in their own niceness, looking no further, turned away from God, would be just as desperately in need of salvation as a miserable world—and even might be more difficult to save.[2]

British journalist Malcolm Muggeridge turned to Christ late in his life. Like Lewis, he concluded that we have a deep-seated problem with sin. Muggeridge wrote,

> It is precisely when you consider the best in man that you see there is in each of us a hard core of pride or self-centeredness

---

2. Lewis, *Surprised By Joy*, 181.

which corrupts our best achievements and blights our best experiences. It comes out in all sorts of ways—in jealousy which spoils our friendships, in the vanity we feel when we have done something pretty good, in the easy conversion of love into lust, in the meanness which makes us depreciate the efforts of other people, in the distortion of our judgment by our own self-interest, in our fondness for flattery and our resentment of blame, in our self-assertive profession of fine ideals which we never begin to practice.[3]

## Survival or Salvation?

In the movie *Castaway*, Tom Hanks plays Chuck Nolan, an efficiency expert for FedEx. His life consists of work and a relationship with a girlfriend. Just before he boards a FedEx flight to the South Pacific he proposes to her. He kisses her goodbye and assures her he'll be back in a week, but his plane goes down in a terrible storm and he washes up on a deserted island. He is the lone survivor and a modern-day version of Robinson Crusoe. The differences between the movie *Castaway* and Daniel Defoe's novel *Robinson Crusoe* illustrate the gap between survival and salvation and a modern scaled down view of life.

It is fitting that *Castaway* is a movie that looks at Chuck Nolan's struggle to survive, while *Robinson Crusoe* is a novel that explores the mind and soul of Crusoe. The medium itself says something about the modern person. That is not to say, that novels don't depict a modern persona, but in the case of Robinson Crusoe, the novel captures his soul better than a movie could. In *Castaway*, we watch a familiar movie star act out a part. We comment to ourselves that Hanks looks heavy in the first half of the movie and about fifty pounds lighter in the second half of the movie. We make a mental note of his bleached hair and beard. From the odd assortment of FedEx packages that wash up on shore we question the value of our materialism. We watch him try to build a fire out of rubbing sticks and extract a tooth with the tip of an ice-skate. The only real clues as to what was on his mind is his habit of looking at his girlfriend's picture and his attempts to draw her likeness on the wall of a cave. When the body of the pilot washes up on shore, Nolan digs a shallow grave and buries the body. We see him standing before the mound, but instead of prayer, he comments, "That's that." The portrayal is entirely one-dimensional. It is

3. Muggeridge, quoted in Yancey, "Sin," 33.

a tale of survival. The greatest hint that he is a relational being comes in the humor and pathos of his conversations with Wilson, conceived when Nolan's bloody hand print left a crude imprint of a face on a volleyball.

As the years drag on, Nolan contemplates suicide and becomes more like a caveman than a FedEx efficiency expert. He just barely clings to survival. Eventually, Nolan builds a raft and sails out to sea, to an almost certain death if it were not for the lucky break of being spotted by a tanker. After being gone for four years, he arrives home to find his fianceé married. He has survived, but he cannot redeem the lost years and the lost relationships. The movie closes with Nolan standing at a four corner crossroads on the Texas Panhandle as lost and directionless as he was on his deserted South Pacific island.

The contrast between *Castaway* and *Robinson Crusoe* could not be greater. In Defoe's novel, Crusoe emerges from his nearly three decades of isolation a much stronger person in the end than he was at the beginning. His isolation proved invaluable. In the providence of God, his solitary life led him to examine himself. Suffering opened his heart and mind to God. Stripped of everything worldly, he saw himself as he really was, "without desire of good or conscience of evil." He began to lament his "stupidity of soul" and his ingratitude to God. Illness led him to pray for the first time in years, "Lord be my help, for I am in great distress." He began to ask, "Why has God done this to me? What have I done to deserve this?" But his conscience checked him, "Wretch! Ask what you have done! Look back upon a dreadful misspent life and ask what you have done. Ask, why you have not been destroyed long before this!"

*Robinson Crusoe* is much more than a story about survival. It is a story about salvation. Like the prodigal son, who ran off to the far country, squandered his inheritance, but came to his senses, Crusoe became deeply convinced and convicted of his wickedness. When he earnestly sought the Lord's help in repenting of his sins, he providentially came to the words in the Bible, "God exalted him to his own right hand as Prince and Savior that he might give repentance and forgiveness of sins to Israel" (Acts 5:31). He describes his reaction, "I threw down the book, and with all my heart as well as my hands lifted up to Heaven, in a kind of ecstasy of joy, I cried out aloud, 'Jesus, Thou Son of David, Jesus, Thou exalted Prince and Savior, give me repentance!' " Instead of praying for physical deliverance he prayed for the forgiveness of his sins. Deliverance from sin was "a much greater blessing than deliverance from affliction."

He came to the sober conclusion that the salvation of his soul meant far more to him than his deliverance from captivity. "I began to conclude in my mind that it was possible for me to be more happy in this forsaken, solitary condition than it was probable I should ever have been in any other particular state in the world; and with this thought I was going to give thanks to God for bringing me to this place." Instead of a slow and fearful descent into despair, Crusoe experienced God's rhythms of grace. He read his Bible and prayed daily. He planted crops, made furniture, baked bread, built a canoe, and established an orderly, disciplined life. He lived a life of mercy, not sorrow, and his singular goal was to "make my sense of God's mercy to me."

The message of *Castaway* is that life is a struggle for survival fueled by the human spirit and the existential self. Love, particularly romantic love, can be a great motivator, but relationships are often disappointing and not enduring. Loneliness and isolation expose the myths of modern life, and in the end we are directionless. The message of *Robinson Crusoe* is that life is a struggle in our soul between self-rule and God's will, and it can only come to resolution by the grace and mercy of God. Apart from the saving grace of the Lord Jesus Christ there is no hope, but with Christ we can experience an abundant life even in affliction and suffering.

The prophet Jeremiah condemned the priests of his day for minimizing sin. He echoed the Lord's complaint: "They dress the wound of my people as though it were not serious." "'Peace, peace,' they say, when there is no peace" (Jer 6:14). We wrestle with the same temptation today. Brian Berquist describes his early experience of church this way:

> I attended a "hip" church in the Bay area. I didn't miss a Sunday. It was great entertainment. It was fun. And it was easy. There was no suggestion that being a Christian would require any effort on my part. Show up on Sunday, watch the show, and off you go. I'm sure that if I had tried, I could have found the message of the cross, the true requirements needed to follow Jesus' message, and the reality of the Christian life. But the message of the cross was never obvious. This was a "drop in" and be entertained for an hour so you can say you are "born again."
>
> I attended that church at a critical point in my life; at a time when I would be asked to make many serious decisions about life. I bear full responsibility for choosing that church, but it was the worst possible place for me. I got the message that all of life was meant to be easy and entertaining, including the center of my life, my faith. As you might guess, almost every decision I

> made was based on a fast-food, convenience store, quick-fix get-rich and above all *feel good all the time* mentality. Fifteen years ago I found myself in a non-marriage, making lots of money, addicted to alcohol, and miserable because of all those quick-fix decisions.
>
> It's wonderful that no matter what mistakes we make Jesus forgives us and is waiting for us! No matter how many wrong turns we take, God is waiting for us. I realize now how far I had drifted from the ten year old boy who accepted Jesus as his savior. I don't like the phrase "born again" because it reminds me of the fast-fix lifestyle that got me where I was. I returned to God and I began to make decisions based on what Jesus would have me do. The changes have been remarkable. The un-wife is gone, the money is gone, the alcohol is gone, and above all the misery is gone. It has been replaced by joy. Joy was something that was gone from my life; it is back.[4]

Many today find Paul's dead-in-our-sins realism too pessimistic. But the gospel we need is the one that comes to us from the Bible—the revelation of the Spirit of Christ, not the spirit of the times. In 1751 John Wesley defended his conviction that people needed to hear the gospel in the light of the commands of God. He wrote:

> I mean by preaching the gospel, preaching the love of God to sinners, preaching the life, death, resurrection, and intercession of Christ, with all the blessings which, in consequence thereof, are freely given to true believers. By preaching the law, I mean, explaining and enforcing the commands of Christ, briefly comprised in the Sermon on the Mount. I think, the right method of preaching is this: At our first beginning to preach in any place, after a general declaration of the love of God to sinners, and his willingness that they should be saved, to preach the law, in the strongest, the closest, the most searching manner possible; only intermixing the gospel here and there, and showing it, as it were, afar off.[5]

Without a true conviction of our great need, Wesley believed that we deal with sin too casually. To be convinced of one's own sin was a prerequisite for a true personal application of the gospel.

---

4. Used by permission.
5. Wesley, "Letter on Preaching Christ," 486.

*The Life of Christ*

## Living Dead

Which is more shocking, to be told you are already dead or to be told that death ends all? Randy Pausch, a 47-year-old computer-science professor at Carnegie Mellon University, died from pancreatic cancer, but not before capturing the attention of millions of Americans. While he was on palliative chemotherapy to slow the growth of the tumors and ease the pain, he lectured on his experience. Pausch, a father of three, refused to wallow in self-pity. As he told Diane Sawyer of ABC News, "I've never understood pity and self-pity as an emotion. We have a finite amount of time. Whether short or long, it doesn't matter. Life is to be lived." Even though he was dying, Pausch inspired many with his *Last Lecture on Living Life*. He made it clear up front that he was not going to talk about his wife and children, because he would get too emotional. His lecture was seasoned with a delightful sense of humor and a dry wit. "We're not going to talk about spirituality and religion," he promised. "Although I will tell you that I have experienced a deathbed conversion. I just bought a Macintosh, and I knew I'd get 9 percent of the audience with that." He summed up his philosophy of life: "We can't change the cards we are dealt, we have to play our hand."

"I'm not afraid of death," he declared winsomely, but he admitted to being worried about the process of dying. "I think it will be a real challenge to see if I can squeeze the lemons hard enough to still get lemonade the last few weeks." "Life," he claimed, "is about fulfilling your childhood dreams." Randy's dreams included experiencing zero gravity, playing in the NFL, and working for Disney. His quest led him to some important lessons which he sought to pass along to his children: never lose your childlike wonder; learn to have fun ("I'm dying and I'm having fun"); help other people fulfill their dreams; apologize when you screw up; focus on the good in others, because everyone has a good side; work hard; live your life the right way and karma will take care of itself; and be prepared: preparation is where luck meets opportunity.

Randy Pausch's courage in the face of death, coupled with his extraordinary personality and his charming ability to communicate, makes his *Last Lecture* exceptional in many ways. But sadly, his expertise in computerized virtual reality has carried over into the real world. He lived in a virtual reality of his own making. Having scaled everything down to the temporal, finite order, he persuaded himself to live in denial of God. Herein lies the irony. The very man who ruled out self-pity and flashed his brave smile in the face of death is the man who lives in despair and doesn't know it. He has pretended to make life liveable by denying the *meaning* of life and death.

When I was eighteen and in my last year of high school I went for a routine physical. I needed the doctor to sign off on a medical form included in my college application. I felt great, that is until the doctor found a small lump. One minute he was cracking jokes and the next minute he was on the phone scheduling an appointment for me to see a specialist. Two days later I had surgery. I was diagnosed with cancer and I faced more surgery. What has always impressed me is how well I felt with a deadly disease moving through my body. I was seriously sick without knowing it. That is how it is with our souls. We are dead in our sins and seriously clueless to our true state.

The Danish Christian philosopher Søren Kierkegaard described this paradoxical form of despair in his 1849 work *The Sickness Unto Death*:

> . . . One form of despair is precisely this of not being in despair, that is, not being aware of it. . . . Feeling happy does not necessarily mean that you are not in despair, any more than feeling good, means that you are healthy. . . . In the hidden recesses of happiness, there dwells also the anxious dread which is despair; it would be only too glad to be allowed to remain therein, for the dearest and most attractive dwelling-place of despair is in the very heart of immediate happiness.[6]

Paul condenses in three verses what he took three chapters in Romans to explain. He insists that we have to face the fact that we are not good people who need a little assistance and affirmation. "As for you, you were dead in your transgressions and sins . . ." Mottoes like, "be all you can be," and "living up to your potential" gloss over the desperate depravity of the human condition. Even "good people" are bad. We have violated and transgressed God's boundaries. We have sinned. We have fallen hopelessly below God's standard of goodness and rightness. "All have sinned and fallen short of the glory of God" (Rom 3:23).

The NIV translates "nature" for the Greek word "flesh," because Paul's point was that our whole being is given over to sin. The "highest intellectual and devout religious performances" can be included under "flesh."[7] Paul elaborated on this truth in his letter to the church at Philippi, when he said, "If others think they have reasons to put confidence in the flesh, I have more." He proceeded to tick off all those things that would impress

---

6. Kierkegaard, *The Sickness Unto Death*, 156–59.
7. Barth, *Ephesians*, 230.

any high-minded religious Jew—his circumcision, family heritage, Torah perfectionism, and religious zeal—but the conclusion he reached was shocking: "I consider them *garbage*, that I may gain Christ and be found in him, not having a righteousness of my own that comes from the law, but that which is through faith in Christ—the righteousness that comes from God on the basis of faith" (Phil 3:7-9).

If we think cancer is insidious, sin is all the more. If we think AIDS is awful, sin is worse. Paul's description underscores the pervasive, persistent and pernicious character of sin. When we were dead in our transgressions and sins, we "followed the ways of this world and of the ruler of the kingdom of the air, the spirit who is now at work in those who are disobedient" (Eph 2:2). Paul makes a case for the complexity of evil. Sin is a way of life as big as the world and as pervasive as the air that we breathe. The devil is described as the ruler of the kingdom of the air, suggesting that the immediate inspiration for evil is as close and as penetrating as the air that we breathe. Like a cloud of pollution hanging over the city, the kingdom of the air reigns over its followers. His spirit "is now at work in those who are disobedient." Evil's immediacy is like working in an office with thick second-hand smoke or living around radioactive material. Danger pervades the atmosphere.

## Demonic Rule

In other cultures, there is a profound sense of the devil and the demonic inhabiting space, creating fear among those who sense the demonic presence. Yet the devil's inability to incarnate itself into the physical world may be cause for constant provocation. The demonic is limited to insinuation and is denied incarnation. The devil can infiltrate but the devil cannot embody. The "Word was made flesh" but the devil remains disincarnate, incapable of assuming what he did not create. To preside over the "kingdom of the air" underscores this limitation and is indicative of the ethereal nature of the devil's being and work. Evil is the negative unreality of God's created good. The metaphor has nothing to do with breathing in fresh air. It signifies the pervasiveness of evil. This metaphor, "kingdom of the air," is even suggestive of the pervasiveness of the accessibility of evil over the airways. On the Internet, I am only a few clicks away from the raunchiest pornography or the vilest hate speech. Lust is in the air, but the choice to click my way into pornography still remains my responsibility.

The insidious nature of evil is described by Kathryn Stockett in her novel *The Help*. In the racially segregated deep South, white women punished a black maid that crossed them in a manner altogether different from how a man would do it. They would never beat them with a stick. No. White women kept their hands clean. The weapons of punishment were like the tools laid out on the dentist tray. They inflicted pain in a subtle, manipulative way. After they fired the maid, they would make it impossible for the maid to work for any white woman in the town. Then, they would go after the maid's home and husband. An eviction notice would arrive in the mail, the car would be repossessed, and the husband would be laid off from work. The white woman worked behind the scenes, using her friends to destroy her enemy.[8]

The complexity of evil helps explain the diabolical nature of our addictions and perversions. Theologian Richard Mouw observes, "Sin is not necessarily sustained at every point by individual decision. That is clear from Romans one that we rebel against God and suppress the truth in unrighteousness, and that we are then 'given over' to it—given over to evil thoughts, to the worship of false gods, to our lusts and our sinful desires." We are responsible for our decisions and choices, but the will to choose is often conditioned by biological and psychological factors that seem to render us powerless to choose the good.

Richard Mouw uses alcoholism as one example. The decision to drink can be conditioned on at least three levels. "It can be a chemical dependency, a physical thirst in the body crying out for that stuff. But it's also a psychological addiction that has to do with compulsive behaviors and rescuing patterns. Third, it's a spiritual addiction. It's idolatry." Mouw continues, "We have also been insensitive to the ways in which one person's bondage can be passed on to another person without their necessarily having control over it. There are babies who come into the world screaming for heroin because of what their mothers did. There is a more complicated way in which tendencies to certain addictions—including certain sexual misbehaviors—seem to run in families."[9]

On the subject of the devil the Bible gives us enough information to be on guard, but not enough to indulge our curiosity. Markus Barth observes, "Though [the devil] is often mentioned in the Bible, it is impossible to derive an ontology, phenomenology, and history of Satan sufficiently complete to create a 'satanology' which in the slightest measure

---

8. Stockett, *The Help*, 188.
9. Mouw, "The Life of Bondage in the Light of Grace," 41–42.

corresponds to the weight of biblical 'theo-logy.'"[10] We were meant to be aware of the devil and the power of evil, but never engrossed in the subject. For example, no one need be a student of pornography to be on guard against pornography. To dwell on pornography would be to become its victim. Likewise with the devil, demonic power is real, but should not be fixated on. C. S. Lewis strikes the balance between insight and scorn in *The Screwtape Letters*, his literary expose of covert demonic temptation. Lewis quoted Martin Luther's line and then followed it: "The best way to drive out the devil, if he will not yield to the text of Scripture, is to jeer and flout him, for he cannot bear scorn."[11] The spirit of the antichrist pervades the world but as John reminds us, "Greater is he that is in you than he that is in the world" (1 John 4:4).

Paul began by focusing on the reader, "As for you," but now he includes himself and "all of us." At one time we were all immersed in this spiritual world of sin, "gratifying the cravings of our sinful nature and following its desires and thoughts" (2:3). The first time C. S. Lewis examined his life with "a seriously practical purpose" he discovered what appalled him: "a zoo of lusts, a bedlam of ambitions, a nursery of fears, a harem of fondled hatreds. My name was legion."[12]

The movie *Good Will Hunting* is a story about a young man named Will who experienced a terribly abusive childhood. In a climactic scene, Will comes to see that his fear of love and his expectation of abandonment are the painful result of the horrible treatment he received from his father. After months of therapy sessions, this break-through moment begins when his counselor says to him, "It's not your fault." At first the young man acts as though he didn't hear him. The counselor repeats, "It's not your fault." He ignores it. The counselor moves closer to him and repeats, "It's not your fault." Will laughs nervously and tries to change the subject. The therapist moves closer and repeats, "It's not your fault." Tears well up in his eyes and he begins to grow angry. "Don't mess with me, man," he says. But his counselor moves even closer. They stand together eye-to-eye. "It's not your fault." Will begins to sob as he embraces his counselor. It is a wonderful, powerful scene, a tremendous model of effective, caring therapy.

I imagine that most moviegoers identify with Will. They do not see themselves as a counselor exposing evil, but as a victim in need of care. The pop psychology saying of the 1980s, "I'm OK, You're OK," sounds

---

10. Barth, *Ephesians*, 228.
11. Lewis, *The Screwtape Letters*, vii.
12. Lewis, *Surprised by Joy*, 181.

trite today. "It's not your fault" implies at least that it is somebody's fault. It admits that evil exists and damages lives. But even if there are fears and impulses in our lives that we are not responsible for, we need ultimately to hear something more than "It's not your fault." We need more than affirmation. We need deliverance. We need more than a perspective on the evil all around us; we need forgiveness for the evil within us.

Instead of saying, "It's not your fault," Paul would say, "We all have sinned and fallen short of the glory of God" (Rom 3:23). As much as we might resist the idea, we are by nature deserving of wrath. This is offensive to some and confirms their worst fears of "fire and brimstone" old-time religion. C. S. Lewis observed:

> Speak about beauty, truth and goodness, or about a God who is simply the indwelling principle of these things, speak about a great spiritual force pervading all things, a common mind of which we are all parts, a pool of generalized spirituality to which we can all flow, and you will command friendly interest. But the temperature drops as soon as you mention a God who has purposes and performs particular actions, who does one thing and not another, a concrete, choosing, commanding, prohibiting God with a determinate character. People become embarrassed or angry. Such a conception seems to them primitive and crude and irreverent.[13]

But to argue that the wrath of God is obsolete would be to argue against the teaching of the Bible, the nature of God, and even the moral sensibilities of what it means to be human. Yale theologian Miroslav Volf asks us to imagine giving a lecture in a war zone to people "whose cities and villages have been first plundered, then burned and leveled to the ground, whose daughters and sisters have been raped, whose fathers and brothers have had their throats slit." The subject is "a Christian attitude toward violence" and the thesis is that "the practice of nonviolence requires a belief in divine vengeance." Volf, himself a Croatian who lived and taught in Croatia during the war in former Yugoslavia, argues that non-retaliation and the possibility of reconciliation is grounded in the reality of God's judgment. If there is no divine accountability for sin and evil, it is impossible to live out the gospel of Christ. To deny the wrath of God often means that one has not experienced the horrors of war and the tragedy of evil.[14]

---

13. Lewis, *Miracles*, 83–84.
14. Volf, *Exclusion and Embrace*, 304.

Let's be clear on the meaning of wrath. Wrath does not mean "the intemperate outburst of an uncontrolled character. It is rather the temperature of God's love, the manifestation of his will and power to resist, to overcome, to burn away all that contradicts his counsels of love."[15] The wrath of God is not an embarrassment but a blessing.

I remember one time in particular when I provoked the wrath of my father. I had convinced my younger brother that it would be fun to set our car models on fire by pouring gasoline over them. The smell of burnt plastic must have traveled farther than we thought, because my father came out to the garage to check on the odor. He caught us in the act; uncapped gasoline can and matches in hand. He exploded in anger. He never touched me, but I felt his wrath. At first I wondered why he was making such a big deal about it, but that only made my father angrier. I pictured a little mischief, some harmless fun. He pictured my brother and me in a burn treatment ward. Before the afternoon was over I had gotten the picture; now I can't look at a red gasoline can without thinking of that incident and my father's wrath.

The wrath of God means that there are consequences for evil. There is real accountability and judgment. Eliminate the wrath of God and you eliminate the need for the gospel. The wrath of God provokes the necessity for the gospel. This is why C. S. Lewis said, "The hardness of God is kinder than the softness of men, and His compulsion is our liberation."[16]

## But God! Saved by Grace!

Having described the unimaginable gulf between the risen Christ and a depraved humanity, Paul quickly turns to the powerful, positive message of the gospel. His emphasis on God is emphatic: "But because of his great love for us, God, who is rich in mercy, made us alive with Christ even when we were dead in transgressions" (2:4–5). In the first three verses, we are the subject of sin and depravity, but in the next six verses God is the subject of love and salvation. The stark contrast between sin and salvation was intended by Paul to heighten our appreciation for the necessity and reality of God's grace. The intervention of God's grace is "set in contrast to the bankruptcy and doom of a humanity left to itself, left to what it is 'by nature.'"[17]

15. Barth, *Ephesians*, 231–32.
16. Lewis, *Surprised By Joy*, 183.
17. Lincoln, *Ephesians*, 104.

## The Christ Letter

What is missing in Paul's discussion is any reference to procedure or method or formula for accepting this great love of God in Christ. There is no step-by-step process for acquiring this relationship. Paul applied no pressure here to make a decision. We are not advised to do anything. Our action is implied, and even then it is passive. Repentance for sin is assumed. Belief in the power of God's redemption is accepted. Only God's action is stated. All attention is given "to the special nature of God's saving action as one of gratuitous generosity to an undeserving sinful humanity."[18] Our role is passive. We are receptive to the gift. Grace and mercy are not something we can earn or engineer. No matter what the story of our acceptance of God's grace may be it was never meant to eclipse the wonder of God's grace. All grounds for boasting are removed. We hear echoes of Jeremiah 9:23–24: "Let not the wise boast of their wisdom or the strong boast of their strength or the rich boast of their riches, but let those who boast boast about this: that they understand and know me, that I am the Lord, who exercises kindness, justice and righteousness on earth and in these I delight." In contrast to the vocabulary of death and depravity (*transgressions, sins, ruler of the kingdom of the air, disobedience, the cravings of our sinful nature*, and *wrath*), Paul stacks up the words of the gospel: *mercy, love, grace, kindness*, and *gift*. Each word underscores the undeserved nature of this gift.

In a consumer society, it is not surprising that the free gift of salvation is misconstrued as another commercial product. On a recent Easter Sunday, a Texas megachurch offered two million dollars worth of prizes, including cars, flat-screen televisions, club memberships, and furniture sets, to attract the unchurched and build excitement. The pastor explained, "We hope to show people that while it is exciting to receive free stuff here on Earth, the greatest free gift of all time is something we haven't yet seen, but can enjoy for all eternity. The entire giveaway leads to the Grand Prize available to all, salvation through Christ, if simply received . . . with no strings attached (Eph 2:8–9)." His defense against critics was that if only one person comes to Christ it was worth the two million dollars worth of door prizes. "They're coming for the loot and they're going to leave with Jesus." But by equating the free gift of salvation to the Grand Prize, this particular church has desecrated the costly grace of Jesus Christ. One imagines that they have done this unwittingly, but selling Jesus in any form to religious consumers ruins the impact of the gospel. By their cheap materialistic gimmicks they have trivialized the gospel. Is this any different

---

18. Lincoln, *Ephesians*, 103.

## The Life of Christ

than the church's sale of indulgences in the sixteenth century that led Martin Luther to call for reformation? Only now, instead of selling indulgences to get out of purgatory, we bribe people to accept Jesus. Sacrilege robs God of what belongs to him: true repentance and confession, deep conviction and understanding, costly discipleship and life-transformation.

The chasm between us and the risen Christ has been bridged. Beyond all expectation and merit, we have been raised up, not only from death and from the hellish depths of depravity, but we have been raised up with Christ to be seated with him in the heavenly realms. Grace—God's unmerited favor—is responsible, not only for our forgiveness and freedom from guilt, but for our fulfillment and freedom for good works. Our status is beyond all imagining: we are seated with Christ in the heavenly realms. "The history of God's victory over the devil is narrated with the help of a surprising *chronology*. Not only death, which seems to be the future of every living person, but also resurrection are described as events already accomplished."[19]

What does Paul mean by this seemingly exaggerated portrait of salvation? First, like the prophets, Paul was so impressed by the certainty of our resurrection in Christ that he could speak of it as a present experience. Second, our enthronement with Christ can be embraced and realized, before it is literally actualized. Third, the imagery of being seated with Christ is a metaphor that signifies our status as a "chosen people, a royal priesthood, a holy nation, God's special possession" (1 Peter 2:9). We are not only saved from death but set up for life!

The purpose of this grace and mercy is not for *individual* glorification. God raises us up and seats us in the heavenly realms, "in order that in the coming ages he might show the incomparable riches of his grace, expressed in his kindness to us in Christ Jesus." Markus Barth writes, "It is the nature of the church to exist not for its own sake, but to reflect God's glory (5:27). Her very life is God's glorification (1:6, 12, 14; 3:20–21). No one is reached by God and converted for his own benefit only."[20] This truth ought to eliminate pride and motivate good works.

> Nothing in my hand I bring, simply to thy cross I cling; naked, come to thee for dress, helpless look to thee for grace. (*Rock of Ages*, Augustus Toplady)

---

19. Barth, *Ephesians*, 252.
20. Ibid., 241.

## God's Workmanship

We are God's work of art, his masterpiece, created in Christ Jesus, to do good works. We are saved by faith alone, but saving faith is never alone. In the words of the Reformers, "Faith alone justifies, but not the faith that is alone." [21] Luther said it well: "True faith will no more fail to produce good works than the sun can cease to give light." Early American theologian Jonathan Edwards wrote, "We are not saved on account of our works and yet we are not saved without works." The danger implied in Paul's statement on faith and works is not that the saints are relying on their own good works for salvation but "that their lives are being conformed to the surrounding mores and are not holy enough."[22] Paul's concern relates to the question raised by James, when he said, "What good is it to have faith without deeds?" He proceeded to answer it three times, like a refrain:

> "Faith by itself, if it is not accompanied by action, is dead" (James 2:17).
>
> "Faith without deeds is useless" (2:20).
>
> "As a body without the spirit is dead, so faith without deeds is dead" (2:26).

Dietrich Bonhoeffer insisted that the great truth of justification by faith must not be turned into a justification for cheap grace. He wrote: "Cheap grace is the grace we bestow on ourselves. Cheap grace is the preaching of forgiveness without requiring repentance, baptism without church discipline, Communion without confession, absolution without personal confession. Cheap grace is grace without discipleship, grace without the cross, grace without Jesus Christ, living and incarnate."[23]

Salvation by grace through faith destroys boasting but produces the fruit of salvation. The gift of salvation leads to the fruit of the Spirit. It is not that faith is rooted in grace and works are rooted in effort. Both faith and works find their source in God's grace. The action of God is complete. God "made us alive in Christ," "raised us up with Christ," and "created [us] in Christ Jesus to do good works." This is why Paul said that these good works have been prepared in advance for us to do. "So good works are

---

21. Bloesch, *Essentials of Evangelical Theology*, 232.
22. Lincoln, *Ephesians*, 113.
23. Bonhoeffer, *Cost of Discipleship*, 55, 47–48.

## The Life of Christ

not the source but the goal of the new relationship between humanity and God. Salvation is not *by works* but *for works*."[24]

To recap what Paul has said about salvation:

1. There is no formula for acceptance; no step by step process or pat procedure for becoming saved. All the emphasis falls on what God in his mercy has done for us. We are simply receptive to his free gift of salvation.

2. There is no hierarchy of saints. There are no mediocre saints and there are no elite saints. All the saints have been raised up and seated with Christ in the heavenly realms. There is no status or stature for which to aspire. In Christ we have been promoted to the highest rank already.

3. There is no separation between faith and works. We are not saved by works righteousness; we are saved for the work of righteousness.

These three negatives add up to one very powerful, positive view of salvation.

Preaching the Christ Letter means preaching salvation by faith alone and the social gospel. Salvation is both personal and social, involving deep changes in our thinking and feeling as well as practical changes in our relationships and social commitments. The gospel of the new humanity is as social as it is personal. We preach justification and justice, peace with God and the peace of God. This is the peace of Christ that turns away the wrath of God and overcomes racial, social, class, and tribal hostilities.

The context for this preaching is important and not arbitrary. The church is the place where this personal transformation and social justice finds its true home. Both the Christ-focused message and the Christ-focused community are essential for the personal and social impact of the gospel. We were meant to grow in the grace and knowledge of our Lord and Savior Jesus Christ, in the fullness of all that this means, in the household of faith. Paul was intent on a whole new humanity relearning how to live life, and the place where this personal and social transformation was to take place is in the church. In Christ, we become a new society where sin's propensity and perversity are dealt with; where insecurities and guilt feelings are healed; where pride and prejudice are exposed; where the rich learn to sacrifice their wealth and the poor learn the dignity of their work;

---

24. Lincoln, *Ephesians*, 114.

where racial reconciliation and mutual respect and support find their true home.

## The Preaching Paradigm

Paul's preaching pattern offers a powerful model for us to emulate. There is an organic flow to his preaching that moves from worship to salvation to mission to church. He has all the reason and logic of a systematic theology without compartmentalizing these crucial truths into lifeless abstractions. The order and integration of these truths is essential to the gospel. Paul weaves together this full-orbed theology of Christ in an integrated sequence that by the power of God's grace we can embrace holistically. Paul's spiraling theological vision expresses the biblical vision for each and every household of faith. What is said here was never limited to the church of Ephesus but was meant for the Church universal. When churches hunger for vision, let them turn to Paul's Christ Letter and hear the preaching that was meant for them.

| *Worship* → | *Salvation* → | *Mission* → |
|---|---|---|
| eulogizing praise and eucharistic prayer | personal and social transformation | the global reach of the manifold wisdom of God |

| *Church* → | *Society* → | *Family* → | *Employment* |
|---|---|---|---|
| living worthy of the calling in the body of Christ | living for Christ in culture | mutual submission and love in Christ | serving others as unto the Lord |

# 4

# The Peace of Christ

*"For he himself is our peace, who has made the two one and has destroyed the barrier, the dividing wall of hostility . . ."*

EPHESIANS 2:14

The most profound relational reconciliation and sociological realignment ever imagined takes place in Christ. From the depths of human depravity we are raised up in Christ to the heights of salvation, and from the hostility of human enmity we are delivered by the peace of Christ into the household of God. In Christ, the unbridgeable chasm between God and humankind is bridged and the irreconcilable differences between us are reconciled in Christ.

Chapter two divides into two sections and each section begins with a remembrance of what life was like apart from Christ. The first section begins, "As for you, you were dead in your transgressions and sins, in which you used to live . . ." (2:1–10). The second section begins, ". . . Remember that formerly you who are Gentiles . . . were separate from Christ, excluded from citizenship in Israel and foreigners to the covenants of the promise, without hope and without God in the world" (2:11–22).

Each section has a redemptive turning point: "*But* because of his great love for us, God who is rich in mercy, made us alive with Christ even when we were dead in transgressions" (2:4). "*But* now in Christ Jesus you who once were far away have been brought near by the blood of Christ" (2:13). We not only have been brought back from spiritual death but we have been formed into a spiritual community. Eternal reconciliation with the Father and social reconciliation between all races and classes is accomplished through "the blood of Christ."

Finally, each section concludes with a picture of who we are in Christ: "For we are God's workmanship, created in Christ Jesus to do good works, which God prepared in advance for us to do" (2:10). And we are "members of [God's] household," "a holy temple in the Lord," and "a dwelling in which God lives by his Spirit" (2:19–22). We are a new creation and a new society in Christ.

The symmetry and symphony of truth expressed here was designed to encourage confidence and build strength. Having contrasted the risen, exalted Christ with the depravity of our human condition, Paul moves on to contrast the hostility of the human community with the unity of the household of God. The chasm between God and sinful humanity can only be bridged by the saving grace of Jesus Christ. And the barriers of hostility between people can only be broken down by the cross of Jesus Christ. The peace of Christ embraces the vertical dimension between God and humanity (highlighted in the twofold reference to the heavenly realms) and the horizontal dimension between people (signified by the reference to being "far off" but now "brought near").

Sometimes it is wise to reflect on what we were, in order to know who we are, and how far we've come. *Or how far we should have come.* We remember the past, not to live in the past, but to be fully alive in the present and to anticipate the future. There is a difference between being *haunted by the past* and being *liberated from the past*. Paul saw it as a healthy exercise to remember our sinfulness before God and our alienation from one another so that we would appreciate all the more the amazing grace of the Lord Jesus Christ. "I once was lost, but now am found, was blind, but now I see."

Many Christians concentrate their attention on the first half of this chapter. We stress the importance of personal salvation. Many of us have memorized Ephesians 2:8–10, because it is such a beautiful summary of the gospel. But the second half of this chapter is equally important. We should be as quick to commit the following words to memory: "His purpose was to create in himself one new humanity out of the two, thus making peace and in one body to reconcile both of them to God through the cross, by which he put to death their hostility" (2:15–16). The social, racial, economic, and global implications of the gospel of peace are absolutely crucial to living for Christ. We cannot allow reaction to the early

## The Peace of Christ

twentieth-century social gospel movement or the late twentieth-century liberation theology movement to distance ourselves from the true personal and social impact of the gospel. Paul was not just talking about Jews and Gentiles in this letter. He was preaching the gospel against the dividing wall of hostility that exists on so many levels.

(2:11–18) *"Therefore, remember that formerly you who are Gentiles by birth and called 'uncircumcised' by those who call themselves 'the circumcision' (which is done in the body by human hands)—remember that at that time you were separate from Christ, excluded from citizenship in Israel and foreigners to the covenants of the promise without hope and without God in the world.*

*But now in Christ Jesus you who once were far away have been brought near by the blood of Christ. For he himself is our peace, who has made the two one and has destroyed the barrier, the dividing wall of hostility, by setting aside in his flesh the law with its commands and regulations. His purpose was to create in himself one new humanity out of the two, thus making peace and in one body to reconcile both of them to God through the cross, by which he put to death their hostility. He came and preached peace to you who were far away and peace to those who are near. For through him we both have access to the Father by one Spirit."*

## The Dividing Wall of Hostility

We have in this passage a foundation for all social and racial reconciliation in the church. Whatever separates us from one another must be overcome in Christ. The most profound social alienation known to Paul was the hostility between Jews and Gentiles. In an effort to preserve the purity and integrity of their heritage, the Jews built a moral and spiritual barrier between themselves and the rest of humanity. Nowhere was this moral, spiritual, ceremonial, and racial wall more evident than in the literal stone wall that surrounded the temple in Jerusalem. The outer court of the Gentiles surrounded the temple and excluded Gentiles from entering the temple. The Jewish historian Josephus in his *Wars of the Jews* indicates that there were signs posted on pillars in Greek and Latin warning foreigners not to enter. Archeologists have discovered two of these signs, one of which is on display in a museum in Istanbul and reads, "No foreigner may enter within the barrier and enclosure around the temple. Anyone who is caught doing so will have himself to blame for his ensuing death."[1]

Undoubtedly Paul grew up with powerful feelings of contempt for Gentiles. They inspired his racial pride and fueled his hatred against foreigners. Paul's pre-conversion Pharisaical contempt for Gentiles may be likened in some ways to today's Islamic extremism. Although I would like to say that his commitment to the Old Testament law prevented him from waging war against Gentiles, in all likelihood Paul approved of militant action against Gentiles on the basis of the law. His zeal for the law (Gal 1:14) legitimized hatred against those he considered apostate.[2] To use a politically loaded term, but one nevertheless accurate, Paul's attack against the church was in his mind a holy jihad against Jewish Christians and Gentile believers. Undoubtedly he believed that he was gaining God's approval and commendation by killing Christians.

## Paul's Experience

After his conversion Paul became a victim of Jewish hostility against Gentiles. He almost lost his life because of his effort to bring the gospel to the Gentiles. If Paul had gone about quietly believing in Jesus as the Messiah, he would hardly have raised a stir, but because he insisted on bringing the gospel of the Jewish Messiah to the Gentiles he was a wanted man. This is the single most important reason for the extreme Jewish antagonism against Paul. If Paul had been content to lead a splinter group of nonconformist Jews who believed in Jesus, he might have been ignored. This is true for ourselves as well. If we contain the gospel within the confines of our own culture and limit the gospel to our own group we acquiesce to the dividing wall of hostility. Christianity as its own little cultural subgroup is rarely a problem. But when the gospel crosses cultural barriers and divisions of hostility and calls for the conversion of Jews and Arabs, Asians and Latins, whites and blacks, then it stirs up the world's antagonism. For Paul to declare, "There is neither Jew nor Gentile, neither slave nor free, neither male nor female, for you are all one in Christ Jesus," was explosive truth, not only in his day but in our own (Gal 3:28).

Several years before Paul wrote Ephesians, he returned to Jerusalem with a delegation of Gentile converts. Even though Paul bent over backwards to respect Jewish purification laws, the very fact that he was

1. Stott, *God's New Society: The Message of Ephesians*, 92.
2. Longenecker, *Galatians*, 29.

seen with Trophimus the Ephesian in the city caused an uproar. Jews from Asia Minor stirred up the crowd, saying, "People of Israel, help us! This is the man who teaches everyone everywhere against our people and our law and this place. And besides, he has brought Greeks into the temple and defiled this holy place" (Acts 21:28). Even though Paul had not taken Trophimus into the temple, the fact that they had been seen together was enough to incite the crowd. Paul was dragged from the temple and beaten. If the Roman soldiers had not arrived when they did, he would have been killed.

## The Uncircumcised

One spiteful word, spit out by Jews, summed up the Gentiles. They were *uncircumcised*. This mocking nickname for the non-Jew was used by Jews who referred to themselves as being of *the circumcision*. *Uncircumcision* had the force of a shameful swear word. It was a racial slur. This one derogatory word stood for all the hostility that existed between Jews and non-Jews. *Uncircumcised* meant that Gentiles were excluded from all status and fellowship among the people of God.

Paul weighed into this terribly divisive issue by saying that the only difference between Jew and Gentile is skin deep. Circumcision "is done in the body by human hands." Salvation by grace through faith removed all grounds for boasting. Paul recalled the words of the prophet Jeremiah, "let those who boast boast about this: that they understand and know me" (9:24). But more was on Paul's mind from this Jeremiah text than the issue of boasting. For the prophet continued,

> "The days are coming," declares the Lord, "when I will punish all who are circumcised only in the flesh... For all these nations are really uncircumcised, and even the whole house of Israel is uncircumcised in heart." (Jeremiah 9:25–26)

The implications of circumcision and the heritage that accompanied the ritual go well beyond ethnic and cultural differences. The absence of circumcision represented a fundamental strangeness to the benefits of salvation history. The Gentile—the *uncircumcised*, was ostracized as an outsider, excluded from citizenship, ignorant of the promises, and without hope and without God in the world. Paul managed in two verses to cover the emotive and the practical dimensions of this divide. By calling the Gentiles *uncircumcised*, Paul was alluding to the deep animosity between

Jews and Gentiles. But at the same time he acknowledged the very real benefits belonging to the Jews that the Gentiles missed out on. They were "foreigners" to "the covenants of promise, without hope and without God in the world." The wall of hostility has many angles from Jewish arrogance to Gentile ignorance and from a deceptive status to a deprived status.

In the first section (2:1–3), the apostle compressed his message on depravity to three verses. In Romans, he elaborated on sin and depravity for three chapters. In this second section (2:11–12), Paul described the Jewish/Gentile divide in two verses. In Romans, he worked on the Jewish/Gentile issue for three chapters. On both subjects, humanity's depravity and the dividing wall of racial hostility, the message in Romans and Ephesians is the same, but in Ephesians the truth is compressed, allowing the flow of Paul's manifesto on the power of the gospel to build momentum.

## But in Christ!

The redemptive turning point can't come fast enough for Paul. He was eager to get to the good news. "But now in Christ Jesus you who once were far away have been brought near by the blood of Christ." The sole source of reconciliation and peace is Jesus Christ. Alienation can only be overcome in and through him, by his blood, in his flesh and in his body. Nothing else will bring down the dividing wall of hostility but Jesus Christ. The implications of this single truth are radical. In Paul's mind the Jewish/Gentile divide is a prototype of all divisions caused by race, religion, tradition, class, nation, or culture.[3] Only in Christ are these divisions overcome. For all the animosity and hate, estrangement and alienation, discord and division, divorce and brokenness in this world, there is only one saving solution, Jesus Christ. Peace cannot be achieved through education, health care, democracy, or economics. Neither can it be achieved through military action, dictatorial control, iron-fisted leadership, or genocide.

Andrew Sullivan has a brilliant mind. Educated at Oxford and Harvard, former editor of *The New Republic*, writer for *The New York Times*, and popular gay intellectual, Sullivan has articulated a position that many in our culture find compelling. He argues that there are two alternatives, either religious fundamentalism or spiritual humility. "The resurgence of religious certainty," observes Sullivan, "has deepened our cultural divisions. And so our political discourse gets more polarized, and our global

---

3. Lincoln, *Ephesians*, 161.

discourse gets close to impossible."⁴ Religious zealotry has fostered extremism and fanaticism.

The apostle Paul would not debate Sullivan's description of the walls of hostility and I think he would agree with Sullivan's description of "the secular-fundamentalist death spiral" and the arrogance of political and religious extremism. But I'm certain the apostle Paul would reject Sullivan's proposed solution. According to Sullivan the way out of the crisis is "sincere religious doubt." Confidence and certainty need to be replaced by humility and doubt. For Sullivan our only hope is in "moderate Muslims, tolerant Jews and humble Christians." His solution is to lower the walls of hostility, tone down the rhetoric, cut out the zealotry, and scale back the certainty. Read the Koran and the Bible as moral fables; look to Mohammed and Jesus as spiritual guides. Take what appeals to individual conscience and leave the rest behind. Embrace doubt. Admit that no one knows God's truth. Distance yourself from truth claims. Doubt and faith are the flip side of the same coin. "We do not know. Which is why we believe."⁵

Sullivan is right about needing humility, but the humility we need is the kind that acknowledges God's authority and submits to God's will. G. K. Chesterton said it well: "What we suffer from today, is humility in the wrong place. A man was meant to be doubtful about himself, but undoubting about the truth; this has been exactly reversed. Nowadays the part of a man that a man does assert is exactly the part he ought not to assert—himself. The part he doubts is exactly the part he ought not to doubt—the Divine Reason."⁶

Paul was not interested in lowering the walls, because he believed that in Christ the walls were destroyed. Obliterated. Peace is not a product of lower expectations, softened convictions, and a friendlier rhetoric. The truth of the matter is that even if we had the will to lower the walls of hostility we can't. We simply don't have the capacity and the power—only Christ does. The history of humanity stands as sufficient proof that systemic depravity and alienation forces us apart, polarizes the races and persists in setting up class divisions.

Christ alone is our peace. Peace is not an idea or a policy or a program. Peace is in the person of Christ. "For he himself is our peace, who has made the two one and has destroyed the barrier, the dividing wall

---

4. Sullivan, "When Not Seeing Is Believing," 59.
5. Ibid., 60.
6. Chesterton, *Orthodoxy*, 31.

of hostility." Paul begins with our depravity—the distance between sinful humanity and the Holy God, and moves on to the dividing walls of hostility—the alienation between people caused by a host of factors (racism, sexism, consumerism, nationalism, tribalism, and selfism). The span of perversity from personal sin to international conflicts is great, but at each and every point along the span there is only one hope, Christ.

The specific means in and through Christ for overcoming alienation is the atoning sacrifice of Christ on the cross. The blood of Christ overcomes the distance between God and man, and the hostility between people. In his flesh, Christ sets aside the law with its commands and regulations and breaks down the wall between races and traditions and religions. The cross of Christ destroys any sense of moral merit or ethnic privilege or pride of race or outward show of purity. In Christ himself, one new humanity out of two was created. Reconciliation between God and man was achieved through the cross of Christ and hostility was put to death. Because of Christ and his cross there is no basis for any person, group, race, tribe, nation, or nations to feel superior. If depravity is overcome, no one can boast. If alienation is overcome, no one can boast. We have no grounds for feeling morally superior to others.

This one new humanity in Christ is not part Jewish and part Gentile, nor is it part black and part white. This new race is an act of creation, not a mixture of Asian and Arab, Latin and European. Christ's purpose was "to create in himself one new humanity out of the two." "This distinguishes it from sheer transformation or improvement, or from unification of diverse elements by revealing or adding a common feature."[7] The third race is a resurrection of dead people (2:1, 6), who were formerly Jews and Gentiles, who have now been created to be one new person at the cross of Christ. True unity and social harmony depends upon the cross, for it is only at the cross that all of our hostility and animosity can be put to death.

Racial pride and prejudice are deeply rooted sins that, if not overcome, endanger our life in Christ. Racism in any form is absolutely incompatible with this single new person created in Christ Jesus.

Gene Paisley, a Canadian farmer, is one of the most sincere Christian men you will ever meet. But when his only daughter, Brenda, fell in love with David Mensah, a black African from Ghana, he was upset and bewildered. Gene had first met David, a Bible college student, when David spoke in Gene's small country church. He was moved by David's genuineness and their friendship began to grow. He invited David to work on his

---

7. Barth, *Ephesians*, 308.

farm one summer. They learned they had a lot in common. They loved Christ and they loved the land. It was a beautiful thing to see: a lean, wiry, very black African who had competed internationally in track, working alongside a big, hearty, ruddy-faced Canadian dairy farmer. They talked a lot about crops, cows, and the Great Commission. Gene was profoundly impressed with David's spiritual maturity and his ability to share Christ with others. But he also noticed that his daughter, Brenda, and David were growing closer and closer as friends.

It was the last thing in the world that either David or Brenda had expected, but their friendship, over time, grew into love. They began to talk of marriage—something Gene had not bargained for. It went against his cultural sense of what was right and proper. Gene was upset, but he didn't know how to oppose it. He had already accepted David as his brother in Christ.

As time went on, Gene became convicted about his attitude. He and his wife, Laura, talked and prayed and struggled with the realization that they had no Christian reason for objecting to David as Brenda's husband. After several more months, Gene's view shifted even further. Rather than oppose or reluctantly accept David as his future son-in-law, he decided to give his wholehearted approval to the marriage. And to show his acceptance, he traveled to David's remote village in northern Ghana to meet David's father and to express the honor he felt in receiving David into his family. Gene is a powerful testimony to the oneness of this new humanity created in Christ and forged at the cross.

Jesus "came and preached peace to you who were far away and peace to those who were near. For through him we both have access to the Father by one Spirit" (2:17–18). The social agenda of the world is represented by the Tower of Babel; the social agenda of the church is best illustrated by the preaching at Pentecost. Fear and power drove the Tower project; the Holy Spirit inspired Pentecost. Everyone speaking in their own tongue is different from everyone hearing the gospel in their own language. In the world, the highest goal is to tolerate one another and respect each other's individual rights. In Christ, the greatest blessing is being reconciled to God and to one another.

Peace and unity are the two themes that dominate this paragraph, and both themes depend exclusively on Christ. Christ himself is our peace. Christ on the cross makes peace. Christ came and preached peace. The message was too important to be entrusted to someone else. The distinction between those who are "far away" and those who are "near" is drawn from Isaiah 57:19 and refers to Gentiles and Jews respectively. But this spatial analogy does not stop there. The gospel continues to be proclaimed to those who are "far away" and to those who are "near." Evangelism extends to the ends of the earth and to the next-door neighbor. The gospel is good news for the atheist and for the religious. Those who never attend church and those who have sat in the pew for years need to hear the gospel. And the message preached is not sectarian, religious, or political. Isaiah captured the essence of the good news this way: " 'Peace, peace, to those far and near,' says the Lord. 'And I will heal them'" (Isaiah 57:19).

In Christ, God has become accessible. "For through him we both [Gentile and Jew] have access to the Father by one Spirit" (2:18). The walls of rules and rituals, commands and regulations, pride and prejudice, have been destroyed at the cross. No man-made meritorious means provides access, only the grace of Christ opens the way and allows us to "approach God's throne of grace with confidence, so that we may receive mercy and find grace to help us in our time of need" (Heb 4:16).

## A Church without Walls

(2:19–22) *"Consequently, you are no longer foreigners and strangers, but fellow citizens with God's people and also members of his household, built on the foundation of the apostles and prophets, with Christ Jesus himself as the chief cornerstone. In him the whole building is joined together and rises to become a holy temple in the Lord. And in him you too are being built together to become a dwelling in which God lives by his Spirit."*

The solidarity of the saints is a consistent theme throughout Ephesians. The TNIV refers to Christ creating in himself "one new humanity," but in the Greek it is literally, "one new person." So real was the oneness of this new humanity that Paul spoke of the church as being one new person. Paul was not interested in individual players as much as in the whole team. Everything he says concerns the family, the holy ones, the community of God's people. The imagery of citizenship, household and temple imply strength and security, but above all solidarity. In rapid succession, Paul stacks the metaphors: God's kingdom, God's family, God's temple. His purpose is not to preach a three-point sermon, but to deliver a single message: our identity in Christ is not individualistic but corporate. We are this third race—holy ones, members of God's household, and joined together to become a holy temple. We used to be foreigners and strangers but now we have immigrated to a new country, we have been adopted into a new family, and we belong to a holy temple in the Lord.

You won't find a single word about church facilities in the New Testament, but the apostles enjoyed elaborating on the images and metaphors that describe the community of God's people. Their strength and solidarity was not reflected in church buildings but in their union with Christ Jesus and in the presence and power of the Holy Spirit. Early Christians had a sense of place, a feeling of being at home, not in a facility but in a family of shared faithfulness to the Word of God. There was no outward temple or tall steeple to symbolize their place, but as they met together there was a powerful presence of the risen Lord Jesus. The early Christians knew that "the Most High does not live in houses made by men" (Acts 7:48).

All the metaphors in Ephesians 2 are relational, even the building metaphors. The foundation is made up of people—the apostles and the prophets. Most likely this is a reference to the limited group of disciples who witnessed the risen Lord Jesus together with the expanding circle of preachers and prophets who declared the gospel. The chief cornerstone is Christ Jesus. The "chief cornerstone" is not a ceremonial cornerstone, inscribed with the date of the building, nor is it likely that Paul intended it to refer to the keystone or capstone crowning the top of the building. "Cornerstones in ancient buildings were the primary load-bearing stones that determined the lines of the building. Such stones have been found in Palestine, one weighing as much as 570 tons."[8] The third relational metaphor is "the holy temple in the Lord" described as a dwelling in which God lives by his Spirit. Paul had in mind the people of God, not the Jerusalem temple built by Herod. He used the same imagery with the believers at Corinth, when he said, "Do you not know that your bodies are temples of the Holy Spirit, who is in you, whom you have received from God?" (1 Corinthians 6:19). In each case the meaning of the metaphor is personal and relational.

With the literary care of a poet, Paul orchestrated a wordplay on the Greek word for "house" (οικος). In Christ we are no longer *aliens* (πάροικοι), but members of God's *household* (οἰκεῖοι), *built on* (ἐποικοδομηθέντες) a sure foundation, and the *building* (οἰκοδομὴ) is *built together* (συνοικοδομεῖσθε) into a *dwelling place* (κατοικητήριον) of God.[9] Paul's intentional selection of the household of faith language underscores the relational nature of the church.

8. Snodgrass, *Ephesians*, 137.
9. Ibid., 136.

The relational and spiritual character of this "house," built by God *of people*, is no less material, temporal, spatial, and concrete, than if it had been built with stone and steel. "The accent of Ephesians 2 lies not upon intangibleness but upon the fact that the church of God is made of people, rather than of bricks."[10] The good news is proclaimed and lived through the local church, through the community, rather than through the individual. In a world of hostility the church is an alternative society, a visible sign of the kingdom.

Since the walls of ritual, tradition, laws, and regulations, have been broken down in Christ, we must be careful not to re-erect those old walls. Our relationship to the world is essentially positive. The gospel is not about what we are against, but what we are for. We must never lose sight of the glory of God and this wonderful news that the walls of hostility have been broken down in Christ. Paul pictures open borders in the kingdom of God, a more-the-merrier household of God, and an organically growing temple in the Lord. People who are saved by grace through faith ought not dwell on their denominational distinctives.

When faithful followers of Christ are defined more by what divides them than by what unites them, then their praxis is heretical even if their theology is orthodox. I find it disappointing that disagreements over the sacraments or the role of women or worship music hinder ministry and fellowship. I have been a pastor in four different churches in four different denominations and I am grateful that my ministry has not been limited by denominational distinctions or marginal differences. What is important is that we know Christ and seek to follow him and obey his word. Those who have become one new humanity, this third race in Christ, don't make it hard for others to follow Christ. They don't erect "dividing walls of hostility."

Several years ago one of our church members wrote to me about her experience in our church in San Diego. She started her letter with a verse from Psalm 27: "Though my father and mother forsake me, the Lord will receive me." She explained how she had grown up in a mean-spirited, negative home environment. She identified with those who have felt forsaken by father or mother. "Even as adults," she said, "the pain may linger. But God can take that place in our lives, fill that void, and heal that hurt. He can direct us to adults who may take the role of father and mother for us. His love is sufficient for all our needs."

---

10. Barth, *Ephesians*, 320.

*The Peace of Christ*

Her parents made life more difficult by wrapping up their twisted and negative attitudes "in their brand of Christianity." Over time she absorbed their negative and condemning attitude, which made it extremely difficult for her to relate and find her place in the body of Christ. But because of God's help, she has slowly overcome this deeply rooted judgmental attitude. She concluded her letter with these words, "So many people in this church have been so loving, caring, and kind to me. Their behavior is truly Christ-like. Because of my fellow church members, I am slowly letting down the walls I've built around myself over the years. Please continue to pray for me."

God's purpose is that we not divide along ethnic, cultural, racial, social, gender, and generational lines. We were meant to be fellow citizens with God's people and members of God's household, built on the foundation provided by the apostles and prophets, with Christ Jesus himself as the chief cornerstone. "The church gathers around the character of Christ, not the characteristics of people."[11] It is important to maintain the distinction between being in Christ and being of the world. It is the difference between being guided by God's indwelling Spirit for the good of the world and being shaped by the spirit of the times. Paul became all things to all people "so that by all possible means [he] might save some" (1 Cor 9:22).

This is different from becoming all things to all people in order to win their favor. Paul insisted on doing everything for the sake of the gospel. His refusal to be judgmental did not discredit discernment. His rejection of prejudice did not sanction disobedience. This is why he said to the Ephesians, "So I tell you this, and insist on it in the Lord, that you must no longer lives as the Gentiles do, in the futility of their thinking. They are darkened in their understanding and separated from the life of God because of the ignorance that is in them due to the hardening of their hearts. Having lost all sensitivity, they have given themselves over to sensuality so as to indulge in every kind of impurity, and they are full of greed" (4:17–19).

Since the Christian community is founded solely on Jesus Christ, it is a spiritual reality. Our life together is not based on a sociological or psychological compatibility, but on the relationship created by the Holy Spirit, "who puts Jesus Christ into our hearts as Lord and Savior."[12] One of our seminary students credits his wife with reshaping his experience of Christian community. Left to himself, he gravitated to people who shared

---

11. Ibid., 155.
12. Bonhoeffer, *Life Together*, 31.

his small world. For years his mentors, small group Bible study friends, and his accountability group were all guys like himself. They were similar in age, education, and cultural experience, but thanks to his wife, that's changing. He writes,

> The primary catalyst for my growing desire to embrace the larger Christian community has been my wife. She lives with a sense of mission that I admire. Six years ago she introduced herself to a young girl at church who seemed a bit lost. She could not get the girl out of her mind for several days after that and she eventually tracked down her contact information, and gave her a call. The girl was a meth addict, looking for answers in the midst of her seemingly hopeless struggle. I have watched my wife persevere in that friendship, despite suicide attempts, two stints in rehab, a DUI arrest and conviction, and other personal issues that would have driven me away long ago. I have listened as my wife speaks grace and truth into her friend's distressed life. I have also watched my wife cultivate relationships with our neighbors. She is always ready to interrupt her plans for a conversation or to accept an invitation from someone she barely knows. She has demonstrated a willingness to follow Jesus into new relationships, to odd places and to seemingly odd people.

One of my biblical heroes is John Perkins. You won't find him in the Bible, but you will find the Bible in John Perkins. In college, I read his story, *A Quiet Revolution*, and the eyes of my heart were opened. I saw the transforming power of Christ's love in the life of a man who had reason enough to hate. In his book, he describes the night he was brutally beaten by the police in Brandon, Mississippi. He had participated in a nonviolent civil rights march earlier in the day and had been arrested. He describes how God moved him from hate to love:

> During my night in the jail at Brandon, God began something new in my life. In the midst of the crowded, noisy jailhouse, between the stomping and the blackjacking that we received; between the moments when one of the patrolmen put his pistol to my head and pulled the trigger—"click"—and when another later took a fork and bent the two middle prongs down and pushed the other two up my nose until blood came out—between the reality and the insanity, between the consciousness and the unconsciousness that would sweep across my dizzy mind, between my terror and my unwillingness to break down, between my pain and my fear, in those little snatches of thought when in some miraculous way I could at once be the spectacle

and the spectator, God pushed me past hatred. Just for a little while, moments at a time.

How could I hate when there was so much to pity? How could I hate people I suddenly did not recognize, who had somehow moved past the outer limits of what it means to be human? . . . But I don't think it was just the pity I had or the deep sickness I saw alone that pushed me past hatred. It was also the fact that I was broken . . . The Brandon experience just might have been a way of God bringing me to the place where he could expand his love in me and extend my calling to white people as well as black people . . . And I believe that it was in my own broken state that the depth of the sickness in those men struck home to me, and the fact that I was like them—totally depraved. I had evidence before me and in myself that every human being is bad—depraved. There's something built into all of us that makes us want to be superior. If the black man had the advantage, he'd be just as bad. So I can't hate the white man. It's a spiritual problem—black or white, we all need to be born again . . .

The failure, the frustration, the powerlessness of my situation as a black person in the South pressed me. What it was squeezing out of me was more and more bitterness. Like a lemon—so fresh and sweet looking on the outside but hiding such a sour taste. And the bitterness just made the frustration worse.

I saw how bitterness could destroy me. The Spirit of God had a hold of me and wouldn't let me sidestep his justice. And his justice said that I was just as sinful as those who beat me. But I knew that God's justice is seasoned with forgiveness. Forgiveness is what makes his justice redemptive. Forgiveness! That was the key. And somehow, God's forgiveness for me was tied up in my forgiveness of those who hurt me.

"For if you forgive people when they sin against you, your heavenly Father will also forgive you. But if you do not forgive people their sins, your Father will not forgive your sins" (Matt 6:14–15).

We were right. . . . But now God was saying, "Being right is not enough. You must also be forgiving." Reconciliation is so difficult because the damage is so deep.[13]

John Perkins found God's severe mercy in a Brandon city jail pushing him beyond bitterness and hate to love and forgiveness. The sinful opposition of men was miraculously turned into the discipline of his loving heavenly

---

13. Perkins, *Quiet Revolution*, 190–91.

## The Christ Letter

Father. This unusual transformation of raw evil into divine goodness ought to be the common experience of the followers of Jesus. God takes what would break us, if we were left to ourselves, and makes us into his children, reflecting his love and holiness.

After all these years, John Perkins is still going strong. In *Reconciliation Blues*, Edward Gilbreath describes John Perkins' closing words at a racial reconciliation summit held in Indianapolis in 2005. Leaders from a variety of Christian organizations and institutions spent the morning reflecting on the discouraging and difficult task of racial reconciliation. They sat together in a large circle commiserating on the setbacks and failures of racial reconciliation in America. The more they talked the more it looked like they would all leave the summit more disillusioned than they had come. They were singing the reconciliation blues, when unexpectedly John Perkins walked into the room. At seventy-five in 2005, Dr. Perkins was recognized by many as a modern-day evangelical prophet, an elder statesman of Christian ministry. He had earned the respect of these leaders by his humility and faithfulness to the cause of Christ.

Dr. Perkins was asked by the moderator, "What is your sense of God's message for us today?" He stood in the center of the circle and began to sob. But he was not weeping over race relations, he was weeping over his son. John described his profound discouragement over his son Spencer's death from a heart attack, the very son who had led him to the Lord forty-eight years ago. He shared how he was angry with God, but that God quickly "sobered" him and brought to his mind Jim Elliot's quote: "He is no fool who gives what he cannot keep to gain what he cannot lose." After a few seconds, John said, "I love Spencer, but God loves him more..." For John Perkins to talk about the loss of his son in that context rather than focus on racial setbacks, lifted his Christian calling above race and focused it on obedience to Christ. Dr. Perkins concluded, "What is God telling us? I feel he's telling us Philippians 1:6—'He who has begun this good work in you will carry it on to completion until the day of Christ Jesus.' It is God who gave us this ministry, and he will be the one to fulfill it. We just need to continue to give our hearts and souls to loving others and living the gospel in an incarnational way, and then trust God to bring the change."[14] The reason for John Perkins' "long obedience in the same direction" lies in his understanding of the ministry of reconciliation, that God is reconciling the world to himself in Christ. He agrees with the apostle, "For Christ's love compels us, because we are convinced that one died for all,

---

14. Gilbreath, *Reconciliation Blues*, 186.

and therefore all died. And he died for all, that those who live should no longer live for themselves but for him who died for them and was raised again" (2 Cor 5:14–15).

The borders of the kingdom of God are wide open. The gospel message is all encompassing: "whosoever will may come." No matter how deep the depravity or painful the social alienation, there is room at the table of the Lord in the household of faith. There are no walls of hostility keeping anyone out of the temple of the Lord. Markus Barth calls the message of Ephesians two "the key and high point of the whole epistle."[15] In a world of evil and hostility, the gospel of Jesus Christ is an inclusive invitation to an exclusive Savior and Lord. We come as we are but we do not remain as we were. We are new creations created in Christ Jesus. We have a new citizenship, a new family, and an entirely new indwelling Spirit.

---

15. Barth, *Ephesians*, 275.

# 5

# The Mission of Christ

> "... This grace was given to me: to preach to the Gentiles the boundless riches of Christ, and to make plain to everyone the administration of this mystery, which for ages past was kept hidden in God, who created all things."
>
> EPHESIANS 3:8–9

*Mystery* is the key word, but *missions* is the subject as Paul lays out a theology of missions. In this emotional parenthesis, Paul passionately explains his personal calling to the Gentiles. But he does it in such a way as to include us. He presented the mission of the church not as a duty or a burden that others must accept, but as a gift—as a privileged appointment, that he has personally and gratefully received from God. This was Paul's model of how missions ought to be presented to the church. Grace, not guilt, provided the motivation. All believers are called to salvation, service, sacrifice, and simplicity. For his part, Paul led by example, not by coercion. There was no gap between his calling and his work. He was not recruiting missionaries, raising money, or trying to give away his mission field. Missions was not a burden to be imposed on reluctant believers, but a wonderful privilege to be embraced by willing believers.

## The Mission of Christ

*(3:1–13) "For this reason I, Paul, the prisoner of Christ Jesus for the sake of you Gentiles—Surely you have heard about the administration of God's grace that was given to me for you, that is, the mystery made known to me by revelation, as I have already written briefly. In reading this, then, you will be able to understand my insight into the mystery of Christ, which was not made known to people in other generations as it has now been revealed by the Spirit to God's holy apostles and prophets. This mystery is that through the gospel the Gentiles are heirs together with Israel, members together of one body, and sharers together in the promise in Christ Jesus.*

*I became a servant of this gospel by the gift of God's grace given through the working of his power. Although I am less than the least of all the Lord's people, this grace was given me: to preach to the Gentiles the boundless riches of Christ, and to make plain to everyone the administration of this mystery, which for ages past was kept hidden in God, who created all things. His intent was that now, through the church, the manifold wisdom of God should be made known to the rulers and authorities in the heavenly realms, according to his eternal purpose that he accomplished in Christ Jesus our Lord. In him and through faith in him we may approach God with freedom and confidence. I ask you, therefore, not to be discouraged because of my sufferings for you, which are your glory."*

In the third chapter of Ephesians, Paul describes his purpose and prayer for missions. Implicit in his personal account is a paradigm for our mission involvement. Embedded in this model for missions are seven enduring paradoxes:

1. Like Paul, we face the *identity paradox* (3:1). Instead of seeing himself as a prisoner of Caesar, Paul saw himself as a prisoner of Christ. His identity was different from how the world defined him.

2. Administering the mystery calls attention to the *practitioner's paradox* (3:2, 9). How does anyone manage a mystery? But as we will see, this is exactly what Paul did and expects all believers to do.

3. Next, we have the *truth paradox* (3:9). Paul defines the word *mystery* as revealed truth, in contrast to the gnostic mystery cults and modern notions of the unimaginable and ineffable.

4. The *impact paradox* highlights the contrast between the largeness of the apostle's full-orbed gospel and the smallness of the gospel we often offer (3:10).

5. Paul's mission strategy produced suffering, underscoring the *glory paradox* (3:13). The rich benefits of the gospel are rooted in a mission marked by the cross.

6. Paul prays for love, apart from which there could be no true mission. He prays that we would know the love that surpasses knowledge. Far from disparaging knowledge, the *love paradox* (3:19) fulfills all knowledge.

7. The final grace-filled incongruity is the *expectation paradox* (3:20). Paul prays "to him who is able to do immeasurably more than all we ask or imagine . . ." Expect to be surprised by the power of God "that is at work within us."

Over the next two chapters we will explore the apostle's theology of mission and see how these seven paradoxes shape his understanding and strategy.

## Vision for Mission

For nearly twenty years my wife and I received "missionary letters" from Steve and Sue Befus. These one-page letters to family and friends, describing their work in Liberia, were similar in style and substance to Paul's letters. Their unembellished account of their work always conveyed a deep compassion for their brothers and sisters in Christ. They accepted their responsibility as a privilege instead of a burden. Their stories were free from either "look-at-me" heroism or "woe-is-me" pity. And they were always sensitive to the fact that those who received their letters were also engaged in ministry. Reading their letters gave us a sense that we were partners together in the work that the Lord had called us to do. Sue and Steve took the tough times and emergencies in stride. In addition to a sense of privilege, they conveyed a sense of patience with the church and a perseverance with the work. In keeping with the apostle Paul's strategy, these are the truths that a missionary letter should communicate.

Missions is best presented as a personal story, inspired by the Spirit of Christ, rather than as a duty motivated out of guilt. In this letter, Paul has asked nothing from the saints of Ephesus, except that they not be ashamed of his suffering. Yet by way of example he expects everything

*The Mission of Christ*

from them in Christ. Roland Allen, in his classic study of Paul's missionary methods, writes, "It seems strange to us that there should be no exhortations to missionary zeal in the Epistles of St Paul. There is one sentence of approval, 'The Lord's message rang out from you' (1 Thess 1:8), but there is no insistence upon the command of Christ to preach the gospel."[1]

Missionary statesman Leslie Newbigin agrees, when he writes,

> There has been a long tradition which sees the mission of the Church primarily as obedience to a command. It has been customary to speak of "the missionary mandate." This way of putting the matter is certainly not without justification, and yet it seems to me that it misses the point. It tends to make mission a burden rather than a joy, to make it part of the law rather than part of the gospel. If one looks at the New Testament evidence one gets another impression. Mission begins with a kind of explosion of joy. The news that the rejected and crucified Jesus is alive is something that cannot possibly be suppressed. It must be told. Who could be silent about such a fact?[2]

The post-World War II generation was highly motivated out of strong sense of duty. The missions' mandate was something of a spiritual call to arms in the forties and fifties. Wars fought in Europe and the Pacific opened the eyes of the church in the West to the tremendous global need for spreading the gospel. That sense of duty has waned in subsequent generations, but hopefully we can recover a true sense of the privilege and the power of partnership that can be ours in sharing the gospel.

Halfway through this carefully reasoned letter, Paul had what my daughter and her college friends call an RDT with the saints at Ephesus. In case that acronym is unfamiliar to you, as it was to me, RDT stands for a *Relationship Defining Talk*. Paul turned *emphatically* personal, not because he had something to get off his chest or because he wanted to commend himself, but because he wanted to lead by example. He embraced the mission of the gospel of grace with a palpable sense of privilege and passion. He made no attempt to cajole, berate or browbeat people into the work of missions. What he sought to do was compel them by his infectious joy, his profound gratitude, and his sense of great honor. He was truly grateful for the responsibility of administering the gospel of grace.

His opening phrase, "For this reason," gathers up all that Paul has said about worship and salvation as the foundation for what he is about

1. Allen, *Missionary Methods*, 93.
2. Newbigin, *The Gospel in a Pluralistic Society*, 116.

## The Christ Letter

to say about missions. Paul knew the incomparable riches of God's grace. He understood that we have been chosen, predestined, adopted, and redeemed in Christ. He knew the power of God to overcome humanity's depravity and alienation; to raise up those who were dead in their transgressions and sins; and to destroy the dividing wall of hostility. He knew what it meant to be God's workmanship created in Christ Jesus to do good works. Paul believed in the importance of being citizens of God's kingdom and members of God's family. He was convinced "that the whole building is joined together and rises to become a holy temple in the Lord." This theology of grace formed the foundation for what Paul was about to say about missions and relationships. If we are not truly convinced of the truth laid out in the first two chapters (1:1—2:22), there will be no basis for accepting what Paul says about missions and Christian living in the next four chapters.

## The Identity Paradox

Paul begins, "I, Paul, the prisoner of Christ Jesus for the sake of you Gentiles." Although Paul was literally a political prisoner of Caesar, most likely under house arrest in Rome, he saw himself as a prisoner *of* and *for* Christ (3:1; 4:1). In the eyes of the world, Paul was either a victim of Roman injustice or a troublemaker who deserved to be imprisoned. However, in the eyes of the Lord, Paul was a steward of the mystery made known to him by the revelation of God. He was entrusted with the responsibility of administering the gospel of grace. Others may have despised and pitied him, but he saw himself as an ambassador for Christ, albeit in chains (6:20). Instead of languishing in prison, Paul possessed the freedom to approach God with confidence (3:12). This paradox of worldly shame and heavenly glory often characterizes believers engaged in the mission of the gospel.

## *The Practitioner's Paradox*

The second paradox is "the administration of this mystery." To the modern reader the idea of managing a mystery doesn't make sense. The concepts of "administration" and "mystery" don't belong together. How can anyone control, let alone comprehend, what by definition is unknown, unsolvable, and incomprehensible? That which is "mysterious" is vague, inscrutable, and puzzling, definitely not something that can be managed. Commentators are quick to say that the word "mystery" (μυστήριον) refers to the

*The Mission of Christ*

revelation of God, previously hidden, but now made known. This is true, but it doesn't answer why Paul used the word "mystery" instead of "gospel." Why use a word that reminded his readers of the various "mystery" cults?

Paul did this to drive home a very important truth. The "mystery" cults kept secrets that were made known only to initiates "giving them great spiritual privileges unavailable to others without this knowledge."[3] These secret societies were more or less religious clubs or spiritual fraternities. These little elite in-groups were proud of their exclusivity. Paul took over the word "mystery" intentionally, to distance the gospel of Jesus Christ from the mystery cults with their esoteric knowledge and exclusivity. He did so to make clear that the truth disclosed in the revelation of the gospel was meant to be proclaimed to everyone. By suggesting a comparison to the mystery cults Paul was reinforcing the missional character of the gospel. In the mystery cults "administration" meant keeping secrets, but in the church it meant making the gospel of Jesus Christ known to both Jews and Gentiles.

The church today that keeps the mystery to itself is more like the ancient mystery cults than the open-bordered kingdom of God, or the ever-welcoming household of God, or the organically growing temple of the Lord—a dwelling in which God lives by his Spirit. The word for administration (οἰκονομίαν) is the seventh word Paul used in the "house" word group. The thrust of Paul's artful presentation underscores the inclusiveness of the missionary challenge. Missions belongs to the household of God—to everyone in the church, and not to a select group of "missionaries" set aside for this purpose. Of course, the problem does not lie with the "missionary" but with us and how we view missions. We are often guilty of acting like we belong to a mystery cult. Only in our case, we are not as proud of our "secret" as we are embarrassed by it and intimidated by the world.

## The Truth Paradox

The third paradox implied in this passage has to do with the relationship between truth and mystery. Skeptics grab hold of this term, *mystery*, and exploit it for their own purposes. It becomes a convenient way to distance themselves from the truth. This is proof, they say, that Paul didn't have a corner on the truth. Mystery implies that God surpasses our human understanding. God is beyond our human categories. "We cannot know with

---

3. Lincoln, *Ephesians*, 31.

the kind of surety that allows us to proclaim truth with a capital T. There will always be something that eludes us. If there weren't, it would not be God."[4]

The problem with this perspective is that it turns truth into a liability. The skeptic argues that only the arrogant claim to know the truth, because the truth by definition must be unimaginable, ineffable, and incomprehensible. The skeptic is not willing to entertain the notion that God is capable of revelation. In a sense the skeptics are right: Paul would never have claimed to have had a corner on the truth. This is one of the reasons why he used the word *mystery*, so as to underscore the fact that the truth did not come from him but from God. The only reason he knew the truth of the gospel was because of the revelation of God. Knowing the truth was not a matter of Paul's genius but of God's grace. Besides, this knowledge was not for Paul's sake, but for the benefit of others. The reason this was a knowable mystery and an open secret was because God had made it known.

The administration of God's grace was *given* to Paul, not achieved by Paul. It was a mystery made known by revelation. Paul's Spirit-led insight into the mystery of Christ was not something so ineffable and incomprehensible that people couldn't understand it. Paul had not imbibed the modern spirit of "humility" with its refusal in principle to accept the revelation of God. He administered the mystery confidently. Roland Allen comments on Paul's forthright proclamation of the gospel:

> There is no attempt to keep the door open by partial statements, no concealment of the real issue and all that it involves, no timid fear of giving offence, no suggestion of possible compromise, no attempt to make things really difficult appear easy. . . . There is an unhesitating confidence in the truth of his message, and in its power to meet and satisfy the spiritual needs of people.[5]

Paul was confident about the gospel but humble about himself. "Although I am less than the least of all the Lord's people, this grace was given me: to preach to the Gentiles the boundless riches of Christ, and to make plain to everyone the administration of this mystery, which for ages past was kept hidden in God, who created all things" (3:8–9). Paul was fully impressed with his own littleness in contrast to the immensity of this truth.

---

4. Sullivan, "When Not Seeing Is Believing," 60.
5. Allen, *Missionary Methods*, 64.

## The Impact Paradox

The fourth paradox, implied in Paul's theology of mission, is the contrast between the largeness of the full-orbed gospel preached by Paul and the smallness of the gospel we often preach. Our thoughts about personal salvation often clash with the promise of the gospel to work for justice and overcome social alienation. Note carefully the way Paul expressed the meaning of the mystery, when he said, "This mystery is that through the gospel the Gentiles are heirs together with Israel, members together of one body, and sharers together in the promise in Christ Jesus" (3:6). The gospel of grace is the culmination of salvation history, "which for ages past was kept hidden in God, who created all things" (3:9). The purpose of the gospel is nothing less than "to bring unity to all things in heaven and on earth under Christ" (1:10).

That which was hidden, "what neither the Old Testament nor Jesus revealed was the radical nature of God's plan, which was that the theocracy (the Jewish nation under God's rule) would be terminated, and replaced by a new international community, the church."[6] This is why Paul said, "And God placed all things under his feet and appointed him to be head over everything for the church, which is his body . . ." The scope of salvation is well beyond the personal salvation of the individual, as important as that is. The church encompasses "the fullness of him who fills everything in every way" (1:23). God's plan is "to bring unity to all things in heaven and on earth under Christ" (1:10).

The administration of this mystery is far from a simple strategy of getting people to say "yes" to Jesus. Stewards of the gospel of grace preach "the boundless riches of Christ" across all barriers, whether they are ethnic, racial, linguistic, cultural, political, religious, ideological, gender, or generational. We seek Christ and his kingdom in every aspect of life and in every culture. That which was hidden has now been revealed by God. "His intent was that now, through the church, the manifold wisdom of God should be made known to the rulers and authorities in the heavenly realms, according to his eternal purpose that he accomplished in Christ Jesus our Lord" (3:10–11).

Paul's theology of missions is not primarily about sending someone else to a far away place to share the gospel nor is it about building a church that entertains the masses. The mission of the church is to make known everywhere *the manifold wisdom of God* to the principalities and powers

---

6. Stott, *God's New Society*, 118.

in the heavenly realms. The ministry is much greater than we imagined. The call to action is more intense and demanding than we expected. The unity is far deeper and more complex than we thought possible. It is not only a conversion of the heart and mind, but it is a *social* conversion. We cannot be a new creation in Christ without belonging to the new community in Christ. As a concrete, sociological body, the church was meant to be "a sign and proof of a change that affects the institutions and structures, patterns and spans of the bodily and spiritual, social and individual existence of all humanity."[7] We were meant to bear witness to all of creation as well as to the cosmic spiritual powers that Jesus Christ is Lord.

If we embrace the mission of the gospel, we will be placed in an extraordinary position to see "the manifold witness of God." When I think of the manifold wisdom of God I think of my friends, David and Brenda Mensah, who I wrote about earlier. Their work, in solidarity with a strong team of committed co-workers in northern Ghana, is a solid testimony to the multi-faceted nature of God's wisdom. I have been to northern Ghana three times and I have seen firsthand the effectiveness of their work. It is exciting to see arid land turned into usable farm land, new schools and medical clinics built and staffed, thousands of Ghanians involved in several food co-ops, thirty-five churches planted, lay pastors trained, a fish hatchery producing tilapia, acres and acres of tomato plants, and hundreds of people coming to Christ from villages held in bondage to witchcraft and shamanism. In this ministry, faith and faithfulness come together, so that the proclamation of the gospel is accompanied by the improved status of women, nutrition, sanitation, food security, and access to water. What a wonderful witness to the holistic impact of the gospel!

The manifold wisdom of God is a beautiful way of articulating the all-encompassing work of the priesthood of all believers in the body of Christ, the church. God intends for all believers to bear witness to the saving power of Christ and to demonstrate the manifold wisdom of God in all that they do. Christopher Wright affirms the centrality and comprehensiveness of the cross:

> We need a holistic gospel because the world is in a holistic mess. And by God's incredible grace we have a gospel big enough to redeem all that sin and evil has touched . . . Ultimately all that will be there in the new, redeemed creation will be there because of the cross. And conversely, all that will not be there (suffering, tears, sin, Satan, sickness, oppression, corruption, decay and

---

7. Barth, *Ephesians*, 365.

## The Mission of Christ

death) will not be there because they will have been defeated and destroyed by the cross. That is the length, breadth, height and depth of God's idea of redemption.[8]

Missionary statesman David Livingstone viewed "the missionary enterprise" in its "most extended signification." As he wrote in 1855, "All our efforts are overruled for one glorious end." One of the severest shocks to hit David Livingstone, the renowned nineteenth-century missionary to Africa, was when the London Missionary Society withdrew its support for his missionary activity. The Society determined that his geographical exploration, which Livingstone saw as the necessary first step in the missionary enterprise, was only remotely connected to the spread of the gospel. Besides, they stated, "your reports make it sufficiently obvious that the nature of the country, the unhealthfulness of the climate, the prevalence of poisonous insects, and other adverse influences, constitute a serious array of obstacles to missionary effort, and even were there a reasonable prospect of their being surmounted—and we by no means assume they are insurmountable—yet, in that event, the financial circumstances of the Society are not such as to afford any ground of hope that it would be in a position, within any definite period, to enter upon untried, remote, and difficult fields of labor."[9]

Livingstone responded respectfully. He acknowledged the practical rationale of the directors of the London Missionary Society and the purity of their motives, but he reaffirmed his resolve to focus on "*the untried, remote and difficult fields*" to which, he writes, "I humbly yet firmly believe God has directed my steps." His conviction was based on "the simple continuance of an old determination to devote my life and my all to the services of Christ in whatever way He may lead me in Intertropical Africa."[10] As Livingstone explained, his decision to work in Africa was rooted in the will of God and was not dependent on the Society's support and approval. His definition of a missionary may have been out-of-touch with the London Missionary Society but it impresses us today as faithful to the New Testament vision and in keeping with the best of contemporary mission perspectives. Livingstone wrote,

> Nowhere have I appeared as anything else but a servant of God, who has simply followed the leadings of His hand. My views of what is missionary duty are not so contracted as those whose

8. Wright, *Mission of God*, 315.
9. Seaver, *David Livingstone*, 269.
10. Ibid., 270–71.

> ideal is a dumpy sort of man with a Bible under his arm. I have labored in bricks and mortar, at the forge and carpenter's bench, as well as in preaching and medical practice. I feel that I am "not my own." I am serving Christ when shooting a buffalo for my men, or taking an astronomical observation, or writing to one of His children who forget, during the little moment of penning a note, that charity which is eulogized as "thinking no evil"; and after by His help having got information, which I hope will lead to more abundant blessing being bestowed on Africa than heretofore, am I to hide the light under a bushel merely because some will consider it not sufficiently, or even at all, *missionary*? Knowing that some persons do believe that opening up a new country to the sympathies of Christendom was not a proper work for an agent of a Missionary Society to engage in, I now refrain from taking any salary from the Society with which I was connected; so no pecuniary [monetary] loss is sustained by anyone.[11]

Livingstone combined the promise of consummation, "to bring unity to all things in heaven and on earth under Christ" (1:10), with the compelling testimony of "the manifold wisdom of God" (3:10).[12]

We need the whole church to manifest the manifold wisdom of God. We need mothers, dentists, homebuilders, politicians, educators, engineers, evangelists—you name it; we need the whole vocational range of *real* missionaries who bear witness to Christ and his cross in their daily lives and work. Paul's mission vision supports the priesthood of all believers, every-member ministry, and the shared gifts of the Spirit. This is why we have said that all believers are called to salvation, service, sacrifice, and simplicity.

The Lord used one particular incident to impress upon me the meaning of the manifold wisdom of God. David and Brenda Mensah were visiting from Ghana and we had gathered at a friend's home for dinner. We had a great conversation about their holistic ministry in Ghana, but I was feeling anxious. Andrew, our son who had spent three months in Ghana working alongside David, was a no-show. At the time, Andrew was working as an ocean lifeguard off the coast of California and usually finished his shift at 6 p.m. Knowing how much he was looking forward to seeing David and Brenda again, I thought that something must be wrong. When he finally arrived at 9 p.m., he said very little. His demeanor was subdued.

11. Ibid., 285.
12. Ibid., 267.

*The Mission of Christ*

His eyes were bloodshot and he looked exhausted. I pulled him aside and asked him if he was okay. He explained,

> Dad, I don't want to talk about it to the group but I just had a difficult rescue. Just before sundown we got a distress call from a boat about a mile off shore. I took off on the jet sky, praying, "Lord help me find this boat." It was getting really dark. Then there was a break in the clouds and some moonlight came through and it reflected off the boat. The guy on board was unconscious, lying on the deck with his guts hanging out. He was a bloody mess. I think he was leaning over the boat engine when it exploded. I took off my shirt and wrapped it around him and duct-taped his chest and stomach to stop the bleeding. Loaded him on the jet ski and radioed for an ambulance. By the time I got to shore the ambulance was waiting for us.

Andrew did not expect the man to live, but the next day he got a call from his captain congratulating him and telling him that the man had survived surgery and was expected to recover. By God's grace, Andrew saved a life. The juxtaposition of the Mensah's ministry in Ghana and Andrew's ministry as a lifeguard reflects something of the range of God's mission. The manifold wisdom of God, made known through the church, calls each and every follower of the Lord Jesus to a life of obedience, witness, and mission. Christopher Wright raises the question we should be asking,

> Is *the church as a whole* reflecting the wholeness of God's redemption? Is the church (thinking here of the local church as the organism effectively and strategically placed for God's mission in any given community) aware of all that God's mission summons them to participate in? Is the church through the combined engagement of *all* its members, applying the redemptive power of the cross of Christ to *all* the effects of sin and evil in the surrounding lives, society and environment?[13]

## The Glory Paradox

The impact of the manifold wisdom of God on a hostile world leads to suffering, not success. Far from sounding a note of triumphalism, Paul prepared believers for his sufferings. He wrote, "I ask you, therefore, not to be discouraged because of my sufferings for you, which are your glory"

---

13. Wright, *Mission of God*, 322.

(3:13). Paul reminds us that true worship and mission centers on the passion of Christ. A church that preaches the cross must itself be marked by the cross.[14]

The testimony of the church is not enhanced by becoming impressive in the eyes of the world. Suffering rather than success is the key to revealing the manifold wisdom of God. Like Paul, prisoners for Christ often end up prisoners of Caesar. Leslie Newbigin describes the impact of the missional church:

> It follows that the visible embodiment of this new reality is not a movement which will take control of history and shape the future according to its own vision, not a new imperialism, not a victorious crusade. Its visible embodiment will be a community that lives by this story, a community whose existence is visibly defined in the regular rehearsing and reenactment of the story which has given it birth, the story of the self-emptying of God in the ministry, life, death, and resurrection of Jesus.[15]

The fifth paradox confronting the church is that this gospel of peace in Christ which is designed to destroy the walls of hostility actually provokes hostility. The old paganisms and the new messianisms fight against the church with everything they have. Newbigin writes,

> Wherever the gospel is preached, new ideologies appear—secular humanism, nationalism, Marxism—movements which offer the vision of new age, an age freed from all the ills that beset human life, freed from hunger and disease and war—on other terms. . . . Once the gospel is preached and there is a community which lives by the gospel, then the question of the ultimate meaning of history is posed and other messiahs appear. So the crisis of history is deepened. Even more significant as an example of this development than the rise of Marxism is the rise of Islam. Islam, which means simply submission, is the mightiest of all the post-Christian movements which claim to offer the kingdom of God without the cross. The denial of the crucifixion is and must always be central to Islamic teaching.[16]

If the church expects to reveal the manifold wisdom of God to "the rulers and authorities in the heavenly realms," the church, like the apostle, will have to be marked by the cross. Once again, Newbigin insists that the

---

14. Douglas, "The Lausanne Covenant," 5.
15. Newbigin, *The Gospel in a Pluralistic Society*, 120.
16. Ibid., 122.

*The Mission of Christ*

church shape its expectations according to the life of Jesus and his apostles rather than on an entrepreneurial or evolutionary model of development.

> The gospel calls us back again and again to the real clue, the crucified and risen Jesus, so that we learn that the meaning of history is not immanent in history itself, that history cannot find its meaning at the end of a process of development, but that history is given its meaning by what God has done in Jesus Christ and by what he has promised to do; and that the true horizon is not at the successful end of our projects but in his coming to reign. One may say, therefore, that missions are the test of our faith.[17]

Paul never conceived of missions as a burden or a duty to be imposed on believers. He did not go around thinking of himself as God's public relations chief, trying to urge lackadaisical believers to get excited about missions. It wasn't his job to lay on the church at Ephesus a guilt trip about missions. On the contrary, he challenged the believers to renegotiate their understanding of success. True success, the kind marked by the cross, involved suffering for the sake of the gospel. Paul did not want them discouraged because of his imprisonment and suffering. He wanted them to see his effort and their partnership as God's "eternal purpose." This was the missionary purpose he embraced with every fiber of his being.

Given what Paul has just said we are not surprised that he gets down on his knees and prays for the Ephesians. His missionary prayer completes the seven-fold series of paradoxes that reveals the apostle's powerful theology of mission. In the next chapter, we will explore the meaning of Paul's prayer for missions. We turn our attention to the *love paradox* and the *expectation paradox*.

---

17. Ibid., 126.

# 6

# *The Glory of Christ*

*"Now to him who is able to do immeasurably more than all we ask or imagine, according to his power that is at work within us, to him be glory in the church and in Christ Jesus throughout all generations, for ever and ever! Amen."*

EPHESIANS 3:20–21

The word "glory" has a triumphal ring to it, but in the light of what Paul just finished saying—"don't be discouraged because of my suffering"—we may need to rethink what "glory" means (Eph 3:13). We tend to associate glory with a visceral feeling of transcendence and majesty. A beautiful sanctuary or a spectacular sunset conveys a feeling of glory. But this is not what Paul had in mind when he said, "to him be glory in the church and in Christ Jesus." It is not our job to replicate the glory days when God's glory came down on the tabernacle and when God's glory filled the temple. The glory that Paul had in mind is best revealed in suffering.

Should we build for God a glorious *building* to declare his glory? I very much doubt that the apostle Paul associated Christ's glory with shrines and cathedrals. Any attempt to feel closer to God's transcendence through vaulted ceilings and stained glass windows fails to grasp what Paul meant by glory. This form of visceral transcendence expressed in stone and glass belongs today to the rock group that spends $150 million on spectacular staging and lighting to produce shock and awe.

*The Glory of Christ*

Paul's prayer was for a demonstration within the believing community of the weighty revelation of God. He anticipates the truth of the gospel shining forth in all of its brilliance through the household of faith. Paul's vision of glory begins with the indwelling Christ, "so that Christ may dwell in your hearts through faith" (Eph 3:17). His powerful benediction is in keeping with the apostle John's description of the Incarnate One. "The Word became flesh and dwelt among us, and we beheld his glory, the glory of the only begotten of the Father full of grace and truth" (John 1:14). What John saw in Jesus, Paul prayed to see in the church.

(3:14–19) *"For this reason I kneel before the Father, from whom every family in heaven and on earth derives its name. I pray that out of his glorious riches he may strengthen you with power through his Spirit in your inner being, so that Christ may dwell in your hearts through faith. And I pray that you being rooted and established in love, may have power, together with all the Lord's people, to grasp how wide and long and high and deep is the love of Christ, and to know this love that surpasses knowledge—that you may be filled to the measure of all the fullness of God."*

Paul claimed that he did not communicate with "eloquence" and "superior wisdom," but judging from this prayer it would be difficult to deny that he wrote with both eloquence and persuasion. Augustine, the well-known early church leader, addressed this issue by distinguishing between eloquence based on classical rhetorical conventions and true eloquence flowing naturally from the wisdom of God. Augustine reasoned that whether or not Paul "was guided by the rules of eloquence" didn't matter, because what he said could not have been said in a better way. Whatever skill and style Paul used to communicate was dictated by the message he was led by the Spirit to deliver. Paul was obviously skilled in "the art of elocution." He knew how to build to a climax and emphasize a truth with a rhetorical exclamation. But he never used art simply for art's sake. His purpose was always to call attention to the truth, not the technique. For Augustine, it was a case of "wisdom not aiming at eloquence, yet eloquence not shrinking from wisdom."[1] Paul's rejection of eloquence and superior wisdom was an emphatic denial of all forms of artificiality, manipulation and deception, but by no means a rejection of careful reasoning and skillful communication. Paul was never a crafty, clever communicator, but neither was he an

---

1. Augustine, "On Christian Doctrine," 577–81.

artless, boring communicator. No one could ever use the apostle Paul to excuse preaching that lacked depth and clarity, wisdom and passion. His eloquence was natural, flowing out of the passion of his heart.

## A Missionary Prayer

Prayer is the sensible response to what Paul has just said about the mission of God. Given his perspective on missions it would be hard to imagine any other posture than on our knees before God the Father, Son, and Holy Spirit. *Prayer*, communion with God, is central to following Jesus and being the church. The administration of God's grace presents a missions agenda so weighty and significant that prayer is a natural response for all who are in Christ. Paul's parenthetical thought on missions is not a digression, but an inspiration. If our aim, like Paul, is to become enveloped by the purposes of God, prayer is the natural response. The apostle's prayer, at the heart of his letter, bridges the theology of worship, salvation, and mission covered in the first half of the letter, with what it means to follow Jesus in the church, family, and society in the second half of the letter.

Paul prays to the Father (πατέρα) "from whom all families (πατριὰ) in heaven and on earth derive their name." The God and Father of the Lord Jesus Christ (1:3, 17) is the God and Father of all the families in the cosmos. Paul's mission-minded prayer is for everyone to come to the realization that their Heavenly Father has made himself known through Christ. All relationships in heaven and on earth have their roots in God the Father. Within the created order there is no ground for racism or sectarianism or selfism. "The built-in arrogance of every race, nationality and clan has no ultimate basis."[2] There is "one God and Father of all, who is over all and through all and in all" (4:6). Paul begins his prayer by stressing the inclusiveness of the exclusive gospel of grace. This conviction was not any more acceptable in Paul's day than our own, but the power of the gospel is dependent on this relationship. Whether men and women acknowledge their God and Father or not, all of us derive our very being, and thus our name and identity, from the Father. This dependence on God is the defining relationship for all people in a personal universe.

Paul was in prison but he prayed for the saints at Ephesus. He was weak, but he prayed for their strengthening. He was in poverty but he focused on their glorious riches in Christ (1:7; 2:4, 7; 3:8, 16). His outer being was wasting away but he was filled with concern for their inner

2. Snodgrass, *Ephesians*, 186.

## The Glory of Christ

being. He prayed that God would strengthen them "with power through his Spirit in [their] inner being, so that Christ may dwell in [their] hearts through faith" (3:16–17). Inner strengthening meant union with Christ in the most deeply personal way possible. The shaping and energizing of the interior self, "the real you," by the love and power of the Spirit of Christ "allows the believer to live in a world dominated by rebellion against God."[3]

In this prayer the work of the Father, Son, and Holy Spirit is simultaneous and symphonic; everything is in perfect harmony. The enriching, empowering, and indwelling work of God leads to a well-rooted and well-established resilient believer. Paul's previous description of the church (2:19–22) parallels this description of the individual believer. His prayer highlights what is most important for us to pray for one another. Let the redundant list-making prayers cease and the worshipful, self-less prayers commence!

Paul prayed for one thing four different ways.

First, he prayed that we would be rooted and established in love, just like a well-rooted tree or a well-built home.

Second, he prayed that we would "have power, together with all the Lord's people, to grasp how wide and long and high and deep is the love of Christ." What better prayer for missions can there be, but to grasp "the extravagant dimensions of Christ's love." Paul's outlook was anything but pessimistic. It was not a question of whether he could find glimpses of God's love here or there, but whether he could keep up with the full range of God's love. Paul's prayer was a call to action: "Reach out and experience the breadth! Test its length! Plumb the depths! Rise to the heights!" (Eph 3:18, *The Message*).

Third, he prayed that we would "know this love that surpasses knowledge." This reminds us of Paul's prayer for the peace of God that passes all understanding (Phil 4:7) and the love that abounds more and more in knowledge and depth of insight (Phil 1:9). God's loving ways are beyond our ways. His thoughts are so much greater than our thoughts. Thankfully, God's love is not limited by our knowledge or controlled by our understanding.

Fourth, Paul prayed that we would "be filled to the measure of all the fullness of God." This is what it means to live life to the full. Jesus said, "I have come that you might have life and have it to the full" (John 10:10).

---

3. Thielman, *Ephesians*, 231.

## The Love Paradox

It is easy to see how Paul's four-fold prayer request pulls the *meaning* of the first half of the letter into the personal lives of the saints at Ephesus. Like a good pastor, Paul worked to integrate theology and life. Prayer is one of the main tools we have for building a relationship with the Lord.

When Paul prayed for the believers to be well-rooted and well-built in love, he used planting and building metaphors to bring home the truth of the body of Christ. To be rooted and established in love connects with being citizens of God's kingdom, members of God's household, and worshipers in God's temple. The two themes are inseparable. In Paul's mind the metaphors for the church connect with the botanical and architectural metaphors he used for the believing community's growth in love. When he prayed this way he expected believers to make the connection. For Paul it would be inconceivable for any believer to think they were well-rooted and well-established in love, yet remain out of fellowship with the body of Christ. We may think of it this way: God's love is foundational to the believer's love for Christ and one another. Paul prays that these two loves will thrive.

To have power, *together with all the Lord's people*, emphasizes the believer's personal experience of the love of Christ in solidarity with the people of God. The power to *grasp* this love involves an ability to lay hold of it—a capacity that requires a certain kind of strength. An ocean lifeguard works out regularly to build up his forearms and strengthen his grasp. There are more than eight muscles in the forearm that wrap around the bone and give it strength. For most of us, these muscle fibers are more like rope, but in lifeguards and carpenters they seem more like steel cables. Any lifeguard or carpenter can identify with Paul's metaphor of the strength to grasp the love of God.

Paul prayed that we would have the power to grasp the multi-dimensional character of God's love. Commentators have had a field-day with these four dimensions. They have speculated on the cubic dimensions of the physical universe, the character of God, and the heavenly Jerusalem. They have equated these dimensions with a moral virtues, such as love, hope, patience, and humility. But the question remains, what did Paul have in mind?

The key to interpreting what Paul meant by the width, length, height, and depth of God's love, may be found in the spatial analogies that Paul has already used in his letter. The *width* reminds us of the inclusiveness of

## The Glory of Christ

God's love and grace that encompasses all people. Jew and Gentile alike are included in the breadth of God's love.

The *length* recalls the spatial analogy of "near" and "far." God has gone to great lengths to bring Gentiles into his fellowship and to break down the dividing wall of hostility. "But now in Christ Jesus," Paul wrote, "you who once were far away have been brought near by the blood of Christ" (2:13).

The *height* suggests the distance between being dead in our transgressions and sins and being raised up with Christ and seated in the heavenly realms. This vertical dimension captures well the height of God's love.

The *depth* suggests the extent to which God will go to redeem us from our depravity and despair. As death camp survivor Corrie ten Boom said so well, "No pit is so deep, but that God's love is not deeper still." If we apply Paul's prayer to the spatial analogies and themes he has already developed we may come closest to understanding his intentions.

This interpretation encourages further reflection and meditation on the multi-dimensional character of God's love. Paul's prayer inspires doxology. We cannot think of the breadth of God's love without thinking of "members of every tribe and language and people and nation" that have been purchased by the blood of Christ (Rev 5:9). "For God so loved the world that he gave his one and only Son, that whoever believes in him shall not perish but have eternal life" (John 3:16). Nor can we contemplate the height and length of God's love without echoing the Psalmist: "For as high as the heavens are above the earth, so great is his love for those who fear him; as far as the east is from the west, so far as he removed our transgressions from us" (Ps 103:11–12). The love of God is long enough to last forever. The great preacher Charles Spurgeon said that God's love is "so long that our old age cannot wear it out, our continued tribulations cannot exhaust it, our successive temptations cannot drain it dry, and like eternity itself it knows no bounds."

The faithful have contemplated the love of God in spatial language throughout salvation history. David prayed, "If I go up to the heavens, you are there; if I make my bed in the depths, you are there. If I rise on the wings of the dawn, if I settle on the far side of the sea, even there your hand will guide me, your right hand will hold me fast" (Ps 139:8–10). There is no limit to the love of God. "Surely goodness and love will pursue me all the days of my life and I will dwell in the house of the Lord forever" (Ps 23:6).

# The Christ Letter

The multi-dimensional character of God's love has special relevance to Paul's theology of mission and the church's responsibility to make known "the manifold wisdom of God" (3:10). God's love is manifested through the broadest range of vocational pursuits from the arts to architecture and from music to medicine; from the factory worker to the flight attendant and from education to farming. The manifestation of God's love through the performing arts or the building trades or the health care industry or the financial world always leaves the testimony that there is much more to this work than "performing" or "building" or "earning." If we work well, as unto the glory of God, there will be a palpable sense of the reality of God. People will come to realize that we do not love money or music or medicine as ends unto themselves, but we love God. In this sense, our work becomes a devotional expression of our love for God.

God's love spans the difference between old and young, rich and poor, educated and uneducated, black and white, and male and female. God's love is intended for everyone, everywhere. God's love raises up the sinner to salvation and heals the broken-hearted. God brings "down rulers from their thrones but lifts up the humble" (Luke 1:52). Such love makes our lives more complex and difficult. If we were to "love" only ourselves, only our own little group, then we would never know the kind of love Paul so earnestly prays for. We would have simplified our lives, but at the expense of our impoverishment. In the household of faith there is bound to be a built-in tension with this expansive love. If the eyes of our heart are enlightened, we will be able to look the homeless and the elderly in the eye. If we know something of the power of God we will be able to overcome our insecurities and reach out to others. We will overcome generational and societal tensions when we embrace the love that embraces all others with the love of Christ.

Given the multi-dimensional love of God it should be difficult for those who are rooted and established in love to be narrow minded, short-sighted, low-energy, and shallow. God's love and wisdom are marked by depth and meaning. Paul sums it up well when he writes, "Oh, the depth of the riches of the wisdom and knowledge of God! How unsearchable his judgments, and his paths beyond tracing out!" (Rom 11:33).

The nineteenth-century pastor of Trinity Church, Cambridge, Charles Simeon, spoke of *the four magnitudes of God's love*. By definition, *magnitude* is the quality of being great: great in rank or position; great in size or sound, great in significance or importance. The seismologist measures the force of earthquakes in magnitudes and the astronomer

## The Glory of Christ

measures the brightness of stars in magnitudes. It is a fitting word to use for the size, scope, significance, and the strength of God's love. Given the magnitude of God's love how can all those who are in Christ, be anything but magnanimous, that is to say, great in courage, superior to petty resentment, generous in disregard to injuries, and confident in the love of God?

Paul's prayer for believers to know the love that surpasses knowledge in no way diminishes the importance of knowing God. Paul prayed in his eucharistic prayer for believers to have the Spirit of wisdom and revelation so that they might know the Lord better (1:17). Knowing God through his revelation was the most important knowledge known to Paul. His point was not to disparage knowledge in any way, but to point "to the immensity and incomprehensibility of Christ's love."[4] The love of Christ is so all encompassing and longsuffering, so far beyond us and in-depth, that we will never be able to fully comprehend it, much less begin to exhaust it. I picture Paul agreeing with Job, "I know that you can do all things; no purpose of yours can be thwarted . . . Surely I spoke of things I did not understand, things too wonderful for me to know" (Job 42:3). Knowing what we do know of the love of Christ, how could we think otherwise?

The love that surpasses knowledge is not the love that disputes the revelation of God. It is rather, the love that embraces God's revelation, knowing that we will never know the full extent of God's love, but we accept what God has revealed about his love. Those who want to distance themselves from doctrinal orthodoxy might use this verse to justify their errant ways. They reason that since God's love surpasses knowledge there is no need to take doctrine seriously. The love of God, they claim, always trumps doctrinal differences. Take for example a pastor who claims that he fully depends on the love of God but cannot accept the doctrine of the atoning sacrifice of Christ on the cross. He argues that it is a barbaric doctrine that may have made sense in the first century among people acquainted with sacrificial rituals but in the twenty-first century it is nonsense. He claims that Jesus illustrated the highest degree of sacrificial love, but he was not the atoning sacrifice demanded by God and confessed by the church through the centuries. For Paul, the only love of God available to embrace is the love revealed in the Incarnate Son of God. This is the love that is the saving and sustaining grace of all other loves. This is the redeeming love of the crucified and risen Savior. As Paul wrote,

> In love he predestined us for adoption to sonship through Jesus Christ, in accordance with his pleasure and will—to the praise

4. Lincoln, *Ephesians*, 213.

> of his glorious grace, which he has freely given us in the One he loves. In him we have redemption through his blood, the forgiveness of sins, in accordance with the riches of God's grace that he lavished on us. (Eph 1:4–8)

We cannot love without believing and we cannot believe without loving. Surely it is the height of sacrilege to believe in the atoning work of Christ on the cross and then refuse to love the very people for whom Christ died! "Believing without loving turns the best of creeds into a weapon of oppression." Eugene Peterson continues, "A community that believes but does not love or marginalizes love, regardless of its belief system or doctrinal orthodoxy or 'vision statement,' soon, very soon, becomes a 'synagogue of Satan' (Rev 2:9)."[5]

The love that surpasses knowledge is more like the covenantal love between a husband and wife than the contractual agreement between two business partners. Covenantal love pledges our all. It is grandly inclusive of all we are and have. On the other hand, a business contract is all about limiting obligation and liability. It is guarded and calculated. Doctrinal affirmations are more like a covenant than a contract. Knowing the love that surpasses knowledge means that there is always more to our relationship with God than we can possibly express, but never less than the truth clearly revealed in the Bible.

## The Expectation Paradox

*(3:20–21) "Now to him who is able to do immeasurably more than all we ask or imagine, according to his power that is at work within us, to him be the glory in the church and in Christ Jesus throughout all generations, for ever and ever! Amen."*

Paul was anything but conservative when he contemplated the believer's utmost for God's highest! No prayer request could ever be bolder. But this is consistent with what Paul has been saying from the beginning of his letter. He began by saying, "Praise be to the God and Father of our Lord Jesus Christ, who has blessed us in the heavenly realms with every spiritual blessing in Christ" (1:3). It made perfect sense for Paul to expect great things from those who had been chosen, predestined, and redeemed, all in accordance with the riches of God's grace.

---

5. Peterson, *Christ Plays In Ten Thousand Places*, 261.

The fullness of God is a theme that runs through the letter. Paul ended his eucharistic prayer by referring to the church, "which is [Christ's] body, the fullness of him who fills everything in every way" (1:23). He spoke of the body of Christ "attaining to the whole measure of the fullness of Christ" (4:13). He challenged believers to "be filled with the Spirit" (5:18). There is an obvious tension here between what the church is in principle and what she is in actual practice. The gap between expectation and realization can be explained, at least in part, in the tension between the "already" and the "not yet." Paul expected believers to live up to their God-given potential and to realize the fullness of God in ever increasing ways. The rest of the letter will help to explain and visualize what the fullness of God looks like in practical day-to-day living.

If the church is going to make known "the manifold wisdom of God" to the rulers and authorities in the heavenly realms, it will have to have a real experience of the love and power of God. Paul had no concept of the church as a beleaguered and fearful minority fighting for its life. He saw the church, which the world saw as nothing, as the concrete expression of the love and power of God in the world. He exudes confidence in God, not in any worldly strategy or secular means or political power. Make no mistake, the mission of the church, in so far as it is the mission of the crucified and risen Lord, will be accomplished, only through the power of the cross. Doxology completely overshadowed any lament that Paul might have felt over his circumstances. The glory of God cannot be conveyed in money and buildings, no matter how grand. God's glory is not expensive, but expressive of the indwelling love of Christ. The architecture of the soul is what matters. The building up of the body of Christ in the love of Christ is all that matters.

# 7

# The Body of Christ

*". . . so that the body of Christ may be built up . . ."*

EPHESIANS 4:12

There is a remarkable juxtaposition between Paul's prayer, "Now to him who is able to do immeasurably more than all we ask or imagine . . ." and his exhortation, "Make every effort to keep the unity of the Spirit . . ." He expected the immeasurable power of God to do the unimaginable and unify the body of Christ. The dividing wall of hostility was destroyed in principle, but Paul was passionately concerned that it be destroyed in practice. We may not call what separates believers a dividing wall of hostility, but we have grown accustomed to living with a dividing wall of denominational distinctives. When Paul gave his memorable doxology he could not have imagined the myriad of issues that would divide us today. Thankfully, God does do more than we could ever ask or imagine through Baptists, Anglicans, Presbyterians, Lutherans, Roman Catholics, Charismatics, Methodists, etc., and most believers acknowledge that God is at work through these believers, even if they focus more on their differences than their shared commitment to Christ. Unity in theory, we may all esteem, but unity in practice calls for a life worthy of our calling. Paul is ready to work out the practical application of salvation.

*The Body of Christ*

## Doctrine and Duty

The momentum of Paul's theology of worship, salvation, church, and mission moves him to exhortation. In the second half of the letter he used the imperative forty times, compared to a single use in the first three chapters (Eph 2:11).[1] Everything Paul has said to this point is foundational for his description of a whole new way of living life. The structure of Paul's letter is important and the order is intentional. The movement from "mind-stretching theology to its down-to-earth, concrete implications in everyday life" is exactly what Paul had in mind.[2] He began with worship: praising God for blessing us in the heavenly realms with every spiritual blessing; praying that the eyes of our heart would be enlightened in order for us to know the hope of our calling, the riches of his glorious inheritance, and his incomparably great power.

Following his eulogizing praise and eucharistic prayer (Eph 1:3–23), Paul explored the depths of salvation, the power of God's grace in Christ to overcome our depravity and our alienation (Eph 2:1–18). We are God's workmanship created in Christ Jesus to do good works. We belong to a new society. We are fellow citizens with God's people, members of God's household and joined together to become a holy temple in the Lord. The power of the cross of Christ to break down the dividing wall of hostility leads the church to make known the manifold wisdom of God. On his knees, Paul prays that we would know the four magnitudes of Christ's love and that God would be glorified "in the church and in Christ Jesus." The first half of the letter concludes with a resounding *Amen!*

Paul's approach differs from our perspective in two significant ways.

1. Paul saw the community first and then the individual. He had a high view of the church, God's new society, tasked with the responsibility of administering the mystery of God's grace and making known the manifold wisdom of God. We, on the other hand, zero in on the individual and tend to forget about the community. We can be individualistic to the point of being self-centered. We take the individual as the starting point and tend to look for what appeals and inspires our private selves.

Pollster George Barna describes a new breed of "revolutionary" Christians who want to be part of something big and important—the church. But these "revolutionaries" don't want anything to do with the inconvenience of the local church. Going to church doesn't make you a

1. Hoehner, *Ephesians*, 499.
2. Stott, *God's New Society*, 146.

Christian, says Barna, any more than going to a baseball stadium makes you a professional ballplayer. Barna predicts that the search for customized personal experiences will lead many to "the personal 'church' of the individual."[3]

Barna encourages individuals to choose the activities and relationships that they find fulfilling and inspiring. He counsels people to leave behind the burden of the local church with all of its commitments and responsibilities. He predicts that church service attendance, budgets, and programs will all decline as people select friends and activities that meet their spiritual needs. People's spiritual lives will become more exciting and intimate as they join "marketplace fellowships," "coaching communities," and worship on line at their "cyberchurch." Sunday morning at Singing Hills golf course may be a more worshipful experience than singing the Doxology in church with a cross-section of humanity.

If by "local church" Barna means a large, impersonal religious institution driven by egotistical pastors intent on programming our spiritual experience, then we may find his predictions appealing. Or if going to church means sitting in a pew for sixty minutes and listening to a boring sermon, then we may like Barna's proposed "personal church of the individual." Or if you find yourself lost in the masses at an all-purpose megachurch, you may find it attractive to skip church and meet a friend at Starbucks. The apostle Paul may have agreed with Barna's criticism of the large, impersonal, program-driven local church, but I am fairly certain he never would have agreed with Barna's solution.

Paul frames everything in terms of the new society—the cross-generational, cross-cultural, community in Christ, marked by the cross. "The gospel is never for individuals but always for a people. Sin fragments us, separates us, and sentences us to solitary confinement. The Gospel restores us, unites us, and sets us in community."[4] Paul knew nothing of a "secret, individualized faith." "Christ is not seen apart from the gathered, listening, praying, believing, worshiping people to whom he is Lord and Savior. It is not possible to have Christ apart from the church."[5] Following Jesus without being in the church is like a soccer player without a team, an actor without an audience, a symphony conductor without an orchestra, a teacher without students—you get the point.

3. Barna, *Revolution*, 66.
4. Peterson, *Reversed Thunder*, 42.
5. Ibid., 44.

2. We tend to shy away from thinking theologically. We may be inclined to skip Paul's first section on worship, salvation, and mission and jump directly to the so-called practical issues. We prefer a lively discussion the "hot" topics to thinking about the "heavenly realms." For many, theology is a subject better left alone and simply assumed, than expounded and explained. To delve into theological issues is to leave people bored and restless, or so it is thought. Sadly, too many believers consider theology to be little more than the inconvenient theory behind the more practical and appealing topics of interest. We want practical advice on money and relationships. We want creative talks on core values, self-esteem, feeling good about ourselves, and making a difference.

Ephesians is an antidote to this soul-dwarfing mindset. Paul handles the Word of truth in such a dynamic and life-penetrating way that his theology of worship and salvation builds us up in Christ. Our lives take root in the truth of the gospel. Paul is a poetic theologian, carefully crafting his exposition of God's Word to inspire passion, build confidence, and bring his message home. "Ephesians contains more specific practical applications for daily life than any other [New Testament] book."[6]

Ephesians does not lend itself to an info-sermon, delivered by a talking Bible-head. If we turn Ephesians into a pedantic and laborious study, it's not Paul's fault, it's ours. How could this well-reasoned, thoroughly prayed over, Spirit-inspired, letter from prison be boring except to those who refuse to enter into it on its own terms. We can kill it and dissect it in the laboratory or we can use it to trigger our own opinions, but if we let the prisoner for the Lord speak to us, we will find the message compelling.

## One Calling

(4:1–6) *"As a prisoner for the Lord, then, I urge you to live a life worthy of the calling you have received. Be completely humble and gentle; be patient, bearing with one another in love. Make every effort to keep the unity of the Spirit through the bond of peace. There is one body and one Spirit, just as you were called to one hope when you were called; one Lord, one faith, one baptism; one God and Father of all, who is over all and through all and in all."*

---

6. Hoehner, *Ephesians*, 500.

The Christ Letter

The power of Paul's persuasion flows from his passion not his position. Without a hint of pity, Paul used his "status" as a prisoner for the Lord to urge, encourage, comfort, and warn believers "to live a life worthy of the calling you have received." Literally, Paul exhorted believers, "Walk worthy of the *calling* with which you were *called*."[7] There is only one all-purpose calling for each and every believer and the call to salvation includes the call to sanctification. The call to redemption includes the call to vocation. The purpose of Paul's exhortation is for believers to live lives consistent with the salvation they have received in Christ. This "calling" is shared by all of us and no believer is more called than any other believer and no believer needs to wait for a special experience to feel called of God. To use the language of Ephesians, those who have been, *by God*, blessed, chosen, redeemed, forgiven, predestined, marked, saved, joined together, strengthened, and filled, are equally called by God.

The implications of this *one* calling are profound for embracing our personal responsibility. Theology and ethics are melded together so thoroughly that there is no option for subjective selectivity. We cannot afford to pick and choose what we want to submit to, anymore than a Navy Seal can decide which orders he wants to obey and which ones he wants to ignore. In time the institutional church distinguished between the counsels of perfection and ordinary commands, but Paul never entertained such a notion. He resisted any hint of elitism. He never envisioned a two or three-tiered hierarchy of spirituality, nor a clergy-laity division, much less the meaningless distinction between "true believers" and "average churchgoers." In Paul's theology of the church everyone in Christ shares the same calling.

Perhaps one way to appreciate the significance of our calling in Christ is to compare it with a person's professional identity. Those who have worked hard to gain certification and acceptance in their chosen career usually have a strong sense of professional identity. They are governed by procedures, protocols, and expectations that they are eager to honor and loathe to violate. Firefighters, bankers, artists, physicians, lawyers, musicians, soldiers, pilots, authors, police officers, actors, etc. are all defined by their professional identity. Their creeds and codes are often demanding and all encompassing. They seek to live a life worthy of their profession. If this is true for a person's career, how much more should it be true for those who are called in Christ?

---

7. The verb περιπατέω, "to walk" is used eight times in Ephesians (2:2, 10; 4:1, 17; 5:2, 8, 15) metaphorically to refer to one's conduct or lifestyle.

Paul began his exhortation to live a life worthy of our calling in a way that would have impressed neither the Greek ethicist nor the Jewish moralist of his day, nor the hard-driving professional of our day. "Be completely humble and gentle: be patient, bearing with one another in love," was hardly the recipe for success in the first century. Humility (ταπεινοφροσύνη) meant "lowliness of mind" and was used by Paul in Philippians to describe the attitude of mind that was in Christ Jesus, who "humbled himself by becoming obedient to death—even death on a cross!" (Phil 2:3–8). "Since humility is not considered a virtue by human beings," writes New Testament scholar Harold Hoehner, "it is understandable why this word did not exist before [New Testament] times."[8] Given the newness of the term and its central significance in this new way of living, we might say that Christians invented the term "humility" or at least took out a patent on the character quality.

Paul's emphasis on "all humility" underscored the subservient attitude that was fundamental to Paul's subversive lifestyle. He took an attitude commonly used of slaves and servants and applied it to the Christian, with an eye toward preserving the unity of the body of Christ. He further elaborated on humility by adding two more qualities. Gentleness or meekness implied a strength of personality that did not have to assert itself. Patience literally meant long-tempered rather than short-tempered, and underscored the need for steadfastness and forbearance. All three virtues are consistent with Jesus' beatitude-based character, foot-washing humility, and cross-bearing discipline.

For Paul everything flows from this character-shaping premise and heartfelt disposition. All of his instructions in Christian living, all of his guidance for Christian households, and all of his counsel in Christian employment, go back to this basic premise of humility, gentleness, and patience. To walk worthily literally means balancing the scales or metaphorically bringing the conduct of one's life into balance with one's call.[9] Preserving the unity of the Spirit meant "bearing with one another in love." In Paul's stewardship of life, these two verses form a key mission statement: "Be completely humble and gentle; be patient, bearing with one another in love. Make every effort to keep the unity of the Spirit through the bond of peace."[10]

---

8. Hoehner, *Ephesians*, 505–6.

9. Ibid., 504.

10. Paul offered similar counsel in Colossians 3:12–15.

Paul makes a point of emphasizing the fruit of the Spirit before he discusses either our unity in the Spirit or the gifts of the Spirit. It is absolutely essential that we keep on remembering our dependence upon God's saving grace and undeserved mercy so that we can "bear with one another in love." The theology of the first half of the letter is essential to the practice described in the second half of the letter. We share one calling in one body, making it mandatory that we make allowance for one another's shortcomings and exasperating behavior. "Bearing with others means fully accepting them in their uniqueness, including their weaknesses and faults, and allowing them worth and space."[11]

The value of the individual is not lost in the growth of the body, nor is the church subservient to the whim of the individual. There is a dynamic relationship between Paul's emphasis on *oneness* and his concern for *one another*. In most units, teams, groups, and companies, the individual is sacrificed for the greater good of the larger body. But that's not how God intended it to be in the church. "Christians are part of each other and are to receive one another, build up one another, bear each other's burdens, submit to each other, and encourage one another."[12] God designed the church to be a unique community that can strengthen the individual and build itself up at the same time. In the Spirit, the church neither takes advantage of the individual nor allows the individual to take advantage of the church.

This is a tall order that requires constant vigilance. Paul was emphatic, "Make every effort to keep the unity of the Spirit through the bond of peace." In English it is hard to do justice to the Greek imperative. It means, "Take pains," "Spare no effort," "Give it all you've got." Obviously Paul intends an all-out effort. A lackadaisical attitude is dismissed. Any hint of passivity or a wait-and-see attitude is excluded. Paul calls for "a diligence tempered by all deliberate speed. Yours is the initiative! Do it now! Mean it! You are to do it! I mean it!—such are the overtones in this verse."[13]

The big question is how do we keep the unity of the Spirit through the bond of peace, when there is so much that threatens to pull us apart? We know that Paul was vigilant against doctrinal error and disobedience, yet he was also patient and forbearing with the foibles, personalities, and eccentricities of individuals in the body of Christ. This is a challenge for us, because we are tempted to look the other way when presented with

---

11. Lincoln, *Ephesians*, 236–37.
12. Snodgrass, *Ephesians*, 197.
13. Barth, *Ephesians*, 428.

*The Body of Christ*

cases of heresy and immorality in the church and yet fixate on petty issues and personality clashes in the church. We tend to ignore what we should deal with and deal with what we should ignore.

John Stott distinguishes between the tolerant *mind* and the tolerant *spirit*. "Tolerant in spirit a Christian should always be, loving, understanding, forgiving and forbearing others, making allowances for them, and giving them the benefit of the doubt, for true love 'bears all things, believes all things, hopes all things, endures all things' (1 Corinthians 13:7). But how can we be tolerant in mind of what God has plainly revealed to be either evil or erroneous?"[14] True humility doesn't mean altering the truth of the gospel to fit the spirit of the age, nor substituting the rhetoric of acceptance for the grace of the Lord Jesus. Humility is an intentional commitment to surrender our will to the commands of God and the needs of others. To make every effort to keep the unity of the Spirit calls the saints to sacrifice for the sake of the truth, not to sacrifice the truth.

The bond of peace does not mean a negotiated settlement between two competing rivals. It doesn't mean acquiescing to other people's demands or meeting people halfway or appeasing warring factions in the church. Nor does the *bond* between believers depend on human creativity and orchestration. The bond is Christ. As Paul said earlier, Christ himself is our peace, because we are brought together by the blood of Christ (2:13–14). Whatever effort we exert and whatever bond we seek to strengthen has to be in Christ. What binds us together is not a common cause or a shared activity. It is not sports or music or a shared concern for our children. Christ alone is our only hope. Apart from Christ we cannot break down the walls of hostility or bridge the gaps that come between us.

## One Body

The unity we are called to keep in the Spirit is emphasized in "a series of seven acclamations of oneness," climaxed in a four-fold repetition of "all."[15] Each creedal acclamation calls attention to the dynamic experience of oneness in the body of Christ. The confession forms three parts of equal length: body-Spirit-hope; Lord-faith-baptism; God the Father of all—over, through and in all.[16] This metaphysical description belongs to the most real world, as surely as any physical formula—only more so. The

---

14. Stott, *Christ the Controversialist*, 17.
15. Lincoln, *Ephesians*, 237.
16. Barth, *Ephesians*, 463.

meaning of the oneness confessed in this three-stanza poetic hymn is the foundation for all meaning and order and beauty and wisdom. It takes the power and wisdom and love of this oneness to make the one new person out of a humankind divided in hostility.[17]

The one body is the "one new humanity," the church, "the fullness of him who fills everything in every way," reconciled to God and to one another in Christ (1:23; 2:15). The one Spirit is the Holy Spirit through whom we have access to the Father and in whom we live together in the body (2:18, 22). The one hope is in Christ (1:12, 18), who has the power "to bring unity to all things in heaven and earth" (1:10). Our hope for the future determines how we live in the present. The one Lord is Jesus Christ whom we confess in one faith and one baptism. Christ is the object of our personal faith and the reason for our public baptism. The one God is our heavenly Father, who is the ultimate source and the ultimate destiny of all things.[18] One God is Father of all, who is over all and through all and in all. By calling God "Father," Paul emphasizes the personal character of God. God is the one with whom we have a personal relationship.

The four-fold "all" does not mean that everything is God and God is everything. The oneness described by Paul is different from monism, the belief that everything is ultimately only one thing. Buddhists, Hindus, materialists, and naturalists differ on how to envision this "everything" but they are together in believing that there is only one substance, whether it be material, mental, or spiritual. C. S. Lewis explained it this way: "The Everythingist, if he starts from God, becomes a Pantheist; there must be nothing that is not God. If he starts from Nature he becomes a Naturalist; there must be nothing that is not Nature." Lewis concluded that this philosophy is "profoundly untrue." "All things come from One. All things are related—related in different and complicated ways. But all things are not one."[19]

We cannot say "that God includes all opposites within himself—good and evil, light and darkness, being and nonbeing." Rather, God "is the perfect good that negates evil and sets it off as an antithesis to his holy will."[20] God the Father is *of all*—"for in him all things were created," *over all*—"all things have been created through him and for him," *through all and in all*—"for God was pleased to have all his fullness dwell in him, and

---

17. Barth, *Ephesians*, 463.
18. Fee, *The First Epistle to the Corinthians*, 374.
19. Lewis, *Miracles*, 169.
20. Bloesch, *Essentials of Evangelical Theology*, 1:34.

through him to reconcile to himself all things, whether things on earth or things in heaven, by making peace through his blood shed on the cross" (Col 1:15–20). What is said of the Father can be said of the Son. God is superior to and supreme over all things and stands over and under, above and beyond his creation.

## Every-member Ministry

All of us share equal responsibility to live a life worthy of the calling we have received. This shared calling—our *one* calling, involves "bearing with *one another* in love." Note that the oneness of the call is in relationship with our responsibility to one another. The individual person does not get lost in the great ends of a religious movement or in the crusading spirit of a great cause. The church is never a mass movement that can afford to use people up for the sake of the cause. No one in the body of Christ is expendable. Our shared calling is always linked to bearing with one another in love. Likewise, the unity of the body—our *one* body, depends on *each one* receiving spiritual gifts.

(4:7–13) *"But to each one of us grace has been given as Christ apportioned it. This is why it says: 'When he ascended on high, he took many captives and gave gifts to his people.' (What does 'he ascended' mean except that he also descended to the lower, earthly regions? He who descended is the very one who ascended higher than all the heavens, in order to fill the whole universe.) So Christ himself gave the apostles, the prophets, the evangelists, the pastors and teachers, to equip his people for works of service, so that the body of Christ may be built up until we all reach unity in the faith and in knowledge of the Son of God and become mature, attaining to the whole measure of the fullness of Christ."*

Everyone who is in the body is gifted to build up the body. We are to bear with one another but everyone is expected to bear their own responsibility. We are a household of faith in Christ not a spiritual welfare state. In a family there are various degrees of maturity but all are expected to be maturing. Responsibilities differ but all are responsible. We are interdependent without fostering dependency. We want to strengthen the weak without perpetuating weakness. We want to empower our brothers and sisters in Christ without enabling immaturity. The goal that Paul had in mind is expressed positively and negatively. He wants all of us "to reach unity in the faith and in the knowledge of the Son of God and become mature, attaining to the whole measure of the fullness of Christ. Then we will no longer be infants, tossed back and forth by the waves..." (4:13–14).

For the sake of this process of growth and maturity, Paul's initial emphasis was not on the gifts but on the giver. Paul used Psalm 68 to present the ascended and exalted Christ as the giver of all spiritual gifts. He paralleled the Israelites in the wilderness with the church in Christ. Psalm 68 rehearses the blessings of God when the Israelites were released from captivity. In the wilderness, God forged a new community, giving the Israelites protection, provision, and most importantly, his word. The Psalmist celebrates God's relational gifts: "A father to the fatherless, a defender of widows, is God in his holy dwelling. God sets the lonely in families, he leads out the prisoners with singing . . ." (68:5–6). God also gave his people material gifts, "You gave abundant showers, O God; you refreshed your weary inheritance. Your people settled in it, and from your bounty, God, you provided for the poor" (68:9–10). But the most important gift God gave his people was his Word. The Psalmist declares, "The Lord announced the word, and great was the company of those who proclaimed it" (68:11). To say that God rules and reigns from Mount Sinai is to say that God's Word rules and reigns. Originally, the gifts alluded to in the Psalm referred to the spoils of war, but Paul carried over the meaning of the Psalm and applied it to the victory of Christ and the gifts given by Christ.

The reason he used this particular Psalm may have been its liturgical association with Pentecost, the Jewish feast celebrating the giving of the law on Mount Sinai. The original meaning of Pentecost had now been eclipsed by the outpouring of the Holy Spirit at Pentecost. For Paul the greater significance of Psalm 68 went beyond Moses coming down from Sinai with the law to the ascended Christ giving spiritual gifts to his body. Paul's emphasis on descent and ascent, fits with the incarnation and ascension of Christ (Acts 2:33) and parallels the humiliation and exaltation of Christ described in Philippians 2. The reference to "many captives" refers to Christ's power over "the rulers and authorities in the heavenly realms" (3:10; see 1:21; 6:12).

The diversity of gifts distributed to the church derives from a single donor, Jesus Christ. No one can give what he or she has not first received from Christ and no one can out-give God. The stewardship of life means that everything we receive is held in trust. These gifts are not ours free and clear to simply do with as we please. We have been entrusted to use them for building up the body of Christ. In Ephesians, Paul's emphasis is on the identity of the Giver, followed by a short list of five gifts. In this case, the gifts are not skills or abilities or talents, but *people* tasked with the responsibility of declaring the Word of God. They are listed as apostles, prophets, evangelists, pastors, and teachers. Only teaching gifts are mentioned here. These are the gifts that introduce, proclaim, announce, nurture, and instruct people in the Word of God.

John Calvin observed, "We see that God, who might perfect his people in a moment, chooses not to bring them to maturity in any other way than by the education of the Church."[21] Therefore, preaching the Word became instrumental in growing strong Christians, not because it was the only way, but because it was the chosen way. God might have used angels or no means at all, but instead he chose humans and the "ordinary method of teaching" to convey his truth, "that he may thus allure us to himself, instead of driving us away by his thunder."[22] God declared his own love and humility towards us by choosing people like us "to be interpreters of his secret will; in short, to represent his own person." The method and the means demonstrates not only the humility of God, but requires our humility as well. Calvin calls it "a most excellent and useful training in humility."

We might think that having described preachers as the mouthpiece of God, "doing God's work by their lips," that Calvin would emphasize the exalted status of the preacher, but he does just the opposite. By divine design, we learn humility by having to listen to God's Word through people like ourselves, "or, it may be, our inferiors in worth." Calvin goes on to say, "When a feeble man, sprung from the dust, speaks in the name of God, we give the best proof of our piety and obedience, by listening with docility to his servant, though not in any respect our superior. Accordingly, he hides the treasure of his heavenly wisdom in frail earthen vessels (2 Cor 4:7), that he may have a more certain proof of the estimation in which it is held by us."[23]

Calvin's perspective on the humility of God, who chooses this ordinary method of teaching to communicate his Word, and the humility of sincere believers, who receive the Word from people like ourselves ("or, it may be, our inferiors in worth"), has implications for the role of women in ministry. We hear in some circles that men are better representatives of the authority of God than women, but if humility is the key concept for

---

21. Calvin, *Institutes of the Christian Religion*, IV:1.5, 284.
22. Ibid., 285.
23. Ibid., IV:3.1, 316.

preaching, then it might be argued, that women are even better than men for the task. I would argue that neither men nor women are inferior or superior in the preaching ministry, but both underscore the humility of God in choosing them to represent his Word. And both men and women train us all in humility in listening to them preach the Word.

We need to resist the temptation to digress from Paul's purpose, by dwelling on the differences between apostles, prophets, evangelists, pastors, and teachers. In my opinion, Paul's concern was not so much to differentiate these five servants as to emphasize Christ's singular purpose, namely, "to equip his people for works of service, so that the body of Christ might be built up . . ." This is another example of Paul piling up the evidence to make his case: first, that all spiritual gifts are dependent upon the Word of God for their effective use. There are no spiritual gifts, no works of service, designed to build up the body that can work effectively apart from the wisdom and guidance of the Word of God. The ministry of the Word is essential in the use of all the spiritual gifts. Second, Paul implies that all believers are without excuse. No one can claim to be ill-equipped to serve, because Christ has provided a variety of ministers of the Word to meet the need.

Suppose a person says, "I need an effective Bible study teacher before I can effectively serve the Lord." And someone else says, "I can't serve the Lord, because I don't have a nurturing pastor." And a third person says, "When someone shows me how to evangelize then maybe I'll be able to talk to others about Christ." Excuses like these misunderstand Paul's point. He is arguing that all the saints are already the beneficiaries of the apostles, prophets, evangelists, pastors, and teachers. Christ has already given these gifts and we have already received their benefits. So instead of lamenting our perceived deficiencies we should acknowledge God's gracious ministry to us.

To equip the saints for works of service involved dynamic *conditioning* rather than indoctrination; it meant meaningful *restoration* in the love of Christ rather than pedantic teaching on procedures and techniques. Paul was not envisioning "how-to" lessons in social justice or creative formulas for church growth or five easy steps for evangelism.

One church member complained to me that the reason he had never served was because he had never been equipped. Although he had listened to forty years of Bible preaching and been involved in countless Bible studies, he lamented that no pastor had ever taken the time to equip him. He had the mistaken notion that equipping the saints meant specialized, how-to-instruction not found in the Bible. He was looking for step-by-step techniques. But the kind of equipping Paul had in mind was designed to cultivate the Christian mind, which would in turn lead to Christian action. His word to Timothy parallels this meaning: "All Scripture is God-breathed and is useful for teaching, rebuking, correcting and training in righteousness, so that all God's people may be thoroughly equipped for every good work" (2 Tim 3:16–17).

The saints who are equipped "for works of service" are those who allow the Word of God to train and condition them "for every good work." Because they have a hunger and thirst for righteousness they feed on the Word of God. Because they have been called to be "salt" and "light" in the midst of decay and darkness, they have a need for the life and light of the Word of God. The equipping process takes two sincere people: an honest, humble teacher who is submissive to the Bible and capable of communicating its truth effectively and faithfully, and a sincere saint who is ready to do works of service, so that the body of Christ may be built up. After many years of preaching, I believe it is those who see themselves as missionaries in the marketplace or in the classroom or in their families who get the most out of the Sunday morning message. *Salt and light* Christians have a hunger for the Word of God and they profit from this equipping ministry.

The diversity of gifts contributes to the unity of the body, not its division. Paul never intended to reduce the bulk of church members to "the rank of mere consumers of spiritual gifts."[24] Nor was his emphasis on teaching gifts meant to produce a division between pastors and people. The responsibility to build up the body of believers belongs to the people as a whole, not to pastors in particular. Paul assumes two important principles, a team-ministry approach for teaching the Word of God and an every-member ministry for building up the church. No single person is responsible for teaching the Word of God. Christ gives his church a variety of people to minister the Word: apostles, prophets, evangelists, pastors, and teachers. The ministry of the Word is indispensable, but never independent from the full-orbed work of the gospel. Strong Bible teaching invariably produces well-equipped servants who demonstrate "the manifold wisdom of God" and the multi-dimensional love of Christ.

---

24. Barth, *Ephesians*, 479.

## Maturity versus Infancy

(4:14–16) *"Then we will no longer be infants, tossed back and forth by the waves, and blown here and there by every wind of teaching and by the cunning and craftiness of people in their deceitful scheming. Instead speaking the truth in love, we will in all things grow up in him who is the head, that is Christ. From him the whole body, joined and held together by every supporting ligament, grows and builds itself up in love, as each part does its work."*

The goal of unity is maturity. Unity in the body of Christ is reached "in the faith and in the knowledge of the Son of God." Maturity involves "attaining to the whole measure of the fullness of Christ." All that Paul has said about worship, salvation and mission comes to bear in his picture of unity and maturity. The two are inseparable. If we think unity can be achieved through any other means than Christ and his Word we are mistaken.

In the absence of this maturity, Christians remain as weak and as vulnerable as infants. Paul concludes this section with a set of contrasts. Those who do not "reach unity in the faith and in the knowledge of the Son of God and become mature, attaining to the whole measure of the fullness of Christ," remain like "infants, tossed back and forth by the waves." If our growth in Christ is retarded we will remain as vulnerable as a baby in a raging sea. Paul pictures the immature Christian tossed around "by every wind of teaching and by the cunning and craftiness of people in their deceitful scheming."

Instead of being held together and built up, they are tossed around and broken down. Instead of being equipped by apostles, prophets, evangelists, pastors and teachers, they are confused and manipulated by impostors—spiritual con artists, who prey on unstable believers. Instead of "speaking the truth in love," these schemers use tricks and gimmicks and deceit to sway unsuspecting believers. Instead of "growing up into him who is the head, that is Christ," they are subject to humanistic, self-serving leadership. Instead of each part of a unified body doing its work, immature believers are passive consumers of deception.

Paul's set of contrasts reminds us of Jesus' conclusion in the Sermon on the Mount (Matt 7:13–27). Jesus contrasted two ways (broad and narrow), two teachers (false and true), two pleas (words and deeds), and finally two foundations (sand and rock). His message ends with a parable about two kinds of builders: one who builds on the rock and one who builds on the sand. The choice is ours: the wisdom of Christ or the foolishness of the world. We either build on shifting sands or we build on the bedrock foundation of Jesus Christ.

In Ephesians, the main metaphor is the body. If we are part of the body we will be growing up into him who is the head, that is Christ. We will be held together by every supporting ligament and we will grow up in love, as each part does its work. The unity of the body of Christ is the gift we have received by grace and the goal of all our work in Christ. John Calvin wrote, "The whole comes to this, that the Holy Spirit is the bond by which Christ effectually binds us to himself."[25]

---

25. Calvin, *Institutes*, III:1, 463.

# 8

# The Ethic of Christ

*"You were taught, with regard to your former way of life, to put off
your old self, which is being corrupted by its deceitful desires;
to be made new in the attitude of your minds;
and to put on the new self, created to be like God
in true righteousness and holiness."*

EPHESIANS 4:22–24

Never one for humorous introductions or pious platitudes, Paul maintains the momentum of his exhortation. Like his Lord in the Sermon on the Mount, Paul had a down-to-earth, tell-it-like-it-is approach that skipped amusing anecdotes and heart-tugging human interest stories. Paul admonished believers to speak the truth in love so that the body of Christ might grow up into him, who is the head, that is Christ. The teaching and counsel that follows is an illustration of speaking the truth in love, but it may be more direct and straightforward than we are used to.

Paul's description of the new humanity in Christ begins with a sharp contrast between the old self and the new self. "So I tell you this, and insist on it in the Lord, that you must no longer live as the Gentiles do, in the futility of their thinking" (Eph 4:17). Our age tends to be seriously unserious, but Paul appears intensely serious. He was authoritative and insistent, without being opinionated and heavy-handed. His style and substance effectively convey that he is being used by the Lord instead of using the Lord for his own purposes.

## Authoritative Preaching

(4:17–24) *"So I tell you this, and insist on it in the Lord, that you must no longer live as the Gentiles do, in the futility of their thinking. They are darkened in their understanding and separated from the life of God because of the ignorance that is in them due to the hardening of their hearts. Having lost all sensitivity, they have given themselves over to sensuality so as to indulge in every kind of impurity, and they are full of greed.*

*That, however, is not the way of life you learned when you heard about Christ and were taught in him in accordance with the truth that is in Jesus. You were taught, with regard to your former way of life, to put off your old self, which is being corrupted by its deceitful desires; to be made new in the attitude of your minds; and to put on the new self, created to be like God in true righteousness and holiness."*

Moved by the apostle Paul's preaching example, the Danish Christian philosopher Søren Kierkegaard distinguished worldly persuasion from divine authority. Kierkegaard highlighted Paul's convictions in the following observations:

1. A genius is born; an apostle is called. A genius adds to the accumulated understanding and science of man, but an apostle proclaims the wisdom of God, not found in the nature of things. A genius' insights are quickly assimilated and superceded by new breakthroughs, but the apostle's proclamation remains true through time.

2. A genius is measured by intelligence, inventiveness, and innate abilities, but an apostle is identified exclusively by divine authority. We do not listen to the apostle Paul "because he is clever, or even brilliantly clever" but because his message comes from God. Authority is not measured in "the profundity, the excellence, the cleverness of the doctrine."[1]

Kierkegaard lamented the artificial style of preachers in his day. "Yet, nowadays, it is seldom, very seldom, that one hears or reads a religious

---

1. Kierkegaard, *Of the Difference Between a Genius and an Apostle*, 96.

discourse which is framed correctly . . . If one had to describe Christian discourse as it is now heard with a single definite predicate, one would have to say it was *affected* . . . the whole train of thought is affected."[2] Kierkegaard argued that we must not accept the truth of God, because it is "clever or profound or wonderfully beautiful, for this is a mockery of God."[3] Don't picture Paul as the dazzling Greek orator on stage, insisted Kierkegaard, picture Paul as the tireless housewife in a needy family who herself hardly has time to eat, so busy is she preparing food for others. He is far more like a parent training his children than a philosopher wooing his audience. When Paul says, "So I tell you this, and insist on it in the Lord," pay attention!

## "Separated from the life of God"

To live worthy of the calling we have received (4:1), means to no longer live as *Californians* live (4:17). Substitute whatever cultural context you would like. After living for fourteen years in southern California this brings the message home for me. I really like California! It may be easier to assume that Paul's message was meant for someone else at another time and place, but it is clear from the force of his message that it remains in effect for today's believer. In the Spirit, Paul's exhortation applies to the church down through the centuries. The purpose of preaching Ephesians is not to have a clearer understanding of Paul for Paul's sake, but to have a deeper understanding of the way we ought to live for Christ today.

Since Paul saw himself as an apostle to the Gentiles, called to preach to the Gentiles the boundless riches of Christ, he intended no disrespect against Gentile *ethnicity*. But Paul saw it as his duty to warn believers against a Gentile *ethic*. The prevailing pagan worldviews and lifestyles represented a grave danger to unsuspecting and immature Christians who might be tempted to fall back into their old patterns of thinking and living.

Before discussing specific issues of behavior, Paul developed a stark contrast between the old self and the new self. He did this by describing the presuppositions behind the Gentile lifestyle and the thinking behind the Christian lifestyle. Christian apologist Francis Schaeffer began his important work in the 1970s, entitled *How Should We Then Live?*, by doing what Paul did in the first century. He argued that the flow of history and culture is rooted in the thoughts of people. Schaeffer's reasoning fits

2. Ibid., 101–3.
3. Ibid., 104.

## The Ethic of Christ

with Paul's indictment of Gentile thinking, or should we say, *California* thinking!

> People have presuppositions and they will live more consistently on the basis of these presuppositions than even they themselves may realize. By presuppositions we mean the basic way an individual looks at life, his basic world view, the grid through which he sees the world. Presuppositions rest upon that which a person considers to be the truth of what exists. People's presuppositions lay a grid for all they bring forth into the external world. Their presuppositions also provide the basis for their values and therefore the basis for their decisions.[4]

Paul was not interested in debating the positive and negative features of the Gentile lifestyle. He could have found signs of God's common grace among the pagans, but instead he chose to examine their moral, intellectual, and spiritual foundation for living. Impressive lives, like beautiful buildings, can be built on faulty foundations. Paul is like a trained engineer, examining the worldview foundation for living. He is not distracted by the beautiful living room decor.

For Paul the heart of the matter can be summed up by the proverb, "As a man thinks so is he." His examination of the fundamental presuppositions of the Californian lifestyle is described in wholly negative terms. People live "in the futility of their thinking." They are "darkened in their understanding and separated from the life of God because of the ignorance that is in them due to the hardening of their hearts" (4:17–18). Their thinking is empty, flawed, and ultimately pointless. "The light has gone out in the seat of [*Californians'*] understanding so that they are no longer capable of apprehending ultimate truth."[5]

What Paul says in Ephesians closely parallels his thought in Romans:

> For although they knew God, they neither glorified him as God nor gave thanks to him, but their thinking became futile and their foolish hearts were darkened. Although they claimed to be wise, they became fools and exchanged the glory of the immortal God for images made to look like mortal human beings and birds and animals and reptiles. (Rom 1:21–23)

From Paul's perspective, there was no excuse for this trained incapacity to think, this learned ignorance, this sophisticated suppression of the truth.

---

4. Schaeffer, *How Should We Then Live?*, 19.
5. Lincoln, *Ephesians*, 277.

## The Christ Letter

"At the center of their thinking, feeling, and volition, [the *Californians*] have hardened themselves to God and to the knowledge of him that was available to them." The result of this hardening was "a progressive insensitivity and obtuseness in relation to God."[6] Because of this ignorance they are "separated from the life of God."

We do well to consider what types of thinking separate us from the life of God. When I lived in Toronto I remember a sign just before the Church of the Redeemer at the corner of Bloor and Avenue Road. It read "Discover the Art of Living." If you were walking west on Bloor, it appeared to be a sign for the church, but it wasn't. It was an advertisement for a new luxury condominium being built next door. The sign captured the wisdom of the age: The art of living is knowing where to live—in a luxury condo—not *how* to live. According to the wisdom of the age, the art of living is making a living.

Commenting on education at Harvard, child psychologist Robert Coles said, "We have systems here to explain everything except how to live. And we have categories for every person on earth, but we cannot explain one person." Novelist Walker Percy said it well, "Students are getting all A's but flunking ordinary life." Consummate intellectual David Brooks writes that it is beginning to dawn on culture's high-achievers that they are shallower than they need to be. "They live in a society that prizes the development of career skills but is inarticulate when it comes to the things that matter most."[7] The life we have lost in the living is the life of wisdom, truth, and justice. Catholic apologist G. K. Chesterton was right, Christian truth has to uneducate the educated, unmake the self-made man or woman.[8] We have lives of convenience and comfort, filled with passionate intensity about things that don't count. When I listen to talk radio, I recall William Butler Yeats' warning in "The Second Coming": "the best lack all conviction, while the worst are full of passionate intensity." Who wins the Alabama versus Auburn football game not only has no eternal significance, it has very little significance at all.

The knowledge explosion has resulted in a fallout of ignorance. In *The Closing of the American Mind*, the late Allan Bloom, former professor of social thought at the University of Chicago, lamented "the disheartening expansion of trained ignorance and bad thought." For Bloom, "the university has become society's conceptual warehouse of often harmful

---

6. Lincoln, *Ephesians*, 278.
7. Brooks, "Social Animal."
8. Ahlquist, *Common Sense 101: Lessons From G. K. Chesterton*, 109.

influences."[9] It is a strange paradox that in an age of growing scientific, technological, military, political, and economic complexity men and women should be so complacent, content to live with such simplistic answers to our moral and spiritual crises.

The art of living measures a man by his income and a woman by her clothes. Today's sacred power is felt in a passion for self-expression. People give themselves to sports, sex, self-styled spirituality, food, drugs, and success. Today's shrines are found at malls, stadiums, resorts, and restaurants. Like the cult of Artemis in Ephesus, there is a sensual fixation on the body. People tend to be more interested in counting calories than in meeting the needs of others. Attending to the meaning of life is all but forgotten. Such living denies the true meaning of life and is inclined to view God's commands as impertinent. The Author of life is ignored in the living, and we are the losers. Anything that counters the dogma of Quiet Desperation which pervades most modern novels is either ignored or scorned. "The serious parts of life gets lopped off," writes David Brooks, "and readers have to stoop to inhabit a low-ceilinged world."[10]

Our understanding of freedom is a good indication of where our mind is at. "The Christian concept of freedom, rooted as it is in the notion of total self-surrender within the family of God, and accompanied as it is by a code of disciplines rigorous in their check upon self-indulgence or self-assertive individualism, is a virtually contradictory concept to that humanist notion of freedom as residing in an unfettered autonomous individualism, which plagues current thinking today."[11] Judging from Jonathan Franzen's novel *Freedom* we may have come to the end of our failed humanistic experiment. The story of our obsession with personal freedom, no matter how artfully written, is boring. Life is no longer about great souls seeking truth, but about quiet lives of desperation. We are both freer and closer to suicide than we have ever been before.[12]

Our understanding of truth is another strong indicator of our mindset. Is truth a matter of opinion and personal preference or an absolute reality that is unchanging and universally valid? Do we live in a split-level universe of facts and feelings: the lower story consisting of rational and verifiable information and the upper story made up of private values and personal opinions? Beliefs and values are socially constructed, rather than

---

9. Bloom, *Closing of the American Mind*, 17–18.
10. Brooks, "The 'Freedom' Agenda."
11. Blamires, *The Christian Mind*, 12.
12. Franzen, *Freedom*, 193.

authoritatively received. Or, do we believe in an integrated, unified understanding of truth, that all truth is God's truth and that truth cannot be compartmentalized? Today's secular worldview believes that Christ is a figment of our spiritual imagination, a product of religious wishful thinking, but Christians believe that Christ is the one in whom are hidden all the treasures of wisdom and knowledge (Col 2:3).

Our understanding of the person is also evidence of how we think. Are we rational agents made in the image of God, entrusted with personal responsibility, accountable for our actions, and endowed with capacities to love, think, communicate, and worship that ultimately defy naturalistic explanation? Or, are we complex thinking machines, the result of impersonal forces and behavioral conditioning? Are we persons created in God's image or *products* made in a biochemical process?

Paul was convinced that the way we think about life, truth, freedom, and the meaning of the person has a profound impact on whether we are "separated from the life of God" or "created to be like God in true righteousness and holiness" (4:18, 24). Keep in mind that what Paul has said about worship, salvation, and mission forms the foundation for his exhortation. In Christ, our thinking must change. Nowhere does Paul say this better than in Romans 12:1–2:

> Therefore, I urge you, brothers and sisters, in view of God's mercy, to offer your bodies as a living sacrifice, holy and pleasing to God—this is true worship. Do not conform to the pattern of this world, but be transformed by the renewing of your mind. Then you will be able to test and approve what God's will is—his good, pleasing and perfect will.

Failure to be transformed by the renewing of our mind leads to the loss of all sensitivity (Eph 4:18–19). Actions issue out of thinking and if one's thinking remains empty, meaningless, dark, and intentionally ignorant, it is only a matter of time before one's heart becomes hardened (πώρωσιν—literally, *petrified*, a word used for marble). And the consequence of having an insensitive, impenetrable heart is moral insensitivity and callousness. This lack of moral feeling—this absence of moral pain, is described by Paul with a Greek participle (ἀπηλγηκότες) that literally means "having ceased to feel pain."

To be pain free is a blessing, but only in a certain sense. If our bodies are insensitive to pain we are in danger. Regardless of what we might think, without the gift of pain, physical health is impossible to maintain. Dr. Paul Brand begins his book on *Pain: The Gift Nobody Wants* by exploring the nightmares of painlessness. Tanya was a four-year old patient of his who had a rare genetic disorder known as "congenital indifference to pain." The first time her mother realized something was wrong was when she discovered Tanya in her playpen fingerpainting red swirls on the white plastic sheet. When she got closer she realized that Tanya was using the tip of her own finger, which she had bitten off to make the designs. From that point on Tanya couldn't help but injure herself. When she twisted her ankle or stepped on a nail or bit her tongue she felt no pain. By the age of eleven, Tanya was living a pathetic existence in an institution. She had lost both legs to amputation and had bitten off her fingers. Her tongue was badly scarred from chewing on it.[13] Life without pain may sound attractive at first, until we realize the necessity of pain as an early warning system designed to protect our bodies.

What is true for our physical bodies is also true for our moral and spiritual selves. C. S. Lewis observed that without pain, "we can rest contentedly in our sins and in our stupidities." Pain proves to be a necessary obstacle against a moral free fall. "God whispers to us in our pleasures, speaks in our conscience, but shouts in our pains: it is His megaphone to rouse a deaf world. A bad man, happy, is a man without the least inkling that his actions do not 'answer,' that they are not in accord with the laws of the universe."[14]

We are all susceptible to strategies of self-deception that pacify and placate our conscience. We excuse evil when we are overexposed to evil, causing our hearts to become callous. When we are around people who think nothing of gossiping or swearing or cheating or mocking, it is easier for us to accept such behavior as the norm. Subtle social forces can cause us to participate in sinful behavior that apart from the persistent "group think" we would condemn as wrong. In some circles moral numbing has become a way of life. Well-educated, socially upstanding suburbanites, who focus on personal peace and pleasure, are not unlike abandoned inner city youth, who have trained themselves to hate. Both groups share in the pathology of painlessness. Morally and spiritually they have lost all sensitivity, which leads "to uncontrolled, outrageous, sinful behavior, especially with regard to sexuality."[15]

The end product of emptiness, idleness, vanity, foolishness, and purposelessness, is a life of obsession, addiction, indulgence, lasciviousness,

---

13. Brand, *Pain*, 3–5.
14. Lewis, *Problem of Pain*, 93.
15. Snodgrass, *Ephesians*, 231.

impurity, and greed. We usually associate "greed" with money, but Paul used the word here to describe an insatiable, gluttonous, and covetous fixation with all types of indulgence: more sex, more money, more power, more ego. Paul elaborated on the "plunge into degrading activities" in his letter to the church at Rome (Rom 1:24–32).[16]

## You Learned Christ

Paul made every effort to develop the sharpest contrast between the old self based on deceit and the new self based on truth. He emphasized the contrast forcefully, "But that's no life for you. You learned Christ!" (Eph 4:20, *The Message*). Instead of living the way Californians do, Paul argued for a whole new way of life in Christ. He used three telling phrases to define this new approach to living.

The first phrase is literally, "You have learned the Messiah," but the idea of learning a person is found nowhere else in the Greek Bible. It suggests a deeper knowledge than learning about Christ, such as the facts of his existence and his doctrines.[17] Instead of head-knowledge about Christ, Paul refers to a personal knowledge *of* Christ.

The second phrase is literally, "to hear Christ," which again implies more than over-hearing information about Christ. Paul said in effect, "You were at the other end of the dialogue with Christ. You heard him for yourself." Of course, Paul was addressing believers who were Gentiles living in Asia Minor, people who had never had the opportunity to hear Jesus in person, but as far as Paul was concerned Christ himself speaks in and through those proclaiming Christ.[18]

The third phrase, "you were taught in Christ," opens up all the possibilities of being in Christ. Christ is not only the message, but the messenger; he is the content of the teaching and the teacher. In the school of Christ, Christ is the medium and the message. He is the principal, professor, curriculum, pedagogy, and practitioner, all rolled into one. Graduates from the school of Christ don't receive diplomas. They get new lives. This education is a far cry from moralistic religious lessons and free-for-all, bull-session Bible studies. It is a school of discipleship running 24/7 under the instruction of Christ himself. There is no pedantic sermonizing in this curriculum. This is real life instruction in what it means to follow Jesus

---

16. Lincoln, *Ephesians*, 279.
17. Barth, *Ephesians*, 529.
18. Ibid., 530.

*The Ethic of Christ*

in the rough and tumble of daily living. Paul's phrase, "the truth that is in Jesus," recalls the Lord's promise, delivered by Jeremiah, "I will put my law in their minds and write it on their hearts. . . . No longer will they teach their neighbors, or say to one another, 'Know the Lord,' because they will all know me, from the least of them to the greatest" (Jer 31:33–34). We are reminded of the words of Jesus, "If you hold to my teaching, you are really my disciples. Then you will know the truth, and the truth will set you free" (John 8:31).

Faith in Christ depends on the truth that is in Jesus. This is a remarkable truth given the tendency by some to divide Jesus and Paul. For many years I was fed a steady diet of verse-by-verse expositions of Paul's letters. A book such as Ephesians took the better part of a year for our pastor to preach through. So little attention was paid to the Gospels in our church that it felt like they were eclipsed by Paul's letters. The impression was given that the theology of justification by faith trumped Jesus' preaching on the kingdom. On the rare occasion when the pastor preached from a Gospel text, it was as if the pastor needed Paul to rescue Jesus from works righteousness. But Ephesians 4:20–21 unites what some mistakenly divide. The Gospels and the Epistles stand together. Jesus preached the gospel and Paul preached the gospel of Jesus. If someone asks, "Did Jesus preach the gospel of Paul?" The answer is, "Yes," because Paul preached Jesus and Jesus preached himself. The gospel according to Paul is the gospel of Jesus. Both Jesus and Paul distinguish between works righteousness and the work of righteousness. Both the kingdom of God and justification by faith depend exclusively on Jesus. Thus the way of life envisioned by Paul is none other than the kingdom ethic preached by Jesus. Beatitude-based belief and justification by faith are two different ways of expressing the one and only gospel of grace.

Paul reminds us that we are expected to become like Jesus. Since "we are God's workmanship, created in Christ Jesus to do good works" (2:10), we need to appropriate our new identity. Paul tied the spiritual, supernatural experience of knowing Christ to a tradition he expected his readers to be fully aware of and governed by: "Surely you heard of him and were taught in him in accordance with the truth that is in Jesus" (4:21). To understand Christ we must follow Jesus.

Our conviction should be as Paul's, the key to knowing Christ is to become like Jesus as he is presented in the Bible. For only as we follow him and allow his work to humble us and motivate us do we begin to understand Christ. Then Jesus' life begins to transform every aspect of our lives. His spirituality becomes the model for our worship. His teaching is the ground for our ethic; his self-understanding, the pattern of our self-awareness; his self-sacrifice, the paradigm for our service; his bodily resurrection, the hope of our resurrection. His method of evangelism becomes our strategy for witnessing, and his call for justice becomes our commitment. Life is transformed by the power and wisdom of the crucified and risen Lord Jesus.

Becoming like Jesus does not just happen automatically. It is a process—an educational process, which allows Christ's life by the Spirit to take shape in ours. The knowledge of Christ rests on the supernatural reality of Jesus' presence in our lives to transform us into his image. The person and work of Christ cannot be divided, just as the Christian faith cannot be separated from the Christian life.

For all who seek to live a life worthy of the calling they have received in Christ, Paul brings the message home with three vital action steps. First, strip off "the rotting garment of the old humanity." Second, build up an entirely new mind-set. Third, put on "the fresh clean clothing of the new humanity with its just and holy living."[19] These three exhortations require our involvement—our personal engagement. From Paul's perspective "divine initiative and human responsibility go hand in hand."[20] And the timing of this dynamic exchange is not limited to our baptism or special times of awakening, but extends to every hour of every day. The memory of having stripped off the old self and put on the new self sometime in the past is not enough. The hope of someday being free of the former life once and for all and being made new forever is not enough. This three-fold imperative is presented as our moment-by-moment challenge and responsibility.

The counterpoint to living like Californians or New Yorkers or Alabamians is not just a new way of thinking, but an entirely new way of living. We strip off futility, emptiness, hardness of heart, moral painlessness, and indulgence in every kind of impurity. We put on the new self, "created to be like God in true righteousness and holiness." Paul offered a beautiful description of the new self in Colossians: "Clothe yourselves with compassion, kindness, humility, gentleness and patience. Bear with each other and forgive one another if any of you has a grievance against someone. Forgive as the Lord forgave you. And over all these virtues put on love, which binds them all together in perfect unity" (Col 3:12–14).

---

19. Lincoln, *Ephesians*, 290.
20. Ibid.

The clarity and boldness of the contrast between the old self and the new self, the former life and the new life, is in keeping with the seriousness of Paul's concern. Christians faced a grave danger of forgetting their true identity in Christ and falling back into the habits and values of a pagan culture. We would be naive to think that we do not face a similar danger today. Paul labored with all his might to strengthen the believers in Christ.

# 9

# The Example of Christ

*"Follow God's example, therefore, as dearly loved children and walk in the way of love, just as Christ loved us and gave himself up for us as a fragrant offering and sacrifice to God."*

EPHESIANS 5:1–2

"You learned Christ." What does it mean for those who have been chosen, blessed, redeemed, predestined, and gifted, to live out their faith in Christ? Paul followed up his admonition for a new humanity with practical, down-to-earth advice. He described what is involved in stripping off, building up and putting on. Paul paints a picture of what real obedience looks like that is as timely today as it was in the first century. He offers clear answers and good reasons for how and why we should live. His simple, but not simplistic, list of seven Do's and Don'ts are grounded in seven theological motivations. From Paul's perspective, ordinary daily life is the battleground for spiritual conflict. To know Christ is to become like Jesus everyday.

*The truth that is in Jesus* leads us to confront the real issues involved in character formation and practical obedience. The moral virtues that we are called by God to practice are for the most part easily understood and uncomplicated. The challenge posed by these virtues, also known as the fruit of the Spirit, has more to do with their practice and implementation than with their description. Paul begins, "Therefore each of you must . . ." To modern ears educated in Western culture this is a strange way of talking. The culture, then and now, is not attuned to "thus, says the Lord," but the Christian should be. Paul is not giving us his opinion. He is issuing God's orders. The divine imperative is not up for debate. The command is clear: follow Jesus.

## The Educated Heart

Virtue must not be confused with values and character is not the same as personality. Values are self-selected according to individual preferences and are often viewed as personal possessions. "Values are good because I prize and choose them."[1] But virtues are good because God commands them. Their goodness is rooted in the very structure of life and lies outside of my preferences and inclinations. Values change with the times. Virtues remain constant according to the will of God. Values conform to what is fashionable. Virtues confirm what it is to be faithful.

Character is not the same as personality. Personalities can vary like the weather and change like the seasons. They can be hot or cold, wet or dry, bright or dark. There is a reason why temperature and temperament come from the same linguistic root. But character cuts across all personalities types and ranges and describes the fundamental foundation and orientation of life in moral terms. We may speak of good and bad personalities, but what we really mean is that some personalities are easier to relate to than others. But when we speak of good and bad character we are discerning the difference between love and hate, purity and lust, fidelity and infidelity, truth and falsehood, reconciliation and retaliation. Character is a matter of the heart that relates God's will to life. The essence of who we are—the real self—was meant to become transformed and inspired by the mind of Christ. Character seeks to apply God's justice and righteousness in every dimension of life. Character formation through prayer and worship is the process of internalizing the wisdom and discernment we need in order to live as we ought to live.

If you think of life as a landscaping job, then New York's Central Park offers a great analogy. The outcropping rock ledges expose the original bedrock and give the park personality. Instead of eliminating these ledges Frederick Olmsted and Calvert Vaux landscaped them. Thanks to their design and massive amounts of hard work, money, and creativity, the character of the park is a work of art. Several natural-looking lakes and ponds were created. The foliage appears natural but almost all of it has

---

1. Augsburger, *Dissident Discipleship*, 73.

been landscaped. Since the original soil was not fertile, more than ten million cartloads of soil and rock were removed and 21,000 tons of topsoil from New Jersey were imported. More than four million trees, shrubs and plants were transplanted to the park. Like the park, our outcropping bedrock personality remains, but our true character is remade in Christ's image.

The question Paul addressed in Ephesians is the same one we must address: Is the quality of spiritual and ethical sensitivity nurtured in our churches sufficient for us to become like Jesus? Are we reversing the Gentile (read "Californian" or "New Yorker") descent into insensitivity? Are we becoming resensitized by the Spirit of Christ and the will of God? Paul has painted a bleak picture of cultural morality (futility → apathy → ignorance → petrification → moral painlessness). Witness the large-scale retreat from serious thinking and the almost universal appeal of style and personality over substance and character. The scandals of a few church leaders are publicized and sensationalized, but the church's widespread insensitivity and moral immaturity are glossed over as non-issues. Many people come to church looking for an emotional lift and black-and-white answers. "Felt needs" have little to do with discerning good and evil but a lot to do with feeling good about yourself. "If Christians cannot communicate as thinking beings," writes Harry Blamires, "they are reduced to encountering one another only at the shallow level of gossip and small talk."[2]

Moral perspectives in the church and the culture vacillate between everyone doing what is right in their own eyes and everyone being told how to think. We sway between moralistic self-righteousness and relativistic permissiveness. Yet from a biblical perspective, self-righteousness and hedonism are much the same in God's eyes. It is no better to be a legalist than a relativist. Both perversions express a willful selfism that neglects the heart of God's commands and the meaning of biblical morality.

An educated heart is informed and transformed by the Spirit of God; it embraces the affections as well as the mind, revealing in word and action through patient endurance authentic Christian character. Educating the heart is synonymous with being "thoroughly equipped for every good work" (2 Tim 3:17). It involves becoming wise for salvation and being trained in righteousness. Educating the heart involves a deep-seated internalization of moral-order character.

True spirituality makes Christian ethics inseparable from authentic love. The choices of the heart proceed from an education motivated by

---

2. Blamires, *The Christian Mind*, 13.

love and abounding more and more in knowledge and depth of insight. Overcoming the habits of the heart that have been ingrained by years of empty thinking, a darkened understanding and hard-hearted indifference does not happen automatically. Choosing between the habits of the heart and the educated heart means rejecting ethical relativism *and* ethical moralism.

Indoctrination is not effective in educating the heart. In Aldous Huxley's *Brave New World* the Controller explains to the Savage, "There's no such thing as a divided allegiance; you're so conditioned that you can't help doing what you ought to do." And just in case something unpleasant should arise a pill is provided, labeled *soma*—designed "to give you a holiday from the facts." In Huxley's futuristic civilization, which had chosen machinery, medicine, and universal happiness instead of God, there is always *soma* "to calm your anger, to reconcile you to your enemies, to make you patient and long-suffering." The Controller praises the drug's benefits:

> In the past you could only accomplish these things by making a great effort and after years of hard moral training. Now, you swallow two or three half-gram tablets, and there you are. Anybody can be virtuous now. You can carry at least half your morality in a bottle. Christianity without tears—that's what soma is."[3]

Nothing can replace the hard work of moral training and dependence upon the Spirit. Ethical sensitivity needs to be nurtured and developed. The deceptiveness of sin needs to be exposed and the lessons of moral pain learned in the crucible of life. That is why the followers of Christ have been given the Holy Spirit to guide them in all truth. But Jesus never promised us an automatic, painless process.

What does the world see in the life of the follower of Jesus? The apostle Paul's social ethic follows the pattern laid down by Jesus in the Sermon on the Mount. Jesus' description of beatitude-based obedience, the kind that surpasses the righteousness of the scribes and Pharisees, focuses on our relationship to others. Jesus does not lead with the spiritual disciplines, such as prayer, giving, or fasting. Later he will discuss idolatry, profanity, and Sabbath keeping, but first he emphasizes visible righteousness—the way we treat others.

Jesus' revolutionary strategy for living, "You have heard it said . . . but I say to you," highlights a way of life that is antithetical to both religious and secular thinking. Yet he follows it with an even more shocking

---

3. Huxley, *Brave New World*, 190.

statement: "Be perfect, therefore, as your heavenly Father is perfect" (Matt 5:48). A follower of Jesus understands that becoming like our heavenly Father has much more to do with simple honesty and truthfulness than with heroic accomplishments. Living out our God-centered identity in love and honesty may run against the grain of our depravity, but it fits well with who we really want to be and what the world longs to see. The compelling splendor of God's holy righteousness is revealed in the disciples of Jesus. They are to be loving as their heavenly Father is loving; pure as their heavenly Father is pure; faithful as their heavenly Father is faithful; truthful as their heavenly Father is truthful; forgiving as their heavenly Father is forgiving. The culture may equate being holy with being "holier than thou," but Jesus did not. He equated holiness with a radical new approach to relationships—reconciliation rather than alienation.

## Christian Social Ethics: *Visible Righteousness*

(4:25—5:2) "*Therefore each of you must put off falsehood and speak truthfully to your neighbor, for we are all members of one body. 'In your anger do not sin': Do not let the sun go down while you are still angry, and do not give the devil a foothold. Those who have been stealing must steal no longer, but must work, doing something useful with their own hands, that they may have something to share with those in need.*

*Do not let any unwholesome talk come out of your mouths, but only what is helpful for building others up according to their needs, that it may benefit those who listen. And do not grieve the Holy Spirit of God, with whom you were sealed for the day of redemption. Get rid of all bitterness, rage and anger, brawling and slander, along with every form of malice. Be kind and compassionate to one another, forgiving each other, just as in Christ God forgave you. Follow God's example, therefore, as dearly loved children and walk in the way of love, just as Christ loved us and gave himself up for us as a fragrant offering and sacrifice to God.*"

Perceptive readers discern that Paul is not giving a haphazard list of instructions, but he is being practical.[4] He is not taking a moralistic short-cut and insisting on thoughtless compliance, but he is being clear

---

4. Snodgrass, *Ephesians*, 248.

and authoritative. True to the Word of God, Paul's do's and don'ts are double-edged, cutting through moralistic self-righteousness and relativistic permissiveness. What Paul says here is completely in line with Jesus' beatitude-based character and the ethic of the Sermon on the Mount. Paul's *exhortations—what* believers should and should not do, and his *motivations—why* believers should obey these imperatives, dispel both legalistic conformity and apathetic indifference.

There are several reasons for this: First, believers are compelled to wrestle with these moral imperatives because of their reasonable consistency with what Paul has said about worship, salvation, mission, and humanity. Theology and ethics are distinct but inseparable in Paul's mind. Second, the nature of these exhortations calls for thoughtful discernment. These imperatives have a completely different effect on our thinking than the old short list of taboos, like not smoking, drinking, or dancing. Paul cannot be accused of zeroing in on peripheral matters, like the Pharisees who worried about tithing their spices. His exhortations deal with the weightier matters of obedience from the heart (Matt 23:23–24). Third, the seven motivations outlined by Paul are neither superficial, self-righteous, nor ego-gratifying. His intent was to neither coerce by heavy-handed pressure nor coax by offering people-pleasing incentives. The seven motivations behind his seven imperatives are all deeply theological. True moral order is motivated by the body of Christ, victory over the devil, meeting real needs, extending God's grace to others, living in the Spirit, forgiving as we have been forgiven, and imitating Christ's offering and sacrifice. We make much of a church preaching the gospel. Why invite people to a church where the gospel is not being preached? But why invite people to a church where the gospel is not being practiced?

## Seven Imperatives: What It Means to Strip off, Build up, and Put on

Paul's description of a Christian social ethic is personal, practical, and sensible. Spirituality and ethics go hand-in-hand. In the Sermon on the Mount, Jesus put a priority on visible righteousness (love instead of hate, purity instead of lust, honesty instead of deception, etc.). Jesus emphasized the virtues that interface with the world before he discussed the hidden righteousness of prayer and fasting and giving. It makes sense that Paul would follow the same line of reasoning—the truth that is in Jesus.

## The Christ Letter

Paul understood the negative and positive dynamic of a Christian social ethic. For every *no* there is a *yes* and for every *yes* there is a *no*. Falsehood is a *no* and speaking truthfully is a *yes*. Unrestrained anger is a *no*; refusing to give the devil a foothold is a *yes*. Stealing is a *no*; working to provide for others is a *yes*. Unwholesome talk is a *no*; building others up is a *yes*. Grieving the Holy Spirit is a *no*; being kind and compassionate to one another, forgiving each other, just as in Christ God forgave you is a *yes*. Following God's example, walking in the way of love, imitating Christ—his love, his offering, and his sacrifice to God, are all *yes's*; but even the hint of sexual immorality or any kind of impurity or greed, are all definitely *no's*. Obscenity, foolish talk, and coarse joking are all *no's*; thanksgiving is an absolute *yes*.

Paul's dialectical approach underscores the "either/or" choice that confronts believers who are serious about stripping off and putting on. He deftly lays out the practical parameters of a social ethic. Yet not a single line is a pedantic bullet point. Each imperative invites meditation, in-depth discussion, and prayerful application. Paul proves himself the Spirit-led poetic ethicist, speaking to the young and engaging the old, with wisdom simple enough to understand and equally challenging to apply.

The seven imperatives are matched by seven motivations. We are exhorted to truthfulness because "we are all members of one body." Anger must be limited, lest the devil gain an advantage over us. Work must be done so we have something to share with those in need. Speech is for the benefit of those who listen. We forgive because God in Christ forgave us. We follow God's example because we are his dearly loved children. We imitate Christ because he loved us and gave himself for us.

Paul meant for the force of these ethical imperatives and theological motivations to define the difference between our former selves apart from Christ and our new selves in Christ. Although each imperative and motivation deserves careful attention, we can only give a brief reflection on each one here.

### *Truthfulness*

Simple honesty will do more for the cause of Christ than complex arguments for the nature of truth. For those who have given up on truth in principle, truthful people are the only way they may see the truth. Being truthful liberates the believer from manipulation and posturing. We refuse to mimic "the cunning and craftiness of people in their deceitful scheming. Instead, speaking the truth in love, we will in all things grow up into him who is the head, that is, Christ" (4:14–15).

Truthfulness requires careful work. There may be no greater laboratory for learning how to communicate with care than in the church. "Truthfulness," writes Walter Wangerin, "hides nothing in lying; it neglects nothing important; it distorts nothing, either consciously or unconsciously; it communicates as accurate a picture as possible of anything it chooses to offer . . ."[5] Telling the truth, simply and carefully, is a labor of love requiring two cares: "care for the topic, to get it right; and care for the person receiving your message, that she/he hear it right. That's work."[6] The reward for this simple, truth-telling lifestyle is invaluable. When a disciple's yes and no can be depended on; when her words are honest and caring, the fruit of her labor is trust and friendship, security, and intimacy. The gift she receives is the solidarity of truthfulness. "Untruthfulness destroys fellowship," wrote Bonhoeffer, "but truth cuts false fellowship to pieces and establishes genuine brotherhood. We cannot follow Christ unless we live in revealed truth before God and man."[7]

Truthfulness is important for Christians of all ages, but Christian teenagers face a special challenge in this area. Their peers have no trouble admitting that they lie regularly while claiming to be honest. In a two year study of teenagers, Chap Clark came to some startling conclusions. He writes, "I rarely encountered a midadolescent who believed lying was unethical. Midadolescents reshape the idea of lying to the point where a justified deception, including an outright, bald-faced lie, is not actually lying. Nearly every student admitted to lying regularly, without remorse. Yet these same students actually believed that they were highly moral, ethical, and honest people!"[8]

From the perspective of common culture rather than common grace, simple honesty places one at a distinct *dis*advantage. It is generally assumed that politicians do not practice it, advertisers deny it, entrepreneurs ignore it, academics rationalize it, and entertainers joke about it. Is it any wonder then that Jesus chose truth as his *modus operandi*? He laid aside *deceptive language*, refusing to say what he did not mean to say; *flattering language*, resisting the temptation to say what the other person wanted to hear; *manipulative language*, rejecting the impulse to control others;

5. Wangerin, *As For Me And My House*, 123.
6. Ibid.
7. Bonhoeffer, *The Cost of Discipleship*, 155.
8. Clark, *Hurt: Inside the World of Today's Teenagers*, 151.

*flowery language*, choosing to communicate, rather than impress; and *misleading language*, denying the option to betray the truth.

The motivation for being truthful, "for we are all members of one body," is certainly not the only reason for being truthful, but it is an important one. Conceivably some might interpret this motive as an appeal to tribal solidarity, that we are only under moral obligation to be truthful to those who are in our group. But if this were the case, truth would inevitably suffer and our neighbor would be deceived. Paul is not implying that Christians are only expected to tell the truth to Christians. Instead of restricting the scope of truth-telling to our own kind, Paul is insisting that all people deserve the truth just as if they belonged to our inner circle of friends. Our truthfulness or lack there of is a direct testimony to the body of Christ. Paul's bottom line is clear: "Members of Christ's body do not lie!"[9]

## *Anger Gone at Sundown*

Speaking the truth in love is clearly better than speaking the truth in anger. But Paul acknowledges that there is a valid form of anger rooted in love, compassion, sacrifice, and righteousness. This is not the anger rooted in pride, vanity, hatred, malice, and revenge. One type of anger is born of hate and the other of holiness. The difference between righteous anger and evil anger is the difference between the anger that stirs up alienation and the anger that seeks reconciliation—one leads to hate, the other to justice.

Anger is a dangerous emotion, because it makes us more susceptible to sin. Paul is not saying that all anger is bad, but he is saying that nothing good comes from an anger that is allowed to metastasize. Anger quickly becomes a carcinogen that robs the soul of its life and vitality and replaces it with bitterness and malice. One of the tell-tale marks of righteous anger is its quick dissipation of emotion, leaving only the enduring and persevering commitment to righteousness. Our anger becomes suspect when we allow it to fester and grow into bitterness. Even righteous anger can quickly grow into an evil anger that is nursed and cherished as one's dearest possession. Why give the devil an easy advantage over you, to manipulate you? Why allow the devil a foothold to climb all over you? Angry believers are easy game for the devil who "prowls around like a roaring lion looking for someone to devour" (1 Pet 5:8).

---

9. Barth, *Ephesians*, 513.

## Work Ethic 101

Stealing comes in many forms. Paul may have had in mind low-class thieves who stole to survive. Or he may have been thinking of those who earned a living by ripping people off. Stealing is not limited to petty criminals who prey on the weak. The obscene salaries of pinstriped executives and the excessive profits of high-flying entrepreneurs who make a "killing" qualify as stealing. Presumably some of the new converts in Ephesus had to find new jobs, because their previous line of work was not compatible with following Jesus.

One thing is for sure, Paul commended a hardworking, blue-collar spirituality. Do something useful with your hands was his directive. He reiterated this message in previous letters. Work would sooner win the respect of the world than talk. "Make it your ambition to lead a quiet life," wrote Paul. "You should mind your own business and work with your hands, just as we told you, so that your daily life may win the respect of outsiders and so that you will not be dependent on anybody" (1 Thess 4:11–12).

Paul opposed any tendency to rationalize or spiritualize sloth and laziness. He laid down the rule: "Anyone who is unwilling to work shall not eat." Paul continued, "We hear that some among you are idle and disruptive. They are not busy; they are busybodies. Such people we command and urge in the Lord Jesus Christ to settle down and earn the bread they eat" (2 Thess 3:10–12).

The motive for work goes beyond supporting oneself to working to meet the needs of others. Paul's social ethic always includes the other: the neighbor, the poor, the needy, the stranger.

## Healthy Communication

Can you imagine what it would be like for all Christians to refrain from gossip, slander, rumor, backbiting, and trash talking? Just think how much healthier our churches would be. "Unwholesome talk" refers to "foul" speech. Speech that comes across like rotten fruit or putrid meat or spoiled milk.[10] What if our negative speech actually carried an odor?

The accent of this imperative is on speaking the truth *in love*. Every conversation presents the Christian with a choice to either build up or tear down. On the subject of speech and communications, Proverbs is as

---

10. Ibid., 518.

timely in the twenty-first century as it was a millennium before Christ. It is still true: "The tongue of the wise commends knowledge, but the mouth of the fool gushes folly" (15:2). The importance of the tongue can hardly be overstated. "The tongue has the power of life and death, and those who love it will eat its fruit" (18:21). The worldwide web and the Internet have only intensified the need for wisdom. The medium has changed but the message remains the same. "The tongue that brings healing is a tree of life, but a deceitful tongue crushes the spirit" (15:4).

Technology's amazing reach and the ability to preserve everything and anything communicated on tape or on a hard-drive has only accentuated the need for truth and the danger of deception. "The lips of the wise spread knowledge; not so the hearts of fools" (15:7). Proverbs believes in the power of communication for good and evil. "With his mouth the godless destroys his neighbor, but through knowledge the righteous escape" (11:9). "The words of the wicked lie in wait for blood, but the speech of the upright rescues them" (12:6). The daily demand to communicate, not only personally, but by cell phone and computer, has compounded the impact of both wisdom and perversity. The "reckless words" that "pierce like a sword" can be transmitted globally in seconds (12:18). Technology only intensifies the truth of Proverbs. "The speech of a good person clears the air; the words of the wicked pollute it" (Prov 10:32, *The Message*).

Now more than ever we need the wisdom of Proverbs. The perverse and penetrating impact of gossip, slander, lying, flattery, and foolish talk are no less acceptable today when they are communicated by satellite and Internet, than when delivered face-to-face. The impersonal medium of technology does not justify lowering the standards of personal communication, in either the words we speak or in the messages we receive. Proverbs declares, "Stay away from a foolish man, for you will not find knowledge on his lips" (14:7), and warns against "a chattering fool" (10:10). These are pertinent proverbs for disciplining our access to music, movies, television, and Internet chat rooms. Proverbs insists that all communication is personal and reflects the heart. "The mouth of the righteous is a fountain of life, but violence overwhelms the mouth of the wicked" (10:11). "The tongue of the righteous is choice silver, but the heart of the wicked is of little value" (10:20). The real source for true and effective communication is not technological, but spiritual. "A wise man's heart guides his mouth, and his lips promote instruction" (16:23). Wisdom advises us to choose our words well. "A gentle answer turns away wrath, but a harsh word stirs up anger" (15:1). "He who guards his lips guards his soul, but he

## The Example of Christ

who speaks rashly will come to ruin" (13:3). "The wise in heart are called discerning, and pleasant words promote instruction" (16:21). We need to keep the wise counsel of Proverbs in mind when we write on Facebook or when we tweet on Twitter.

Christians have only a limited free speech mandate. We are not at liberty to vent our frustrations and get whatever is bothering us off our chest. The purpose of communications is not to make us feel better but to build others up. The focus is on the *listener not the talker.* Our concern is for his or her emotional welfare and spiritual edification.

## Filled with the Holy Spirit of God

The opposite of grieving the Holy Spirit is being filled with the Holy Spirit. Paul has more to say about being intoxicated with the Holy Spirit in the next chapter (5:18), but first he must describe the attitudes and actions that grieve the Holy Spirit. The list of six terms forms a negative counterpoint to the nine-fold fruit of the Spirit (Gal 5:22–23). It is wrong for a believer to be anywhere along this continuum of evil: "bitterness, rage and anger, brawling and slander, along with every form of malice."

Paul is not concerned with what *provokes* negative reactions. He is dealing here with the believer's response, not the cause. Whether the aggravation is deliberately evil or grossly unjust is beside the point. He is only concerned here with the attitude and action of the believer. There is no excuse for the behavior he describes. No matter what, "Get rid of all bitterness!" This is important, because when we have been attacked, abused, mistreated, cheated, and slandered, it is our natural tendency to fight back and meet evil with evil. This is why Paul takes the weapons of the world out of the believers' hands, or I should say out of their mouths! Paul's strategy is this: "Do not be overcome by evil, but overcome evil with good" (Rom 12:21).

Sometimes the greatest catalyst for this negative behavior comes from Christians and the hardest place to live may be in the Christian community. This is why it is easier to attend a mega-church and remain a part of the audience than it is to belong to a local church where we feel the pressure to get to know people and relate to them. Large scale Christian movements and events are easier to experience, because we do so on our own terms, than it is to actually participate in the fellowship of the household of faith. We are often disappointed when we get to know one another, because we suffer from what Dietrich Bonhoeffer called our "wish dream" of Christian community.[11] The very people whom we expect to display the fruit of the Spirit and the wisdom of Christ seem determined to upset us and not surprisingly we seem to do the same to them with little effort. "We might define true community," writes Parker Palmer, "as that place where the person you least want to live with always lives."[12] To be fair, we are often guilty of attributing to malice what can be better explained by incompetence. Yet each one of us has sufficient reason to be angry and upset with somebody in the community, but that is no excuse for being bitter and malicious. The Quakers have a proverb: "True community exists when the person you dislike most dies or moves away and someone worse takes their place."[13] Regardless of how difficult people may be, we are warned against grieving the Holy Spirit. It makes no sense to offend the Holy Spirit, "with whom [we] are sealed for the day of redemption," because we have been offended by others.

The positive motive, greater by far than the power of the negative provocation, is based on the cross of Christ. The impact of Paul's imperative, "Be kind and compassionate to one another, forgiving each other," depends not on our will power, but on the power of the cross. "Bear with each other and forgive whatever grievances you have against one another. Forgive as the Lord forgave you" (Col 3:13).

## *Following God's Example*

The trinitarian thrust of Paul's exhortation continues with a series of staccato imperatives. Because we are dearly loved children we are commanded to follow the example of our heavenly Father. Because of Christ's love we are commanded to walk in the way of love. We are motivated to strip off, build up, and put on, because he gave himself up for us "as a fragrant offering and sacrifice to God." Paul's words are reminiscent of Jesus' imperative: "Be perfect as your heavenly Father is perfect" (Matt 5:48). Apart from being blessed "with every spiritual blessing in Christ" the Christian social ethic outlined here by Paul would be impossible. The difference between

11. Dietrich Bonhoeffer famously said, "Every human wish dream that is interjected into the Christian community is a hindrance to genuine community and must be banished if genuine community is to survive. He who loves his dream of community more than the Christian community itself becomes a destroyer of the latter, even though his personal intentions may be ever so honest and earnest and sacrificial." *Life Together*, 27.

12. Palmer, *A Place Called Community*, 20.

13. Augsburger, *Dissident Discipleship*, 57.

*The Example of Christ*

living under the law and living under grace is relational. It is the difference between laying down the law for a group of prison inmates and living out the law of love in a loving family. In prison the goal is to keep the inmates from hurting one another. In a family the goal is to show love to one another.

This sixth imperative, expressed three ways (follow God's example, walk in love, be like Christ), is not a pious rhetorical flourish but sound theological reasoning based on what God in Christ has done for us and what Christ in God has given to us. In two words, offering and sacrifice, Paul encompasses the priestly and prophetic work of Christ. He gave his life in total obedience as an atoning sacrifice. The reference to Christ's offering and sacrifice to God has a double function, pointing first to the "saving event that cannot be duplicated or imitated" and then to the "example which is to be followed."[14] Christ is not only the Savior who redeems us, but our Lord who calls us to follow him in sacrificial love.

## Thanksgiving

Before the seventh imperative, Paul lists six things that have no part in a Christian's life. His directives leave no room for ambiguity. His admonition "must not be taken more lightly than the proclamation of the gospel. His exhortation is as radical and uncompromising as his preaching." For Paul, "imperatives are an indispensable way of describing God's will."[15] His simple, clipped sentences are emphatic. There should not be even the hint of sexual immorality and nothing to do with impurity or a greedy desire for more. Nor should there be any obscenity, foolish talk, or coarse joking.

Over and against this negative lifestyle which is improper for the Lord's people, Paul declares a one word alternative: eucharist (εὐχαριστία). Instead of a vulgar mind and foul mouth, the believer's way of thinking is grateful and his or her speaking is gratifying. "Thanksgiving is our dialect" (Eph 5:4, *The Message*). Gratitude is singled out "as the basic structure of the Christians' ethic."[16] All that Paul says here about the believer's lifestyle is rooted in his eucharistic prayer at the beginning. Thanksgiving is the key. It is impossible for people who know the love of God in Christ and whose eyes and heart have been enlightened, not to be grateful. If they know the hope to which they have been called and the glorious riches of

14. Barth, *Ephesians*, 559.
15. Ibid., 587.
16. Ibid., 563.

## The Christ Letter

his glorious inheritance how could they be anything but thankful? Paul never tired of this truth, which he expressed so often and effectively. I especially like the way he expressed it to the believers at Colossae:

> Let the peace of Christ rule in your hearts, since as members of one body you were called to peace. And be thankful. Let the word of Christ dwell in you richly as you teach and admonish one another with all wisdom, singing psalms and hymns and spiritual songs with gratitude in your hearts to the Lord. And what ever you do, whether in word or deed, do it all in the name of the Lord Jesus, giving thanks to God the Father through him. (Col 3:15–17)

Robert Gagnon, New Testament scholar and author of the acclaimed book, *The Bible and Homosexual Practice*, offers a prayer for the church in words taken from and inspired by Ephesians 4:1—5:20:

> Lord, may we walk in a manner worthy of our calling, with all humility and gentleness, with patience, bearing with one another in love. May we earnestly endeavor to keep the oneness of the Spirit and of the faith by means of the bond of peace and common adherence to the apostolic teaching in sexual holiness, as on other matters. May we as Your body arrive at an adult knowledge of Christ, no longer being blown about by teachings that depart from Your word. May we put off the old humanity, deluded into approving forms of sexual desire that You have rejected, and clothe ourselves with the new humanity, embracing with a renewed mind the standard for sexual wholeness that You have established for our benefit. For, as You have warned us, no one who engages unrepentantly and repeatedly in a form of sexual intercourse deemed immoral by apostolic teaching will have any inheritance in Your kingdom of light. Help us, Lord, to expose to the light of Your word the lie that diversity in types of sexual unions is an absolute good, remembering our own sin and need for daily repentance. May your church quickly restore the penitent, thereby maximizing salvation to the many. Amen.[17]

---

17. Gagnon, "The Bible and Homosexual Practice: Theology, Analogies, and Genes," 13.

# 10

# The Wisdom of Christ

*"Be very careful, then, how you live—
not as unwise but as wise..."*

EPHESIANS 5:15

Paul began his Christ Letter with three fundamental subjects: Worship (praise and prayer); salvation (personal and social); and missions (purpose and prayer). The apostle's orthodoxy pulsates with life and energy. He lays out not only a solid, but a beautiful foundation for discussing the body of Christ (gifts and goal) and the new humanity (old self and new self). Paul's aim is for the gospel we preach to be the gospel we practice.

We want to invite friends to a church where they are going to hear the gospel message, a church that lifts Jesus up in its worship. But if we are honest that's not enough. Not only must the gospel be preached, it must be practiced. If orthodoxy does not lead to orthopraxy, then the church is in trouble. The theology we joyfully affirm in church calls for a Christian ethic that is practiced with wisdom and passion in the world.

## Living in Tension

Paul challenged the church at Ephesus *to live a life worthy of the calling they had received.* Throughout this section the apostle paints a picture of two contrasting lifestyles: the way of life that is separated from God and the way of life learned from Christ. He makes his point emphatically. The acceptable mores of the culture are different from the ethic of Jesus. The believer must put off the old self and put on the new self, "created to be like God in true righteousness and holiness" (4:24). We can either grieve the Holy Spirit or we can be filled with the Holy Spirit (4:30; 5:18).

In rapid succession, Paul fires off a series of non-negotiable imperatives. His spiritual direction on these matters is authoritative and unequivocal. "Get rid of all bitterness, rage and anger, brawling and slander, along with every form of malice. Be kind and compassionate to one other, forgiving each other, just as in Christ God forgave you" (4:31–32). We sense that we are building to a conclusion. Paul declares, "Follow God's example, therefore as dearly loved children and walk in the way of love, just as Christ loved us and gave himself up for us as a fragrant offering and sacrifice to God" (5:1–2). He has made his point in the most powerful way, yet it seems that Paul is unsatisfied. He is not confident that he has gotten through to the believers. Are they truly hearing what he has to say?

Paul comes at this crucial topic again, continuing to emphasize the stark contrast between the way of the world and the way of Christ. This time he focuses on sexual immorality and greed.[1]

*(5:3–7) "But among you there must not be even a hint of sexual immorality, or of any kind of impurity, or of greed, because these are improper for the Lord's people. Nor should there be obscenity, foolish talk or coarse joking, which are out of place, but rather thanksgiving. For of this you can be sure: No immoral, impure or greedy person—such a person is an idolater—has an inheritance in the kingdom of Christ and of God. Let no one deceive you with empty words, for because of such things God's wrath comes on those who are disobedient. Therefore do not be partners with them."*

The spiritual direction that is laid out here is absolutely clear and timely. There is nothing new about living in a sex-crazed, money-driven culture. The people of God have always been resident aliens living in the "burbs" of Babylon and strolling the streets of Corinth. We all live east of Eden, outside the Garden.

The apostle Paul's spiritual direction draws a sharp line between biblical sexual morality and cultural sexual morality. Today's mainstream culture has severed the link between sex and morality while shifting the moral focus to sexual harassment. There is passive approval of premarital

---

1. Thielman, *Ephesians*, 328–29.

sex, adulterous affairs, homosexual practice, and pornography. Our culture is callously indifferent to the sin of consensual extramarital sex but sensitive to sexual innuendo in the work place. Sexual activity among minors is accepted as a fact of life, but consensual sex with a minor is a felony. Homosexual practice is celebrated. Pedophilia is condemned. Abortion is a popular form of birth control amidst growing sensitivity about child abuse. Pornography and violence are big box-office draws, but rape is a serious crime.

As a culture, we have the good sense to know that some things are wrong but it is a fragmented, selective sense of right and wrong. "Not even a hint" underscores how seriously Paul took this admonition. He was not joking. His moral sensitivity extended to how we talk about sex and the jokes we tell. "Obscenity, foolish talk or coarse joking" are out of place. They don't belong in the Christian's life.

We hear an emphatic tone in Paul's warning, like a doctor discussing a life-and-death decision with a patient. Paul insists, "Be sure you understand this: No immoral, impure or greedy person—such a person is an idolater—has any inheritance in the kingdom of Christ and of God." The believer cannot be defined by both sexual promiscuity and the rule of God. The disciple of Christ cannot give himself or herself to pornography and still be under the Lordship of Christ. The ambition to acquire wealth and to find one's self-worth in wealth is incompatible with being a slave of Christ. We have to live *in* two worlds, but we cannot be *of* two worlds. Unless sex and money are dethroned from the center of our lives, we will not experience the kingdom of God either now or in eternity.

The proof of conversion lies in the converted life. In Christ we are meant to be holistic, integrated human beings. Light dispels the darkness. We cannot follow the example of Christ and simultaneously live a life separated from God. We cannot be children of our heavenly Father and subject to "the ruler of the kingdom of the air" at the same time. We cannot be both sexually immoral and spiritually alive.

Christians in the early church faced a double threat. Gnostic dualists despised the body and promoted a spiritual elitism that despised the ordinary activities of life, such as marriage, family, and physical labor. False teachers were laying down rules: "Do not handle! Do not taste! Do not touch!" (Col 2:21). They were, in Paul's words, "hypocritical liars, whose consciences have been seared as with a hot iron. They forbid people to marry and ordered them to abstain from certain foods, which God created to be received with thanksgiving by those who believe and who know the truth" (1 Tim 4:2–3).

The church was plagued by a distorted message of *sexual aversion*, and at the same time exposed to the threat of *sexual immersion*. Hedonists claimed that all forms of sexual promiscuity were permitted because the body had nothing to do with the soul. Sexuality and spirituality operated in two separate realms. This form of sexual perversion may have been in Paul's mind when he warned, "Let no one deceive you with empty words . . ." Christians believe there is a physical side to being spiritual and a spiritual side to being physical. The correlation belongs to the fact that we are made body, mind, and soul in God's image. We are neither bodyless souls nor soul-less bodies, but bodies and souls in community. We cannot give ourselves to sexual immorality and expect to be in a relationship with Christ. The wrath of God comes on those who ignore the Word of God.

The Christian life is a life lived in tension. For those intent on following Jesus tension is unavoidable, but there are different kinds of tension. Aerobics is designed to stretch and strengthen your muscles without straining your muscles. We know the difference between being in good shape and suffering shin splints, tendinitis, and stress fractures. Negative tension in life is the result of disobedience, ignorance, and resistance to the will of God. Positive tension comes from obedience, biblical integrity, faithfulness to the will of God, and costly discipleship. We want to reduce negative tension in our lives and ministries and embrace positive tension. This is easier said than done. To keep negative tensions at bay, while thriving on positive tensions, requires the grace of God giving us discernment, humility, and courage. Living in tension distinguishes the followers of Jesus from the admirers of Jesus—from being almost Christians to being altogether Christians.

Like resistance training in a physical workout, certain tensions are *good* for us. They are necessary for our growth and obedience. Where there is no tension, there is no spiritual growth. Positive tensions come from being in the world but not of the world. Negative tensions come from being in the world and of the world. We want to be free from negative tensions but we don't want to be tension-free. When the apostle Paul wrote to the church at Corinth and told them not to associate with sexually immoral people, he was referring to believers who were continuing to live sexually immoral lives (1 Cor 5:9). His aim was to minimize the negative tension of unrepentant sexual immorality in the body of Christ, but the Corinthian believers misunderstood what Paul meant. They thought he wanted them to have nothing to do with sexually immoral people *outside* the church as well. This of course would have eliminated the positive tension of sharing

*The Wisdom of Christ*

the gospel with the very people for whom Christ died. As Paul wryly said, "In that case you would have to leave the world" (1 Cor 5:10). The church seeks the positive tension of being in the world but not of the world. Truth is held in tension. The promise of Christ, "I have come that you might have life and have it more abundantly," is in tension with, "My grace is sufficient for you, for my power is made perfect in weakness" (John 10:10; 2 Cor 12:9).

## Living as Children of Light

Once again the apostle Paul reaffirms the truth that is at the heart of his Christ Letter. In Christ, we are no longer what we were apart from Christ. "For you were once darkness, but now you are light in the Lord." The expectation—more than that, *the fact* of utter, radical transformation is fundamental to every dimension of his spiritual direction.

(5:8–14) *"For you were once darkness, but now you are light in the Lord. Live as children of light (for the fruit of the light consists in all goodness, righteousness and truth) and find out what pleases the Lord. Have nothing to do with the fruitless deeds of darkness, but rather expose them. It is shameful even to mention what the disobedient do in secret. But everything exposed by the light becomes visible—and everything that is illuminated becomes a light. This is why it is said: 'Wake up, sleeper, rise from the dead, and Christ will shine on you.'"*

"But now" is the phrase that underscores the decisive new reality in the believer's life. Paul refers to this redemptive turning point twice before. First, when he was discussing personal salvation: "We were by nature deserving wrath. *But* because of his great love for us, God, who is rich in mercy, made us alive with Christ even when we were dead in transgressions—it is by grace you have been saved" (2:4–5). Second, when he spoke of the social impact of salvation: "Remember that at the time you were separate from Christ . . . foreigners to the covenants of the promise, without hope and without God in the world. *But now* in Christ you who once were far away have been brought near by the blood of Christ" (2:12–13).

In exchange for the fruitless deeds of darkness, the children of light produce the fruit of light which consists "in all goodness, righteousness and truth." "Dearly loved children" (5:1) reflect their parents' nature.[2]

---

2. New Testament scholar Frank Thielman writes, "The step from 'children' to

## The Christ Letter

Thoughtful parenting educates the heart of the child. Indoctrination lays down the law and insists on conformity. But love instills a character that is able to face unexpected challenges. Paul has moved away from a religious heritage that sought to lay out legalistically how a person should respond in every conceivable situation. Casuistic legalism has been replaced by heart righteousness. Paul's admonition, "find out what pleases the Lord," is wonderfully maturing and freeing. He "intentionally left room for believers to make decisions by using their own renewed thinking (Rom 12:2)."[3] The best way to overcome susceptibility to deception is to actively cultivate the ability to discern the will of God. This is why Paul prayed the way he did for the church at Philippi:

> This is my prayer: that your love may abound more and more in knowledge and depth of insight, so that you may be able to discern what is best and may be pure and blameless until the day of Christ, filled with the fruit of righteousness that comes through Jesus Christ—to the glory and praise of God. (Phil 1:9–11)

The most striking aspect of Paul's prayer is his insistence on uniting what we often separate, namely love and knowledge. May "your love abound more and more in knowledge and depth of insight." The apostle's prayer is for discerning love, insightful love, righteous love. To the apostle, love minus the knowledge of the holy is mere sentiment and opinion. For many people, love is distinct from biblical love and is divorced from knowing and doing the will of God. Even in the church, love has become synonymous with acceptance, an excuse for moral compromise. The loving thing to do, we are told, is to lay aside our "prejudice" and accept and affirm people regardless of their actions. Paul disagreed. The penetrating, discerning light of God's love exposes evil. We are not helping people if we pretend that sexual immorality and greed are not hurting them. The medical doctor who refuses to give the true diagnosis is guilty of malpractice.

The educated heart shares God's deep love for justice and righteousness and applies these convictions to ordinary life. Life is placed in orbit around a quality of being that reflects spiritual devotion, ethical discernment, and a teachable spirit. Character is not assembled, it is nurtured. Christians with an educated heart do not fall off an assembly line. They are grown in the soil of spiritual transformation and the whole counsel of God.

---

'fruit' is natural for someone familiar with the LXX, where children are sometimes metaphorically described as 'the fruit of the womb.' " In *Ephesians*, 339.

3. Ibid., 341.

True character is reflected in the lives of those who have learned the moral will of God by heart. They work out the will of God the way a gifted musician plays a complex musical score. It is played not only with masterly precision but from the heart. There is a palpable sense in which the music has been internalized. What music is to the musician, Christ's ethic is to the Christian.

Paul brings his point to a climax by quoting a line of what was apparently a popular worship song: "Wake up, sleeper, rise from the dead, and Christ will shine on you." Whether he was calling unbelievers to conversion or believers to live in the light of their conversion does not make a great difference. In either case, the message was the same: we must live in the light of Christ. Musician and songwriter Keith Green turned Paul's piece into a prophetic ballad. One stanza of "Asleep in the Light" is especially powerful:

> The world is sleeping in the dark
> That the church just can't fight
> 'cause it's asleep in the light.
> How can you be so dead
> When you've been so well fed?
> Jesus rose from the grave,
> and you can't even get out of bed.

Paul used three simple phrases to capture his vision for discipleship: walk in the way of love, live as children of light, and find out what pleases the Lord and do it. But the apostle is still not finished making his point. He has more to say.

## Living the Dual Imperative

(5:15–20) *"Be very careful, then, how you live—not as unwise but as wise, making the most of every opportunity, because the days are evil. Therefore do not be foolish, but understand what the Lord's will is. Do not get drunk on wine, which leads to debauchery. Instead, be filled with the Spirit, speaking to one another with psalms, hymns, and songs from your heart to the Lord, always giving thanks to God the Father for everything, in the name of our Lord Jesus Christ."*

Paul calls for a *dual imperative*: "Be very careful how you live" and "Be filled with the Spirit." The responsibility for being wise and making the most of every opportunity, because the days are evil, belongs to the believer.

This call to discipleship is consistent with being filled with the Spirit and inconsistent with getting drunk. Diligence and debauchery are polar opposites. Carelessness holds little regard for wisdom, ignores opportunities, and rejects moral urgency.

Any form of spirituality that makes the Christian feel less responsible and separates the experience of the Spirit from personal discipline, determination, and diligence is foreign to the apostle Paul. To be filled with the Spirit causes the believer to embrace the challenge of ordinary life, not evade it. To be very careful how we live is consistent with being filled with the Spirit, and really much more like its prerequisite than its impediment. Whenever the focus is on us it is about our responsibility to be faithful, wise, obedient, and open to the work of the Spirit *for the sake of others*. The part of us that is self-conscious was meant to be concerned with humility, sacrifice, and faithfulness.

To walk in wisdom is to "find out what pleases the Lord" (5:10) and do it. Paul envisions a practical real world soulcraft that is able to discern, apply and enjoy the wisdom of God in every aspect of life. "Making the most of every opportunity" (5:15) is an appealing and positive admonition. Paul is using the language of the marketplace. His challenge to "make the most of every opportunity" or to "redeem the time," means literally to "buy up this time." The Christian faces a unique investment opportunity.

For Paul this is a *kairos* moment. In Greek there are two words for time, *chronos* and *kairos*. Our English word chronology comes from *chronos*. It is time measured in seconds and seasons, days and decades, months and millennia. *Kairos*, as it is used here, describes time framed by God's blessing. *Chronos* measures the length of time. *Kairos* measures meaning in time. It conveys meaning and purpose. *Kairos* is a point in time that calls for reflection and action. Time can seem to stand still in a kairos moment. Instead of a stream of undifferentiated time, *kairos* punctuates the linear line of minutes with the pulsing heartbeat of meaning. Paul insists that this is a *kairos* moment for the church at Ephesus. They cannot afford to simply put in their time and merrily go about their lives without a sense of urgency and purpose. This is a defining moment and Christ's followers must capitalize on the opportunity. His vivid description of evil's futility and darkness serves as a stimulus to spiritual maturity rather than an excuse.

The apostle's exhortation to "be filled with the Spirit" builds on the fulfillment theme that runs through Ephesians. In chapter one, Paul prayed for Christ's body to experience "the fullness of him who fills everything in

## The Wisdom of Christ

every way" (1:23). His longing was for the church to be filled by Christ who is himself "continually and completely filled by God."[4] In chapter three he prayed "that [we] may be filled to the measure of all the fullness of God" (3:19). In chapter four, he gave the purpose of the gifts, so that the body of Christ may attain "to the whole measure of the fullness of Christ" (4:13). For Christ's followers this is the new language of self-fulfillment. We are filled and fulfilled by the three-personed God—Father, Son, and Spirit.

Paul's *dual imperative* has a *double relational impact*. To be filled with the Spirit inspires our horizontal and vertical communication. We speak *to one another* with psalms, hymns, and songs from the Spirit and we sing from our heart *to the Lord*. This is a wonderful description of fellowship and worship because it stresses "a horizontal and corporate dimension" and "a more vertical and individual focus."[5] Instead of falsehood and "any unwholesome talk" coming out of our mouths, we speak to one another "only what is helpful for building others up according to their needs" (4:25, 29). The motivation for our interpersonal communication is not self-expression, but the edification of the other person.

The apostle James addressed the disharmony between our horizontal and vertical communication when he wrote, "With the tongue we praise our Lord and Father, and with it we curse human beings, who have been made in God's likeness. Out of the same mouth come praise and cursing. My brothers and sisters, this should not be" (Jas 3:9–10). Paul focused on the harmony between our relational conversation and our devotional communion and brought out both dimensions in the context of worship. To be filled with the Spirit meant making the most of every opportunity and that meant every time we open our mouths!

Paul contrasted alcoholic intoxication with being filled with the Spirit. "Do not get drunk on wine, which leads to debauchery. Instead, be filled with the Spirit. Speak to one another with psalms, hymns and spiritual songs" (5:18–19). The evidence of being filled with the Spirit is an outpouring of praise and gratitude. "Sing and make music in your heart to the Lord, always giving thanks to God the Father for everything, in the name of our Lord Jesus Christ" (5:19–20). Internalizing the Word of God not only nourishes the soul but it also makes the heart sing.

In a parallel passage, Paul said to the believers in Colossae, "Let the Word of Christ dwell in you richly as you teach and admonish one another with all wisdom and sing psalms, hymns and spiritual songs with gratitude

---

4. Thielman, *Ephesians*, 115.
5. Lincoln, *Ephesians*, 346.

in your hearts to the Lord" (Col 3:16). The inspiration for worship music depends on the filling of the Holy Spirit and the indwelling of the Word of Christ. In the mind of Paul, there is no separation between the Spirit of God and the Word of God. Faith in Christ seeks both in-depth understanding and heartfelt expression. Worship is a matter of thinking and feeling. It is both intellectual and emotional, because it engages the mind and expresses the heart. Teaching and singing the Word of God in the household of faith are two actions that belong together. When the church teaches with wisdom and sings with gratitude, our minds and our hearts are informed and inspired by the Word of God.

Paul's three-fold description of musical expression, "psalms, hymns, and spiritual songs," encourages variety and flexibility in worship music. Most scholars agree that it is not possible to come up with tight definitions and categories for these three terms because their meanings overlap. Their common purpose is for the praise and adoration of the living God. Paul's intent was not to limit worship music but to allow for the full expression of praise. Paul might have disagreed with Calvin's conclusion that singing should be based exclusively on the Psalms. Paul ignored issues of musical style, form and accompaniment, and focused on the heart of worship. He probably did not envision choir robes for the church's music ministry, but he expected the congregation to be robed in "compassion, kindness, humility, gentleness and patience" (Col 3:12). Before they could sing in harmony they needed to live in harmony; before they could sing the melody of love they needed to practice love. Paul repeatedly stressed that joy and gratitude are the underlying emotions behind our worship in song. If our hearts are right with God our voices will sing praise to God. If we are being very careful how we live, making the most of every opportunity, and if we are filled with the Spirit, it will be impossible to keep from singing. All believers were meant to participate in singing psalms, hymns, and spiritual songs with gratitude in their hearts to the Lord.

The apostle Paul's spiritual direction is not for exceptional disciples or extraordinary believers. There is no spiritual elitism here. He is describing what the wisdom of Christ produces in the life of the ordinary Christ follower. Everyday spirituality and ethics are forged together in a character that consists of "all goodness, righteousness and truth." The proof of conversion lies in the converted life.

# 11

# *The Relational Christ*

*"Submit to one another out of reverence for Christ."*
EPHESIANS 5:21

True relationships depend on believers submitting first to the Lord Jesus Christ and then to one another in Christ. Reciprocity is a key theme in Paul's Christ Letter: "Be kind and compassionate to one another, forgiving each other, just as in Christ God forgave you" (4:32). Mutuality is the goal: "Be completely humble and gentle; be patient, bearing with one another in love. Make every effort to keep the unity of the Spirit through the bond of peace" (4:2–3). Everything Paul says is oriented around the "togetherness" of the body of Christ. His spiritual direction is focused on "we" not "me" and "us" not "them." Nothing is said to the lonely autonomous self. He is building a household of faith, not leading a mass movement. Paul's call for mutual submission, to renounce one's own will for the sake of others, is consistent with the spiritual direction he gives elsewhere:

> If you have any encouragement from being united with Christ . . . then make my joy complete by being like-minded, having the same love, being one in spirit and of one mind. Do nothing out of selfish ambition or vain conceit. Rather, in humility value others above yourselves, not looking to your own interests but each of you to the interests of others. In your relationships with

> one another, have the same attitude of mind Christ Jesus had. (Phil 2:1–5)

Faith in Christ means living life the Jesus way. The way to know Christ is for women and men to become like Jesus. The new covenant envisions reconciled and restored relationships. Men and women are forgiven and freed to live the way God intended for humankind before the fall. The Jesus way is crucial to our understanding of the relationship between men and women. The upside-down value reversal of the kingdom of God renegotiates our understanding of power and authority. Instead of taking our cues from the world we need to model our lives after Jesus.

Life in the Spirit means the freedom to "serve one another humbly in love" (Gal 5:12). Paul challenges believers, "Do not think of yourself more highly than you ought, but rather think of yourself with sober judgment . . . Love must be sincere. Hate what is evil; cling to what is good. Be devoted to one another above yourselves" (Rom 12:3, 9–10).

## The Work of Ministry

> *(5:21) "Submit to one another out of reverence for Christ."*

Paul explores what it means "to live a life worthy of the calling" we received in Christ (4:1). He puts forth the case that relationships are built on service and sacrifice rather than social convention and tradition. Making the most of every opportunity is based on serving one another in Christ rather than striving to be superior to one another. As a rule, rulers lord it over their subjects, but Jesus said to his disciples, "Not so with you. Instead, whoever wants to become great among you must be your servant, and whoever wants to be first must be your slave—just as the Son of Man did not come to be served, but to serve, and to give his life as a ransom for many" (Matt 20:26–28).

Mutual submission in Christ does not mean the loss of authority in the household of faith or order in the family. It doesn't mean that everyone gets their way or that everyone does whatever they want to do. Pastor David Mains, speaking from personal experience, warns that a common mistake made by pastors today is to minimize their leadership role. When he was pastor of Circle Church in Chicago he tried to make everyone in the church feel like an equal. He stressed every-member ministry, the gifts of the Spirit, and servant leadership, but what he failed to emphasize was the proper role of leadership and spiritual maturity. He stressed the team concept to the neglect of his leadership. As a result, when key decisions had to be made or conflicts resolved people ignored his leadership. Everybody felt like they were on the team, but they had trouble recognizing the authority of the coach. Pastor Mains is concerned that the prevailing "anti-authoritarian bias" has seriously affected our willingness to respect and submit to leaders in the body who have been called to exercise authority in the church.

The apostle Paul is an interesting case in point. His leadership was challenged and even ridiculed in the church of Corinth, but he refused to back down. When Corinthian believers questioned his authority and demanded proof that God was speaking through him, he claimed the authority of Christ. Christ "is not weak in dealing with you," wrote Paul, "but is powerful among you. For to be sure, he was crucified in weakness, yet he lives by God's power. Likewise, we are weak in him, yet by God's power we will live with him in our dealing with you" (2 Cor 13:3–4). Mutual submission in Christ is consistent with authoritative leadership as long as we embrace the weakness of the cross and the power of the resurrection.

The words "submission" and "reverence" are not the problematic words that many people think they are, although they may run counter to how our culture thinks and acts. "Reverence" literally means "fear" as in "The fear of the Lord is the beginning of wisdom" (Prov 9:10). In Romans 12:1, the motivation for living the transformed life in Christ comes from the mercies of God. "*By the mercies of God*, I urge you to offer your bodies as a living sacrifice, holy and pleasing to God." But the motivation in Ephesians is fear and to translate φόβος (phobos) as "reverence" or "respect" (5:33) tends to soften the meaning. The fear of the Lord means "more than deference and less than terror."[1] We cannot precisely define this bound phrase nor shrink it down to a code of conduct. The fear of the Lord involves a way of life "appropriate to our creation and salvation and blessing by God."[2] Our fear is not out of dread, but out of concern that we might displease the Lord.

Mutual submission in Christ leads us into the work of ministry. In Christ, we are all meant to be servant-pastors gifted by the Spirit, set apart for holy vocations and equipped for good works. Congregations appoint a team from within the body of Christ who evidence the gift of teaching and preaching the Word of God and who have the necessary training and discernment to lead the household of faith. This pastoral responsibility

---

1. Thielman, *Ephesians*, 374.
2. Peterson, *Christ Plays In Ten Thousand Places*, 43.

was meant to enhance every-member ministry, not diminish it. We are all called to salvation, service, sacrifice, and simplicity.

When I think of the priesthood of all believers, Lori Meals, a neo-natal intensive care nurse, comes to mind. Several years ago, when I was a pastor in San Diego, we received an urgent call to help a young couple in need. Their newborn was very ill and they were flying from their home in Hawaii to San Diego in order to receive the specialized medical care their baby needed. Our church was asked to minister to this family. Because of Lori's years of experience with gravely sick children and her spiritual maturity, we turned to her to help befriend this family and to minister to them. Lori became a very special pastor to them, sharing Christ's love with them, praying for them, and helping them through what became for all involved a horrendous ordeal. When she was with the family, she laid aside her normal ministry as a nurse and became their pastor—a pastor with a very helpful medical background.

At the outset of my ministry career I doubt if I would have thought of asking Lori to pastor this family. She had her job and I had mine. Even if I had been pulled in twenty different directions, I would have felt it was my responsibility to be there for this family and for others in our congregation facing a crisis. Thankfully, I am older and a little more biblical now. Lori's spiritual depth and willingness to be used made her a natural for this challenging responsibility. There were times throughout that stressful year that I felt guilty for asking her to undertake such a difficult ministry. The daily challenges were great, but each time we discussed the situation, she assured me that she felt called to do it. I had not given her this task, the Lord had. A few nights before the baby's memorial service, Lori called me and we talked through the meditation she was writing. I realized that her deep biblical insights were born of months of praying, befriending, witnessing, and loving. She was standing at the intersection of the mystery of God and the mess of the human condition and preaching Resurrection hope.

The dual imperative: "Be very careful how you live" and "Be filled with the Spirit" leads us to the work of ministry. The priesthood of all believers rests on what Paul has already said about putting "on the new self, created to be like God in true righteousness and holiness" (4:24). All that he has said about being the children of the light, practicing sexual purity, and pursuing moral integrity form a foundation for what he is about to say on relationships.

The grace of forgiveness and the power of spiritual renewal must be experienced before proceeding. The grammar of the text reinforces this

*The Relational Christ*

connection. Paul links five participles to the imperative, "Be filled with the Spirit."

> *Speaking* to one another with psalms, hymns, and songs from the Spirit,
>
> *Singing* and *making* music from your heart to the Lord,
>
> *Giving* thanks to God the Father for everything in the name of our Lord Jesus Christ,
>
> *Submitting* to one another out of reverence for Christ.

Paul's emphasis on devotion to God and worship music segues beautifully into his discussion of the melody and harmony of true relationships. We dare not divorce the meaning of submission from Paul's clear teaching on sexual purity and worship. Any hint of a sexual double standard or spiritual apathy and indifference throws off the meaning of mutual submission.

## The Work of Marriage

In the middle of everything Paul has to say about how wives and husbands ought to relate, he plants the cross of Christ. We cannot possibly speak of marriage and ignore the Christian ethic of self-denial, the biblical call to discipleship, and the very real, costly challenge firmly planted in the center of our lives, called the cross. Paul grounds marriage, family, and work on the cross of Jesus Christ.

The first thing that people see when they enter the sanctuary of Cherry Creek Presbyterian Church in Denver is a twelve-foot, free-standing wooden cross off to the side of the pulpit. I have found it to be a powerful reminder of God's grace and our Lord's call to discipleship. One engaged couple surprised us all by requesting that the cross be removed for their wedding. They complained that the cross was "so religious" and that it was bound to show up in some of their wedding pictures. We were happy to inform them that the cross in the sanctuary could not be removed; it was permanent.

(5:22–33) *"Wives, submit yourselves to your own husbands as you do to the Lord. For the husband is the head of the wife as Christ is the head of the church, his body, of which he is the Savior. Now as the church submits to Christ, so also wives should submit to their husbands in everything.*

> *Husbands, love your wives, just as Christ loved the church and gave himself up for her to make her holy, cleansing her by the washing with water through the word, and present her to himself as a radiant church, without stain or wrinkle or any other blemish, but holy and blameless. In this same way, husbands ought to love their wives as their own bodies. He who loves his wife loves himself. After all, people have never hated their own bodies, but they feed and care for them, just as Christ does the church—for we are members of his body.*
>
> *'For this reason a man will leave his father and mother and be united to his wife, and the two will become one flesh.' This is a profound mystery—but I am talking about Christ and the church. However, each one of you also must love his wife as he loves himself, and the wife must respect her husband."*

If we take a cynical view of this "submission" passage, we will write it off. Wives need not submit to their husbands anymore than slaves need to obey their masters (6:5–9). Since we no longer have slavery, we should no longer have a traditional male-dominated family. But a flippant dismissal of this biblical text misses the radical truth laid down by Paul that undermines both slavery and the patriarchal family.

Relationships in the household of faith are based on the transforming work of the Spirit of Christ. The defensive, competitive, manipulative, and domineering relational strategies of the old nature give way to mutual submission and gift-based, every-member ministry in Christ. The church is no longer bound but free from patriarchal and matriarchal control. Nothing the world has to offer, from traditional male headship to radical feminism, comes close to expressing the new relational dynamic created in Christ Jesus. Marriage is theologically grounded, rather than ideologically driven. There is nothing Victorian or Aristotelian or modern about Christian marriage.

Paul intended this passage to bridge the gender divide, not reinforce it. He was seeking to heal the fracture between belief and behavior, not make it worse. The tension in this text is not between submission and headship, but between submitting to Christ and living for self. This text should not be lifted out of context and turned into a marriage seminar on love and submission. All that Paul has said from the beginning of his Christ Letter until now informs what he says to wives and husbands.

The verb "submit" is missing in verse 22 and needs to be supplied from verse 21, but that is not the only thing that needs to be supplied to

## The Relational Christ

make sense of verse 22. If reverence for Christ is missing then nothing Paul says about marriage is going to make sense. The key to everything is mutual submission in Christ and under Christ. If this is not in the picture, then nothing will work from this point on.

According to theologian Sarah Sumner, the church has often failed to see just how carefully balanced and nuanced Paul's description of marriage is. Sumner identifies three couplets in this passage, designed by Paul to bring out the meaning of marriage:

1. submission is coupled with sacrifice;
2. the body is joined to the head to form one flesh;
3. and a wife's respect for her husband is matched by a husband's love for his wife.

These three correlations expound the meaning of marital mutual submission in Christ and correspond to the dual imperative (being very careful and being filled with the Spirit) and the double impact (speaking to one another with psalms, hymns, and songs from the Spirit and singing and making music from your heart to the Lord).

Interpreters tend to jump to the wrong conclusions here. They have contrasted submission with headship and debated the difference between love and respect. They have ignored Paul's emphasis on "one flesh" and concentrated on hierarchal implications. But I don't believe this is what Paul had in mind. Paul's challenge to make the most of every opportunity calls for wives and husbands to model in the home what Christ has done in the church. Precisely because love can be romanticized, sentimentalized, or spiritualized, Paul uses the verb *submit*. Marital love depends not on romantic feelings or pious feelings but on covenant and commitment. Fidelity does not depend upon feelings, but feelings depend upon fidelity. Romance does not create love; it is love that creates romance.

Paul says, "For the husband is the head of the wife as Christ is the head of the church, his body, of which he is the Savior" (5:23). What does it mean for the husband to represent Christ's authority? Does it mean that his wife does not have Christ's authority over her and that her husband must represent Christ's authority over her? Is the husband placed in the role of mediating Christ to his wife as if she does not have direct access to God? Does she need to wait for her husband, for his instruction and guidance? Does submission mean subservience?

Based on everything Paul has said, it is best to see the radical nature of this *in Christ* relationship. Because the husband is under Christ's authority he exercises his responsibility the way Jesus did. "Greater love has no one than this: to lay down one's life for one's friends" (John 15:13). His contribution to the body life of the marriage and the family will be governed by the principle of the cross—"my life for yours." His headship is modeled on Christ's leadership and is a radical reversal of what the world understands headship to mean. For even if we interpret "head" as "authority over" it could never mean the kind of authoritarian rule that smacks of male chauvinism. It could never mean anything remotely sexist or self-serving. Nor could it mean that the husband is the king of his castle. We would expect that a "headship" modeled after Jesus, who empowered women and was supported by women, would call women to use their Spirit-gifts to serve and teach men and women. The distinction between a life-giving headship and a ruling headship strikes me as an important distinction to be made. We want to affirm the sacrificial responsibility of the man to lay down his life for the woman. We want to celebrate the differences between men and women, but we do not want to impose on the biblical text our traditionalism.

The focus in this passage is on the everyday opportunity *in Christ* for wives to submit to their husbands and husbands to sacrifice for their wives. We should challenge any interpretation that reserves the truth of this passage for extreme situations, such as when a wife's life is endangered or when a husband and wife are at a serious impasse. The very remote possibility of a husband being called upon to give up his life for his wife only serves to fuel the chivalrous fantasy of a macho husband acting heroically. The more likely possibility of husband and wife being at loggerheads implies that there are many more occasions for a wife to submit than a husband to sacrifice. Sarah Sumner writes, "The problem with this model of *emergency-time sacrifice*, and *impasse-time submission* is that it fails to meet the scriptural standards. The Bible says that wives are to be subject to their husbands 'in everything.' Likewise, the sacrifice of husbands is a full-time relational posture."[3]

The thrust of Paul's spiritual direction reverses cultural expectations. Wives were expected to care for their husbands and children and to manage the household well "in order to free the husband from domestic concerns and enhance his social prestige. In contrast, Paul's comparison between the husband's love for his wife and Christ's love for the church implies that the husband's love for his wife should be so broad and long and high and deep (3:18–19) that it includes the sacrifice of his own social

3. Sumner, "Bridging the Ephesian 5 Divide," 61.

prestige and well-being, indeed his life, for the sake of his wife (see Phil 2:5–8)."[4]

Mutual submission "out of reverence for Christ" applies the principle of the cross to the marriage relationship in a million ways. The reason Paul's spiritual direction has caused such debate is because of our sinful tendency to confuse humility with humiliation. The humility Paul has in mind has nothing to do with passivity or subservience, but rather with obedience and faithfulness. A wife's life is not subject to the whim of her husband but is defined in Christ, even as a husband's love is patterned after Christ's love for the church.

"The husband is the head of the wife just in so far as he is to her what Christ is to the Church," writes C. S. Lewis. "He is to love her as Christ loved the Church—read on—'and gave his life for her.'"[5] Lewis rightly observes that what the apostle had in mind was not a husband's superiority but rather his Christ-like sacrifice. Paul gives husbands two high-impact images to shape their understanding of how they should relate to their wives. The first image, Christ's love for the church, calls a husband to love his wife sacrificially, to strengthen and support her. The second image Paul uses is as personal as the first image is exalted: "Husbands ought to love their wives as their own bodies. He who loves his wife loves himself. After all, no one ever hated his own body, but he feeds and cares for it, just as Christ does the church" (Eph 5:28–29). Paul draws on the principle of the cross, "my life for yours," and the principle of creation, "and the two will become one flesh."

In Ephesians 5:21–33, believers are given "the spirit, the shape, and the reason for mutual submission of husband and wife," but not the roles. Paul Stevens writes, "I believe there is an inspired reason for the silence of Scripture on the question of marriage roles. We are invited to write our own play."

> The deepest issues of our life in Christ resist reduction to manageable ideas or stereotyped roles. Biblical teaching is often ambiguous in just these areas. Hence we find ourselves living with tensions individually, maritally, and in the church. These tensions can generate friction and frustration. Or they can be resolved by an artificial choice to live out only one side of the biblical witness. Alternatively, the tension can be embraced in a contemplative manner. The ambiguity can be seen as pointing

---

4. Thielman, *Ephesians*, 382.
5. Lewis, *The Four Loves*, 105.

> to a God-sized issue. The tension can be lived out experientially, incarnationally, by a joyous attention and submission to the triune God who uniquely loves and addresses each individual, marriage, and church, while remaining "one God and Father of all, who is above all and through all and in all." (Eph 4:6)[6]

These three paired references, submission and sacrifice, body and head, respect and love, raise an interesting question: Can what is said to the husband be also said to the wife? Can what is said to the wife be also said to the husband? Is there a unique and distinctive way that submission, body, and respect, apply to the wife, and sacrifice, head, and love, apply to the husband? To answer that question, we have to examine the two-fold thrust of Paul's message. His overarching stress is on mutuality in marriage. It is, as we have said, hard to distinguish between submission and sacrifice, body and head, respect and love. But with that said, Paul places the weight of responsibility for this one-flesh sacrificial mutuality in marriage squarely on the husband. He is meant to take the lead in this cruciform life. The husband is not the king of his castle, lording it over his wife. He is like his Lord and Savior, willing and ready to lay down his life for his wife. The tradition Paul had in mind is radically Christ-centered and Spirit-filled like no other cultural tradition known to humanity.

On a visit to Bhar Dar, Ethiopia, I was teaching from this text and encouraging husbands to share their lives more fully with their wives. I suggested that it was important for husbands and wives to talk over their relationship with Christ, to pray together, and to discuss family matters and issues at work. We explored various ways that God intended for husbands and wives to become soulmates. I offered a few ideas on how husbands could be servant leaders in the home, although I could tell my suggestion that cleaning the dishes after a meal was probably a bridge too far for both the husbands and the wives.

When I finished, my wife Virginia gave her perspective. "I'm here to tell you that Doug is telling the truth." She described the various ways that a biblical view of marriage strengthens a wife and husband. She talked about the ways it deepens the marriage bond and empowers couples to be better parents. Virginia's forthright and slightly humorous approach brought laughter and encouraging openness. One man stood up and shared how talking over his faith with his wife had made him a stronger Christian. Another woman emphasized that relationships centered in Christ are very freeing and encouraging. Instead of a quid quo

---

6. Stevens, "Breaking the Gender Impasse," 31.

pro equation or a winner-take-all mentality she was experiencing mutual love, respect, support, and encouragement. Our twenty-five-year-old son Andrew followed Virginia and described what it was like growing up in our home. Our Ethiopian host Benyamen Yusuf told us that it was the first time a pastor's family had addressed these family issues.

## The Work of the Church

The one-flesh marriage relationship is Paul's vivid analogy for Christ and the church. The love and commitment between a husband and wife is a redemptive analogy for Christ's love for the church. These two loves, marital love and divine love, romantic love and redemptive love, are meant to support and illuminate each other. The lesser love, the love between husband and wife, is meant to help us grasp more completely the personal intimacy and earnestness of God's love for us. The greater love, God's sacrificial, saving, cleansing love, is meant to be the source, strength, and standard for human love. The power and intensity of the oneness experienced between a man and woman points to the greater mystery of our oneness with God in Christ.

What is absolutely clear in Paul's spiritual direction is that husbands and wives cannot be each other's savior. When the pursuit of sexual intimacy in a loving marriage becomes the ultimate quest for love, marriage becomes an idol and each partner a god. Salvation sought within this intimacy always ends in failure. Unless the lesser love is empowered and protected by the greater love, marriage bears an impossible burden. To insist on finding the ultimate, soul-saving love in one's spouse is to drain the energy and joy right out of marriage. We need the greater love. Make no mistake: Jesus Christ is the Savior, without whom we are devastatingly lost. We need the sanctifying, cleansing power of the gospel.

Precautions should be taken to make sure that these two loves do not become rival loves. How can we obey Jesus' command to deny ourselves, take up our cross and follow him (Luke 9:23), and then marry someone who has no interest in following Jesus? I am not speaking here to a person who has come to Christ after being married to an unbeliever, but to a believer who chooses to ignore the meaning and power of God's greater love for the sake of the lesser love. In friendship and dating the first thing people should know about us is that Jesus Christ is our Savior and Lord.

The oneness of the one-flesh relationship is a picture of our oneness with God in Christ. The love between a husband and wife ought to remind

## The Christ Letter

us that there is "one body and one Spirit, just as you were called to one hope when you were called; one Lord, one faith, one baptism; one God and Father of all, who is over all and through all and in all" (4:4–6).

# 12

# The Care of Christ

> *"Fathers, do not exasperate your children;
> instead, bring them up in the training
> and instruction of the Lord."*
>
> EPHESIANS 6:4

The bond that holds marriage and family together is Jesus Christ. Mutual submission out of reverence for Christ is the key to holy, healthy, holistic relationships. That is the easily stated theory anyway, but how does this work out in actual practice? We want our children to know that we have been crucified with Christ and that we no longer live, but Christ lives in us. And the life we now live in the body, we live by faith in the Son of God, who loved us and gave himself for us (Gal 2:20). We want our daily lives to confess Christ to our children. And if anyone can tell the difference in our lives between pious rhetoric and authentic living it is our children.

## Grown-Ups

(6:1–4) *"Children, obey your parents in the Lord, for this right. 'Honor your father and mother'—which is the first commandment with a promise—'so that if may go well with you and that you may enjoy long life on the earth.'*

## The Christ Letter

> *Fathers, do not exasperate your children; instead, bring them up in the training and instruction of the Lord."*

What Paul says about the family is very brief, only four verses. At first glance the Bible seems to say very little about being a parent. One is hard pressed to find much more than a paragraph in Paul's letters on the subject. The apostle's one-line exhortations seem too concise, almost cryptic. If we had only these few lines to work with we would be in trouble, but everything Paul says about living for Christ applies to being a Christian family. This is why the theologically focused first half of Ephesians, which stresses worship, salvation, and mission, is so vitally important to the second half of the letter with its emphasis on ethics and relationships. Behavior flows from belief. To believe is to obey and to obey is to believe. These two dynamics, belief and behavior, are in synergy.

### *Person to Parent*

Everything that Paul hopes and prays for *persons* applies to *parents*. Paul prayed for us as parents, to be "rooted and established in love," and to have "power, together with all the saints, to grasp how wide and long and high and deep is the love of Christ and to know this love that surpasses knowledge—that [we] may be filled to the measure of all the fullness of God" (3:17–19). Paul exhorted parents, "to live a life worthy of the calling [we] have received. Be completely humble and gentle: be patient, bearing with one another in love" (4:1–2). Paul's expectations are clear: "We will no longer be infants, tossed back and forth by the waves, and blown here and there by every wind of teaching and by cunning and craftiness of people in their deceitful scheming. Instead, speaking the truth in love, we will in all things *grow up* into him who is the head, that is Christ" (4:14–15).

Parenting is not defined by matching skills and duties, nor is it a task-oriented job like that of a computer programmer or a surgeon. There is no instruction manual given by God to make us effective parents, no technical guide for expert parenting. "A parent's main job is not to be a parent, but to be a person."[1] I don't ever recall my father addressing his role as a father. I doubt if he distinguished between being a father and being himself. Neither he nor my mother thought of parenting as a task in competition with other responsibilities. They gave my brother and me constant companionship, love, direction, protection, discipline, and support. Good

---

1. Peterson, *Growing Up With Your Teenager*, 18.

parents don't just attend to their children's needs, they carry them in their heart. That's what my parents did for us.

Mature parents appreciate author Jerry Sittser's perspective on this: "I once *performed* as a parent; now I *am* a parent."[2] Being a father or a mother ought to be the most highly integrative calling that we can possibly fulfill. "The parent's main task is to be vulnerable in a living demonstration that adulthood is full, alive and Christian."[3]

Writer Timothy Smith draws out the practical implications of Paul's spiritual direction. He writes:

> Strong parents produce strong kids. Weak parents produce weak kids. Kids pick up what they grow up with. A child who manipulates her parents by whining, throwing fits and sulking won't develop the emotional strength to deal with disappointment, waiting, frustration and boredom and will become more lethal in her teens. How will she have the inner strength and self-control to resist cheating, sex and substance abuse?[4]

## Generation to Generation

Paul expects parents to act like grown-ups, sincere disciples, who care deeply about how they live their lives in Christ. The parent's high calling is to make the most of every opportunity and to be filled with the Spirit. He envisioned the church to be a cross-section of society, made up of different generations, vocations, social classes, and ethnic backgrounds. A congregation primarily made up of people in their twenties will miss out on the dynamic of what Christ has in mind for the household of faith. This is also true of a congregation mainly made up of people in their fifties or older. The Lord of the church did not design churches around singleness, or young families, or senior citizens. Nor did the Lord mean for us to divide along racial and economic lines. "As long as a church is a 'group of our kind,' it fails its mission."[5] We were meant to be a cross-generational, multi-cultural, socially diverse congregation centered in Christ.

---

2. Sittser, *A Grace Disguised*, 90.
3. Peterson, *Growing Up With Your Teenager*, 18.
4. Smith, *The Danger of Raising Nice Kids*, 60.
5. Snodgrass, *Ephesians*, 329.

## The Christ Letter

### *Private to Public*

Paul saw clearly that who we are in the home is who we are. He challenged the difference between our public persona and our private selves. Of all people our children pick up on this fundamental discrepancy the fastest. Sadly, we are often at our worst with the people we love the most. Publicly we may be warm and congenial, but in private we're irritable, judgmental, impatient, and rude. "Christians should have only one persona, or we are no longer living in truth. We need to live tirelessly the humility, tolerant love, and mutual submission of the gospel both in private and in public. The most important witness we have is at stake—the witness within our families."[6]

Moses was given practical instruction in how to overcome the divide between our public and private personas. His admonition to parents is a working pedagogy for everyday spirituality.

> These commandments that I give you today are to be on your hearts. Impress them on your children. Talk about them when you sit at home and when you walk along the road, when you lie down and when you get up (Deut 6:5–7).

Only what is impressed on our hearts can be impressed on our children. The truth of God is so much a part of our lives that it is naturally part of our daily conversation from morning to night. If we want to relay the truth from one generation to another, we should begin not with the pulpit but with the kitchen table. Our table talk is the test of orthodoxy. How we do daily chores demonstrates our humility. Our sense of humor shows our tolerance for others. Love makes itself known in words and deeds, more in the family room than in the sanctuary. Edith Schaeffer writes, "The family is the place where loyalty, dependability, trustworthiness, compassion, sensitivity to others, thoughtfulness, and unselfishness are supposed to have their roots. Someone must take the initiative and use imagination to teach these things."[7]

## Children First

Why does Paul address children first and then parents? One commentator writes, "The text addresses children first because that is the subject of the

---

6. Snodgrass, *Ephesians*, 329.
7. Schaeffer, *What Is a Family?*, 83.

traditional house codes. Ideally parents should be addressed first, for they nurture long before children can obey."[8] Other scholars, however, suggest that the order may be more significant than that. By addressing wives, children and slaves as citizens of the Christ's kingdom and as responsible agents for establishing social order, Paul affirmed their equality before the Lord. "Everyone is subordinated to the same highest authority . . . in this they are equals . . . none is nearer or dearer to God and the Messiah than the other."[9] In Christ the old hierarchies and valuations have changed.

> The vision of "participation" by all members of society in the common good includes the establishment of a common and shared responsibility. When Paul places major emphasis on the contribution of the supposedly "weaker" members, in actuality he takes a revolutionary step. They above all shall and will be the carriers of responsibility, changes, and progress! Yet instead of the dream of a perfect society, it is the knowledge of the crucified Lord's authority which gives Paul the courage to trust in the "power" that "is made perfect in weakness" (2 Cor 12:9).[10]

## Called to Obey

Children are dignified by a calling. They are entrusted with responsibility. They have an important role to play in the health and vitality of the social order. We do our children a disservice when we act as if they are either too cute or too needy to receive this calling. We disrespect them when we do not expect obedience from them. They are made not only to be loved and fed and clothed and educated and signed up for sports, but they are called to obey. They are not passive recipients of what we have to give them, they are active agents of obedience.

Children are called to obey. This is a requirement that flows from mutual submission in Christ but it is not the same as submission. It is important to note that wives are told to submit to their husbands and husbands are told to sacrifice for their wives. Wives are not told to obey their husbands. John Stott writes, "The concept of a husband who issues commands and of a wife who gives him obedience is simply not found in the New Testament. . . . A wife's submission is something quite different

---

8. Snodgrass, *Ephesians*, 329.
9. Barth, *Ephesians*, 756.
10. Ibid.

from obedience. It is a voluntary self-giving to a lover whose responsibility is defined in terms of constructive care; it is love's response to love."[11]

A child's responsibility to obey is related to the parent's responsibility to require obedience. The two obligations are linked. Our children's ability to grow up and mature is tied to their capacity to learn and follow directions, which is directly related to their ability to obey. Obedience to teachers, coaches, and other adults is a reflection of a child's willingness to obey his or her parents. Disobedience disrupts the learning process. Obedience is the foundation for the child's growth and development.

## *In the Lord*

The obedience called for in this imperative is qualified in a significant way: "Obey your parents *in the Lord.*" Paul's earlier description of practical obedience provides an excellent profile of what obedience in the Lord means (4:25—5:4). Obedience involves truthfulness, self-control, hard work, edifying speech, kindness, and love. A child is responsible to obey in these ways and a parent is responsible to require such obedience. Parents who permit lying, tantrums, meanness, and disrespect are hurting their children.

We are confronted by two problems in our day: parental passivity on the one hand and parental abuse on the other. Spanking a young child makes sense when a child needs to be impressed with the consequences of disobedience and when the spanking can be administered by a parent who is emotionally self-controlled. Slapping, punching, and name-calling are always abusive. Calling your child stupid or a jerk or an idiot is always wrong regardless of the offense.

I recall our daughter Kennerly's first spanking, but none after that. She was two at the time and we lived in Toronto. Her brothers were five and seven. I came home from work and walked into the living room. Toys were scattered all over the floor and we were going to have dinner in a few minutes. I said to the boys and Kennerly, "Okay, time to clean up." The boys grudgingly began picking up their toys, but Kennerly stood up defiantly and looked me square in the eye and said emphatically, "No." The boys immediately stopped what they were doing. This was new. Their little sister, still in diapers, was standing up to dad. In a sense it was comical and you had to admire her strong-willed courage. Still in my suit from work—the picture of authority, towering over this two-year-old in diapers

11. Stott, *The New Society*, 238.

whose body was trembling in defiance. Ignoring the first no, I repeated the order, to which Kennerly responded even more adamantly and negatively. Sensing trouble, the boys quickly left the room. After her third and fourth refusal, I spanked her, though I doubt she could have felt much through the diaper, but for hours after it was obvious that I had deeply offended her.

Virginia remembers using a wooden spoon on Andrew's seat. Try as we might we couldn't get him to stop running his army green "G.I. Joe" tricycle into the street. He would race down our narrow driveway peddling as hard as he possibly could and dart out into the middle of the street. We lived on a relatively quiet city street, but we had nightmares of him getting killed right in front of the house. For several days Virginia stood guard at the end of the driveway with a wooden spoon in hand and if he crossed the edge of the concrete where the driveway met the sidewalk he'd get a spanking. Sure enough, Andrew would race to the end as fast as he could go and stop as near to the edge as he possibly could without going over it. He got plenty of spankings, but by the third day he respected the rule and he's alive to this day.

I don't recall needing to spank our children very much. They quickly passed through that phase where spankings were effective. And in no time, we were using "time-outs," restrictions, sanctions, and privations to drive home the point that there were consequences for disobedience.

The Book of Proverbs commends a practical wisdom that will never go out-of-date:

> "Those who spare the rod hate their children,
> but those who love them are careful to discipline them" (13:24).
>
> "Folly is bound up in the heart of a child,
> but the rod of discipline will drive it far away" (22:15).
>
> "A rod and a reprimand impart wisdom,
> but children left to themselves disgrace their mother" (29:15).
>
> "My son, do not despise the Lord's discipline,
> and do not resent his rebuke, because the Lord disciplines
> those he loves, as a father the son he delights in" (3:11–12).

Proverbs also warns those who turn instruction into insults and discipline into abuse:

> "The words of the reckless pierce like swords,
> but the tongue of the wise brings healing" (12:18).

> "Those who guard their lips preserve their lives,
> but those who speak rashly will come to ruin" (13:3).
>
> "The quick-tempered do foolish things . . ." (14:17).
>
> "Those who are patient have great understanding,
> but the quick-tempered display folly" (14:29).
>
> "A gentle answer turns away wrath,
> but a harsh word stirs up anger" (15:1).

Paul offers four motivations to back up his command for children to obey their parents. The first motivation is centered in Christ. Obedience is *in the Lord*. The second is our intuitive sense that this is right and good. This second motivation is based on natural law. We are to obey our parents because it fits with the order of things. Søren Kierkegaard argued that children ought to obey their parents, not because their parents are impressive or eloquent or creative or clever, but because they are their parents. Most cultures recognize this natural law principle. Paul's third motivation is found in the Ten Commandments. The fifth commandment requires children to obey their parents: "Honor your father and your mother, so that you may live long in the land the Lord your God is giving you" (Exodus 20:12). The fourth motivation is the promise of God. Instead of working against the grain of relationships and family life, obedience in the Lord is blessed by the Lord. The fruit of obedience is a harvest of healthy, holy, well-adjusted relationships. The art of living is not knowing where to live but how to live. "Start children off on the way they should go, and even when they are old they will not turn from it" (Prov 22:6).

Another reason why children are addressed first may be because we are all children and we remain someone's child for a long time. The fifth commandment stays in effect for a long time. With parents living into their nineties, children are commanded by the Lord to honor their father and mother in new and sometimes demanding ways. We were meant to honor our parents even when we have children and grandchildren of our own. There is a lot of living to be learned, living between the generations. Honoring parents in the later stages of their earthly lives and training children in the knowledge and admonition of the Lord can feel like a full-time job. But it is in the midst of this family dynamic that we receive the promise of the presence of Christ. It is healthy for us to re-examine our faith in Christ from the perspective of our children's emerging faith and from the perspective of our parents' long-standing faith.

Some see the fifth commandment as the first commandment to deal with our relationship with others, because the first four commandments deal with God and the following six deal with human beings. Another perspective is to see the Ten Commandments as equally divided in focus between God and humanity, which makes honoring parents related to our reverence for God.

In any case, Jesus did not tolerate those who used their alleged reverence for God as an excuse for indifference toward their parents. Apparently the Pharisees argued that if a person pledged a gift to God (Korban) it could not be used to help out needy parents (Matt 15:4–7). The problem persists in our day. Adult children can find many valid-sounding reasons not to assist elderly parents: the time and financial priority of their own children, the pressures of work, and the inconvenience of giving practical help, etc. But the fifth commandment does not allow us to avoid our God-given responsibility to honor our parents in meaningful ways.[12]

## Loving Fathers

Paul admonishes fathers: "Don't exasperate your children by coming down hard on them. Take them by the hand and lead them in the way of the Master" (6:4, *The Message*). Why does he single fathers out for this prohibition? Is it because fathers generally tend to be harsher, less accepting and more demanding of their children? Paul does not remind fathers of their authority, but of their responsibility. In first-century Roman culture fathers had absolute authority in the family. Daughters tended to be ignored while fathers concentrated exclusively on their sons' education and development. Paul challenges this limitation by intentionally referring to "children" rather than "sons." His exhortation to fathers not to make their children angry echoes his earlier concern about anger (4:26–27). If fathers thought they could get away with anger in the home, they were mistaken. What better place to "get rid of all bitterness, rage and anger" than in the home? What better place than in the family to "be kind and compassionate to one another, forgiving each other" (4:31–32)? The home is not the place for fathers to take out their frustrations from work.

Paul zeroes in on fathers, warning them not to come down hard on their children, but instead, to "bring them up in the training and instruction of the Lord."

---

12. Bruner, *The Churchbook: Matthew 13-28*, 85.

> Fathers are made responsible for ensuring that they do not provoke anger in their children. This involves avoiding attitudes, words, and actions which would drive a child to angry exasperation or resentment and thus rules out excessively severe discipline, unreasonably harsh demands, abuse of authority, arbitrariness, unfairness, constant nagging and condemnation, subjecting a child to humiliation, and all forms of gross insensitivity to a child's needs and sensibilities.[13]

As Klyne Snodgrass notes, "The practical consequences of this instruction [in the Lord] include":

1. Creating a context of grace, love, support, respect, and encouragement
2. Always speaking the truth in love
3. Attending to the material and emotional needs of children
4. Teaching, enlightening, warning, holding accountable, and disciplining, all as part of living in Christ; giving them a theology
5. Giving experiences, especially in work and in caring for others
6. Refusing to put down, demean, or damage them (shrill and angry speech does not belong in the home)
7. Rejecting jealousy and contempt
8. Granting freedom and legitimate boundaries
9. Avoiding unhealthy pressure or expectations
10. Refusing to live through the children.[14]

## Unless the Lord

We have to be careful. For even here in this important responsibility of parenting we are tempted to be selfish. Much of our effort as parents may be more for ourselves than for our children. In *Death by Suburb*, David

---

13. Lincoln, *Ephesians*, 406.
14. Snodgrass, *Ephesians*, 329–30.

## The Care of Christ

Goetz warns parents against turning their children into "immortality symbols." We are tempted to bolster our own fragile egos by questing for glory and significance through our children. "Successful children," writes Goetz, "are the ultimate glory in today's Park District and Travel Team culture ... Each child represents real potential for glory in the here and now ... They are the ultimate extension of our selves ... Parenting is hard these days; perhaps it truly is, as the saying goes, today's most competitive adult sport."[15] Goetz argues that if we expect to be of any help to our children we have to overcome what he calls, "Perpetual Spiritual Adolescence."[16] We have to rise above our sinful preoccupation with self, appearances, and success and learn to give ourselves away to others, to forget about ourselves in humble service—the service that may not always make a difference—and to stay put in community for the long haul.

### Family Routine

As I look back on my childhood, my parents did a great job. Part of their effectiveness as parents simply had to do with our family routine. My brother and I grew up faster because we were raised in an adult world. Today, children have their own parallel universe that orbits around an adult world. They have their clothing, food, entertainment, language, movies, music, and symbols. They have their own culture. I grew up in my parents' culture. They set the rhythm of our life together. We were expected to work. Sports was something we kids did on our own in the neighborhood. On Wednesday nights we went to prayer meeting. On Saturday night we got ready for Sunday morning. We studied our Sunday school lesson and wrote out answers to questions on the lesson. We went to bed early so we were ready for worship. Family devotions was also part of our regular routine. Every night after dinner we read the Bible and prayed together.

### Hospitality

Another reason for their effectiveness had to do with how our parents extended hospitality. For years they hosted a large gathering of Chinese students every Friday night for Bible study and fellowship. This had a huge impact on my brother and me. It shaped how we thought of people, the

---

15. Goetz, *Death By Suburb*, 42.
16. Ibid., 138.

church, and mission. You might say that this made us better Christians than we wanted to be.

## *Suffering*

A third reason for their effectiveness was how my parents experienced suffering. Over a span of about five years beginning with my cancer surgery, followed by my father's death from stomach cancer and the deaths of my grandparents and aunt, my mother took the lead in all of the medical, funeral, and legal arrangements. I never recall her complaining or implying that what she was doing was heroic. At the time, my brother and I did not realize what an extraordinary act of love, courage, and strength we were witnessing in our mother.

My parents did not socialize my brother and me to be nice human beings; they trained us to advance the kingdom of God. They didn't expect us to fit into culture very well. They planned for us to be different. They didn't expect society to provide what we needed to flourish. Nor did they expect us to rebel and go through a period of sowing our wild oats. They depended on the Word and Spirit of Christ to accomplish the work of transformation. They felt deeply responsible for that disciple-making process, in themselves and in us. I don't remember them being insecure or nervous about it, either.

Timothy Smith says, "the perfect smile is the icon for today's child." He continues, "We are raising a generation with perfect teeth and twisted hearts. Because of our investment, they have nice teeth, but their hearts are warped. They haven't learned compassion, empathy and initiative. They haven't developed personal convictions and moral standards."[17]

When it comes to building a home and raising a family, Psalm 127 knows no *independent contractors*. Parents cannot out-source their spiritual direction. We are either participating with the Lord in the lead or we are anxiously striving for things that do not matter. Only what is from God is truly strong. Either the work is the Lord's or it is pointless. And nothing illustrates this God-principle better than children. "Unless the Lord builds the house" is another way of saying unless "we submit to one another out of reverence for Christ" we are wasting our time and effort. Children are meant to be a heritage not a liability, a blessing not a burden. The Psalmist likens children to "arrows in the hands of a warrior." The metaphor works well with the picture of the full armor of God described at the end of Paul's

---

17. Smith, *The Danger of Raising Nice Kids*, 23.

letter. Arrows allow a warrior to stand in one place and shoot an arrow far away to have an impact far beyond the warrior's reach. Children multiply our effectiveness as they fight for the kingdom of God in the Jesus way.

# 13

# The Slaves of Christ

> *"Obey them not only to win their favor when their eye is on you, but as slaves of Christ, doing the will of God from your heart."*
>
> EPHESIANS 6:6

The work of mutual submission in Christ continues as the apostle Paul turns his attention to the relationship between slaves and masters. I imagine the apostle Paul agreeing with Bob Dylan, in his 1979 hit song, "You Gotta Serve Somebody." Dylan's lyrics and iconic voice capture the truth: Everyone serves somebody. It doesn't matter who you are. Whether you're an ambassador or a dancer, a fashionable socialite or heavyweight champion, we all end up serving somebody. The master may be the devil or he may be the Lord, but we always serve somebody. One way or another we are slaves, a term few people wish to think about, let alone identify with. In Romans, the apostle Paul declared that we used to be slaves of sin, but now we have been set free from sin to become *slaves of God* (Rom 6:22). In Ephesians, Paul boldly called the followers of Jesus "slaves of Christ."

The horrors of slavery in our national history make the concept of slavery repulsive to us. To buy and sell human beings as if they were a piece of property to be used for economic gain is barbaric. In the early 1600s, Elmina Castle in Ghana, West Africa, became the first slave prison on Ghana's gold coast. At the height of the slave trade in the seventeenth and eighteenth centuries, thirty-five thousand African slaves a year were

## The Slaves of Christ

exported from the fort to the Americas. On a trip to Ghana with my family we visited Elmina Castle and walked through the holding cells where thousands of human beings were imprisoned like animals before boarding a frigate for the dangerous journey west. Many did not survive the harsh and inhumane journey. Thousands died at sea. Slave traders bought their human cargo wholesale in the castle's courtyard. At the auction block they haggled over the price.

There was an eerie silence in the dungeons under the castle and we could only imagine the sights and smells and sounds of what it was like when the dark and dank cells were crowded with Africans who had been sold by Africans to the British or the Portugese or the Dutch. Human beings, image bearers of God, were ripped from their villages, families, spouses, and children and treated worse than livestock.

Directly above these holding cells was a chapel. The inscription above the chapel door is from Psalm 132:13 in Dutch and reads, "For the Lord has chosen Zion, he has desired it for his dwelling." The paradox is beyond comprehension. To think—above the sounds of human suffering, confessing Christians worshiped with Bibles and hymn books in hand oblivious to the grave injustice they presided over.

In first century Roman culture, slavery was the social, legal and economic reality and was not subject to debate. Slavery was central to the economic order as our "service industry" is to our economy. "The institution of slavery was a fact of Mediterranean economic life so completely accepted as a part of the labor structure of the time that one cannot correctly speak of the slave 'problem' in antiquity."[1] In Paul's day, one-third of the population of Greece and Italy were slaves. The Roman Senate debated whether or not to require slaves to wear identifying clothing. They decided against uniforms for fear that the slave population would realize how large and potentially powerful they were.

Unlike American slavery, slaves in the ancient Roman world were not drawn from one race, nor were their duties limited to manual labor. Slaves were responsible for a broad range of economic activities, including administrative positions in the household of the emperor, civil service jobs, medical care, teaching, accountancy, business enterprises, as well as domestic and agricultural work. Some slaves lived very well with a higher status and standard of living than some free people. Some people sold themselves into slavery "in order to climb socially, to obtain particular employment open only to slaves, and to enjoy a better standard of living

1. Westermann, *The Slave Systems of Greek and Roman Antiquity*, 215.

than they had experienced as free persons. Being a slave had the benefit of providing a certain personal and social security."[2] However, slavery under any circumstances is dehumanizing. The Oscar-winning movie *Gladiator*, starring Russell Crowe, tells the story of Maximus, a Roman general who is betrayed and sold into slavery. The movie offers a realistic picture of the brutality and humiliation of slavery in first-century Rome.

## Slaves of Christ

(6:5–9) *"Slaves, obey your earthly masters with respect and fear, and with sincerity of heart, just as you would obey Christ. Obey them not only to win their favor when their eye is on you, but as slaves of Christ, doing the will of God from your heart. Serve wholeheartedly, as if you were serving the Lord, not people, because you know that the Lord will reward each one of you for whatever good you do, whether you are slave or free.*

*And masters, treat your slaves in the same way. Do not threaten them, since you know that he who is both their Master and yours is in heaven, and there is no favoritism with him."*

In spite of its negative connotations, Paul stayed with the title "slave of Christ." He redefined its meaning in the light of the gospel. He emphasized that in Christ, slavery had been abolished. Therefore, we are no longer slaves, but sons and daughters. We no longer live in fear. "The Spirit himself testifies with our spirit that we are God's children" (Romans 8:16; see Galatians 4:7). Our relationship with Christ takes precedence over our social standing. Slaves are free in Christ and those who are free should consider themselves Christ's slaves.

Paul accepted the language and imagery of the slave and used it to define his relationship to Christ. Instead of being a slave to a human master, Paul saw himself as a slave of Christ. He reasoned with the Galatians:

> Am I now trying to win human approval, or God's approval?
> Or am I trying to please people? If I were still trying to please
> people, I would not be a slave of Christ. (Gal 1:10)

He also used the language of slavery to define his mission: "Though I am free and belong to no one, I have made myself a slave to everyone, to win as many as possible" (1 Cor 9:19). He challenged believers not to use their

---

2. Lincoln, *Ephesians*, 418.

## The Slaves of Christ

freedom to indulge the sinful nature, but "to be slaves (δουλεύετε) to one another in love" (Gal 5:13).

> Keeping God's commands is what counts. Each of you should remain in the situation you were in when God called you. Were you a slave when you were called? Don't let it trouble you—although if you can gain your freedom, do so. For those who were slaves when called to faith in the Lord are the Lord's freed people; similarly, those who were free when called are Christ's slaves. You were bought at a price; do not become slaves of human beings. Brothers and sisters, all of you, as responsible to God, should remain in the situation in which God called you. (1 Cor 7:19–24)

Instead of feeling inferior, the believer who was a slave was meant to experience real freedom in Christ. The thrust of Paul's concern is contentment, freedom, and faithfulness. In Christ, there are no second-class Christians. "Were you a slave when you were called? Don't let it trouble you—although if you can gain your freedom, do so" (1 Cor 7:21). The old criteria of social standing based on ethnicity, religion, and social class, no longer control the believer's identity, self-worth, and fulfillment. Far from rendering believers passive to social pressures, Paul sought to make them immune to social pressures. "Believers are not to return to the bondage of an honor-shame culture where everything revolves round what status is achieved in human eyes."[3] "Paul's concern is not with change, one way or the other, but with 'living out one's calling' in whatever situation one is found."[4]

For Paul the bottom line is the cross: "You were bought at a price; do not become slaves of human beings" (1 Cor 7:23). Ultimately the only freedom worth having is the freedom found in Christ, because only that freedom sets us free from the selfish social values of the world, from the dog-eat-dog world of cutthroat competition, and from the law of sin and death.

## Spiritual Direction

Paul's admonition to first-century slaves leads to powerful spiritual direction for all of us who are the slaves of Christ.

---

3. Thiselton, *The First Epistle to the Corinthians*, 562.
4. Fee, *The First Epistle to the Corinthians*, 322.

The Christ Letter

1. The apostle showed them respect by addressing them directly as full-fledged members of the body of Christ. He demonstrated how relationships within the church "embody their Lord's ultimate disregard for any distinctions based on social status."[5] He dignified the slave as a brother or sister in Christ with equal standing before the Lord.

2. Paul applied the gospel to everyday life, to their social and economic realities. Paul emphasized the sanctity of work. Everyday work is related to the Lordship of Christ (Col 3:17). This advice is consistent with his counsel to believers in Thessalonica, when he wrote, "Make it your ambition to lead a quiet life: You should mind your own business and work with your hands, just as we told you, so that your daily life may win the respect of outsiders . . ." (1 Thess 4:11–12).

3. He acted as if their obedience was on par with his own, because their calling was no different from his own. Everyone must work out their salvation with "fear and trembling." Regardless of the situation, obedience, whether by a slave or an apostle is of the same value in the Lord (Phil 2:12).

4. Paul encouraged slaves to focus on their ultimate master—Jesus Christ. They are to relate to their earthly masters as they would to Christ, because their true identity is not as slaves to people, but as slaves of Christ. In the parable of the sheep and goats, Jesus taught that whatever is done for the least of these brothers and sisters is done for him (Matt 25:40). We learn here that what is done for earthly masters is done for Christ.

5. He affirmed the very highest motivation and reward for their work: "Serve wholeheartedly, as if you were serving the Lord, not people, because you know that the Lord will reward each one of you for whatever good you do, whether you are slave or free."

6. And then within their presence, the apostle Paul challenged masters to treat their slaves as their slaves treat them. They may have different social and economic positions but there is only one way to serve others—with sincerity of heart, with an eye toward the Lord, with obedience to the will of God, and with pure motives. In front of Christian brothers and sisters, classified by the world as slaves, Paul emphasized that both masters and slaves are under the same Master in heaven who makes no distinction between slaves and masters.

---

5. Lincoln, *Ephesians*, 428

## The Slaves of Christ

What Paul says here to first-century slaves goes to the heart of *our* motivation for twenty-first-century service. Paul's spiritual direction exposes and critiques the pretend service that is about egotistical self-expression and not about obedience to Christ. Not all so-called service honors Christ. Some service is all about the server's prestige and felt-need satisfaction. This is pseudo-service that is done for self-advancement or for a show of moral superiority. This is service that appears outwardly compassionate and sacrificial, but is really all about power, control, and ego. This is the service that longs to be congratulated as a fine performance. This is very different from the kind of obedient, sacrificial service that Paul is calling for.

William Wilberforce, the eighteenth-century Parliamentarian who led the heroic campaign to end slavery, experienced a gradual conversion. He moved from a nominal nod to Christian tradition and a life of driving ambition to a full-fledged embrace of Christian truth. He called it the "Great Change." Like Nicodemus, who came to Jesus at night, Wilberforce secretly visited John Newton, the former slave trader, now Methodist pastor, who knew firsthand the power of God's amazing grace. Wilberforce expected Newton to tell him that to follow Christ he must leave politics, but instead Newton encouraged Wilberforce to remain in Parliament, convinced that God could use him there.

Wilberforce's social position did not change, but everything else did. He writes: "As soon as I reflected seriously upon these subjects the deep guilt and black ingratitude of my past life forced itself upon me in the strongest colors, and I condemned myself for having wasted my precious time, and opportunities, and talents."[6] The "Great Change" humbled Wilberforce, calmed his soul, transformed his ambition, revolutionized the way he used his money, and reoriented his use of time. He became a slave of Christ in order to abolish the slave trade.

The apostle Paul's spiritual direction to slaves provides a powerful antidote to the many forms of enslavement that threaten us. In the Spirit, Paul gives the slaves of Christ the right attitude for working with unreasonable employers under difficult conditions.

Slaves in Christ who took Paul's counsel to heart may have an advantage over believers today. We think we are in control of our lives, but they knew better. We talk big about freedom but we are slaves to money and debt, technologies and schedules, lusts and leisure. We have our hidden bondage with which to contend.

---

6. Metaxas, *Amazing Grace*, 52.

## The Christ Letter

We think we are what we do and what we own, but they knew better. In Christ, the slaves in Ephesus had an identity beyond the drudgery of work. They refused to confuse their job with their self-worth.

We think we want our neighbor's life, but they knew better. We covet his car, her clothes, his job, her fun, his reputation, her success, but slaves were required to give themselves away. They rejected the temptation to turn things and people into "immortality symbols." They did not have the luxury of contemplating the American myth that you can be anything you want to be.

We think our lives should be easier, but they knew better. They knew life was brutally hard and they accepted it with grace and patience.

We think we need to make a difference with our lives, but they knew better. They were slaves, and their lives could not be defined by results and achievements. Meaning and significance had to be found in Christ and in obedience.

We think we can solve our problems by moving away, switching churches, changing jobs, but they knew better. They couldn't leave; they had to stay. They had to live for Christ under conditions and circumstances over which they had little control.

We think that friendships should enrich our lives and give us something in return, but they knew better. Slaves of Christ befriend fellow strugglers, not for what they can get out of the relationship, but for what they can give.

### Subversive Pastor or Defender of the Status-quo?

Pro-slavery advocates in the American South argued that if the institution of slavery was evil, the apostle Paul would have called for its abolition. The fact that he did not meant that slavery was sanctioned by God. Pro-slavery advocates argued that "the meek and humble Savior of the world in no instance meddled with the established institutions of mankind."[7] Albert Bledsoe in *Cotton is King* (1860) reasoned that if the New Testament allowed slaveholders to be members and leaders in the church then it would be wrong to set up "a different and higher standard of truth and duty" than the Word of God.

There is an unforgettable scene in Alex Haley's movie *Roots* when Fiddler the old slave foreman pleads for the life of Kunta Kinte, a runaway

---

7. Professor Dew, "The Pro-Slavery Argument" (1831), quoted in Swartley, *Slavery, Sabbath, War and Women*, 35.

slave. With the sound of the whip and Kunta's cries in the background, Fiddler rushes to the mansion to the see the master. He is grudgingly permitted to see the master in his study. The master is seated at his desk with a large magnifying glass in hand, poring over the Scriptures. Fiddler tries to reason with the master, but the master refuses to listen. The master insists that Kunta Kinte must be punished. He must be broken. He abruptly dismisses Fiddler and resumes his Bible reading. The scene portrays the master's blindness to the dehumanizing evil of slavery even though he studies the Bible with a magnifying glass.

Thorton Stringfellow wrote an essay entitled "Slavery in the Light of Divine Revelation," published in *Cotton is King*, in which he argued, based on 1 Corinthians 7:20–24, that "one general principle was ordained of God, applicable alike in all countries and at all stages of the church's future history, and that it was this: 'as the Lord has called everyone so let him walk.'"[8] In passages like 1 Timothy 6:1–6, slaveholders found support for the defense of the status quo. Apparently it didn't matter that in the same letter Paul lumped "slave traders" in with murderers, liars, and the sexually immoral (1 Tim 1:10).

On the contrary, anti-slavery advocates reasoned that Jesus and the apostles never approved or condoned slavery. They believed that the doctrine of universal humanity, the command to love your neighbor as yourself, and the prohibition against dominating others, undermines slavery. Abolitionists reasoned that biblical principles of humility, love, and justice lead inevitably to the end of slavery.

Is Paul a subversive pastor or a defender of the status quo? Those who follow Christ have a distinctive understanding and commitment to social change. The inside-out revolution empowered by the gospel is always *personal* before it is *political*, always *relational* before it is *institutional*, always *spiritual* before it is *social*. Beatitude-based believers are salt and light disciples—God's workmanship created in Christ Jesus to do good works. We are called to work out our "salvation with fear and trembling, for it is God who works in [us] to will and act in order to fulfill his good purpose" (Phil 2:12–13). Those who know Christ personally cannot help but have a social impact.

Jesus said to love our neighbor as ourselves and then he redefined the "neighbor" to include those we were least likely to like, let alone love. Such love is bound to have a social impact. He taught us how to pray: "Our Father in heaven, hallowed be your name, your kingdom come, your will

---

8. Swartley, *Slavery, Sabbath, War and Women*, 36.

be done on earth as it is in heaven" (Matt 6:9–10). How can we pray this way and not see the world change? He commissioned us: "Go and make disciples of all nations, baptizing them in the name of the Father and of the Son and of the Holy Spirit, and teaching them to obey everything I have commanded you" (Matt 28:19–20). How can such obedience not have a social impact? How can we seek first the kingdom of God and Christ's righteousness and not change the world? Faith in Christ gets worked into local history and eventually into world history. "Every movement we make in response to God has a ripple effect, touching family, neighbors, friends, community."[9]

The apostle Paul emphasized the sociological impact of the gospel. The "dividing wall of hostility" between Jew and Greek was destroyed in Christ. Christ's purpose "was to create in himself one new humanity out of the two, thus making peace, and in one body to reconcile both of them to God through the cross, by which he put to death their hostility" (Eph 2:14–16). The inclusiveness of the gospel depends exclusively on Christ who is our peace. Breaking down the barriers of social hostility is not based on a negotiated settlement between opposing groups, nor on sentimental spirituality, nor on a tolerant neutrality, but on the cross of Christ, through whom we have "access to the Father by one Spirit" (Eph 2:18). The gospel is not only life-changing but world-changing. The racial, gender, generational, social, and economic divides are being overcome in Christ. "There is neither Jew nor Gentile, neither slave nor free, neither male nor female, for you are all one in Christ Jesus" (Gal 3:28).

"The gospel of Jesus Christ is more political than anyone imagines, but in a way that no one guesses."[10] Likewise, it can be said that the apostle Paul is more revolutionary than anyone imagines, but in a way that no one guesses. Paul's revolutionary word to slaves is essentially, "Do not be overcome by evil, but overcome evil with good" (Rom 12:21). The strategy articulated here is consistent with those who have offered their bodies to Christ as living sacrifices. They bless those who persecute them. They bless and do not curse. They do not repay evil for evil, but they leave room for God's wrath.

On May 2, 1963, Dr. Martin Luther King led a march for freedom and justice in Birmingham, Alabama. Prior to the march he insisted, "If you can't be non-violent, then you need to find another way to offer your support. The integrity of this movement and march depends on your ability

---

9. Peterson, *The Message*, 454.
10. Peterson, *Reversed Thunder*, 117.

to be non-violent." At the Sixteenth Street Baptist Church he gave specific instructions on how to respond if attacked: "If someone knocks you down, stay down. Don't resist the dogs. Just stay there. Don't run from them." Dr. King passed around a huge trash can. "When it's time to march, you'll need to get rid of everything that could be perceived as a weapon—nail files, sharp pencils, everything. Get all that stuff off your bodies."[11]

A friend of mine and graduate from Beeson Divinity School, Carolyn Maull McKinstry, was there that day. When Dr. King asked, "Who's willing to stand for justice, to march for freedom, to take this on?" Carolyn stood, along with a number of other young people. She was only fifteen. Many of the adults, fearful of discrimination, job loss, and retaliation, did not participate in the march. This was a youth movement. On the day of the march, children skipped school and walked to Sixteenth Street Baptist Church. In groups of fifty they left the church to join the peaceful protest march. Waves of marchers, numbering in the thousands, faced tanks, water cannons, and police dogs on the streets of Birmingham. Carolyn was struck by a blast from the water hoses, ripping her clothes and tearing a chunk of hair from her scalp. That night the eyes of the world were on Birmingham. Of the thousands of children who marched that day, 959 were arrested—one of whom was only four years old.

For the followers of Jesus Christ the key to social justice is the principle of the cross—my life for yours. The strategy of the cross is radical, but radical in a way that most "radicals" do not like. People mistake this tough-as-nails willed passivity as acquiescence. At first glance this peacemaking looks like pacification. The seeds of social change are sown in tears. The apostle Peter wrote,

> Slaves, in reverent fear of God submit yourselves to your masters, not only to those who are good and considerate, but also to those who are harsh. For it is commendable if you bear up under the pain of unjust suffering because you are conscious of God. . . . To this you were called, because Christ suffered for you, leaving you an example, that you should follow in his steps. (1 Pet 2:18–21)

## Radical Social Change

Legislation and laws are important for bringing about social change, but ultimately it must be the heart that changes. Slavery refuses to die until

11. McKinstry, *While the World Watched*, 123–24.

human beings embrace as brothers and sisters. The apostle Paul modeled the power of the gospel to bring about this deep change in his brief but compelling letter to Philemon, a brother in Christ and slave owner in Colossae.

Paul wrote regarding Onesimus, a runaway slave who "belonged" to Philemon and who had fled to Rome. Somehow Onesimus met Paul and became converted under Paul's ministry. Onesimus was a common name in antiquity, especially for slaves, and meant "useful, profitable, beneficial." Chances are Onesimus had been given his name at birth by Philemon or Philemon's father.

Paul begins his letter by identifying himself as "a prisoner of Christ Jesus." This is the only time he begins a letter this way, designating himself with a term lower than a slave and used twice for emphasis (v. 9; see Eph 3:1, 4:1; 2 Tim 1:8). Right from the start, Paul bases his appeal on personal sacrifice rather than personal status. The principle of the cross rather than the principle of authority lies behind every word of this letter. Paul also bases his appeal on Philemon's love for the Lord's people, his faith in the Lord Jesus, his partnership in the ministry and in his "deepening understanding of every good thing we share for the sake of Christ" (v. 6).

On the basis of Paul's sacrifice and Philemon's partnership, Paul says, "Therefore, although in Christ I could be bold and order you to do what you ought to do, yet I prefer to appeal to you on the basis of love" (v. 8). The apostle's authority lies behind this letter, but Paul intentionally pushed it into the background to make way for a more powerful, compelling, and personal argument. Twice, he calls Onesimus his son. He who was a slave is now a son; he who was useless is now useful. In Christ, Onesimus has become a son to Paul, a brother to Philemon, and useful to both. Paul calls Onesimus "my very heart" and says to Philemon that Onesimus "could take your place in helping me" (v. 11).

Yet Paul sent Onesimus back to Philemon because he did not want to do anything without his consent. Paul knows that he can change the outward situation by the sheer force of his authority, but what he wants to do is change Philemon's heart toward Onesimus. If Philemon accepts Onesimus as a brother in Christ and as a partner in the gospel, the slave/master status quo is subverted and a whole new relationship is established. Paul makes his appeal personal: "So if you consider me a partner, welcome him as you would welcome me." Paul neither orders nor forces Philemon, but he does everything in his power to persuade Philemon to receive Onesimus as his brother in Christ. Paul's advocacy is based on humility, mutual submission, friendship, and the principle of the cross, "my life for yours." Paul is willing to redeem the situation: "If he has done you any wrong or owes you anything, charge it to me." It is hard to imagine how Philemon could do anything but accept Onesimus, especially after Paul said to him, "you owe me your very self," and "I know you will do even more than I ask," "And by the way, get a room ready for me."

The beauty of Paul's letter to Philemon is that it offers a strategy for meaningful social change. The care with which Paul expressed himself is an indication of the degree of difficulty represented by the deeply entrenched social institution of slavery. The very nature of Paul's persuasion both here and in his letter to the Ephesians is that he does not take this situation of slavery lightly. He makes sure that his first attempt at reconciliation and transformation is his best. We have much to learn from a person who saw himself first and foremost as a slave of Christ.

# 14

# *The Strength of Christ*

> *"Finally, be strong in the Lord and in his mighty power."*
>
> Ephesians 6:10

From the opening benediction to the closing testimony, Paul's Christ Letter is all about growing up in Christ. Faith in Christ means becoming strong in the strength of Christ. The opening challenge, "Be strong," is not an appeal to self-reliance. Paul's imperative is in the passive voice and means "being strengthened." New Testament scholar Lynn Cohick offers a vital perspective, "Believers don't empower themselves, but through Christ they have access to the mighty strength that raised him from the dead and seated him above all powers."[1]

Paul has been building momentum by leading us in worship, expounding on the meaning of salvation, and inspiring us in mission. He has made his case for resilient disciples by describing the new humanity, the new ethic, and the new challenge. Paul's picture of the full armor of God is designed to bring the message home as he climaxes the letter.

If you want to know what the strength of Christ looks and feels like, study Paul's Christ Letter to the Ephesians. The challenge to be strong depends from beginning to end on the strength of God. The question for us is whether we are willing to be made strong with the power that comes from God. If we want the Christians around us to be strong, we can be that

---

1. Cohick, *Ephesians*, 157.

strength in Christ. Ghandi was right, you have to become the change you want others to become.

## A Crisis of Confidence

To a beleaguered minority who felt ostracized and insignificant, Paul brought a message of hope and courage. Like the prophet Elisha's servant, who woke up in the morning to an enemy army that had surrounded the city at night, our natural impulse is fear. The prophet Elisha tried to calm his servant with words, "Don't be afraid. Those who are with us are more than those are with them." Then he prayed, "Open his eyes Lord, so that he may see." When the Lord opened the servant's eyes, "he looked and saw the hills full of horses and chariots of fire all around Elisha" (2 Kgs 6:15–17). Because of the Lord's mighty presence, Elisha's servant had nothing to fear after all. The apostle John made a similar point when he said, "greater is he that is in you than he that is in the world" (1 John 4:4).

It is one thing to know the truth and another thing to put the truth of Christ into practice. The issue for us, as well as for Paul's readers, is not inadequate head knowledge but insufficient life practice. This is why Paul begins with worship rather than apologetics. Instead of presenting a case for faith, he leads his readers in praise (eulogy) and in prayers of thanksgiving (eucharist). To be blessed with the blessings of Christ is to understand in our souls where our strength comes from. Paul's aim is to raise our sights and lift our vision to help us take in the big picture of salvation as a powerful antidote to fixating on our problems.

Paul prays that we would "see" what is really there for us to see: "that the eyes of your heart may be enlightened in order that you may know the hope to which he has called you, the riches of his glorious inheritance in his people, and his incomparably great power for us who believe" (1:18–19). To pray this way is to be strong. Paul is of little help to the believer who insists on living by appearances. His solution for insecurity, low self-esteem, and over-sensitivity is nothing short of full-fledged faith in Christ. If our eyes are looking for audience approval and glued to worldly entertainment, we will not see the world from the perspective of the risen Lord.

Paul impresses us with the scope of personal and social salvation in order to wean us off our preoccupation with ourselves. How can we who have been raised with Christ keep "gratifying the cravings of our sinful nature and following its desires and thoughts?" Impossible! We used to be damaged goods, but now "we are God's workmanship, created in

Christ Jesus to do good works which God prepared in advance for us to do" (2:3, 10). Through Christ, who is our peace, the dividing wall of hostility between people has been destroyed. The church is a place where racial animosities, economic injustices, gender conflicts, and generational divisions are overcome in Christ. Paul envisions a closely-knit, well-built, deeply-rooted household of faith. The church is a picture of strength "built on the foundation of the apostles and prophets, with Christ Jesus himself as the chief cornerstone. In him the whole building is joined together and rises to become a holy temple in the Lord" (2:19–22).

Paul continues to attack his readers' crisis of confidence by embracing the mission of the church—the administration of the mystery of God's grace. Here, he teaches by example. Could anyone picture Paul sitting around feeling sorry for himself, when he was inspired by such a great mission? The Great Commission drives out commiserating. Paul is enthralled by the mission of the church, which he sees in the deepest, broadest terms. God's intent is to make known "the manifold wisdom of God" through the church "to the rulers and authorities in the heavenly realms" (3:10). Could there be a greater, more significant purpose than that? Who really cares about our little personal success stories when compared to the fullness of salvation history? We have a choice: we can either endow our hobbies with immortality status or we can invest our lives in that which is holy. When the game or the trip or the car or the music becomes all about me and is the essence of my value, my significance, my reason for living, then it's really stupid. We're in trouble when we turn the holy into a hobby and a hobby into the holy.

The magnitude of the gospel mission to "every family in heaven and on earth" brings Paul to his knees. He prays for strength: "I pray that out of his glorious riches he may strengthen you with power through his Spirit in your inner being, so that Christ may dwell in your hearts through faith. And I pray that you, being rooted and established in love, may have power together with all the saints, to grasp how wide and long and high and deep is the love of Christ, and to know this love that surpasses knowledge—that you may be filled to the measure of all the fullness of God" (3:16–19).

## A Healthy Body

Following his emphasis on worship, salvation, and mission, Paul focuses on the health and vitality of the body of Christ. Humility, gentleness, patience, and bearing with one another in love describes the mentality of the

## The Strength of Christ

body. Oneness—one body, one Spirit, one hope, one Lord, one faith, one baptism, one God and Father of all—describes the solidarity of the church. The teaching gifts, used to equip the saints for works of service, empower the growth of the body. Christians "blown here and there by every wind of teaching and by the cunning and craftiness of people in their deceitful scheming," are like drowning infants, but grown-ups, who speak the truth in love and "grow up into him who is the head, that is Christ," are a picture of strength.

Paul envisions a new humanity, which puts off the old self, "corrupted by its deceitful desires," and puts on a new self, "created to be like God in true righteousness and holiness." True strength lies in practical obedience: truthfulness, self-control, useful work, wholesome talk, kindness, compassion, and forgiveness. The secret of a strong fellowship of believers is following "God's example, as dearly loved children and walking in the way of love, just as Christ loved us and gave himself for us . . ." (5:1–2).

Living by the grace of Christ empowers purity, gratitude, integrity, and accountability. Grace is hardly an excuse for indifference and disobedience. Instead, grace inspires our earnest desire to "find out what pleases the Lord" (5:10). Being careful how we live is consistent with being filled with the Spirit and how we speak to one another is consistent with how we praise the Lord. The secret for strong relationships in the body of Christ is mutual submission out of reverence for Christ. Wives and husbands, children and parents, slaves and masters respond to each other as they would to Christ.

We are not in the habit of associating submission with strength, but this is the kind of combination Paul envisioned in the new creation. Mutual submission out of reverence for Christ is consistent with the admonition to "be strong in the Lord and in his mighty power." In Christ, human responsibility and divine empowerment converge; great humulity and powerful spirituality rise together; and genuine submission and real solidarity meet. For Paul, human weakness and great strength in the Lord are not incompatible, but inseparable. Paul combined what the old, sinful nature separated: humility and strength, sacrifice and fulfillment, surrender and freedom.

## Finally

(6:10–17) *"Finally, be strong in the Lord and in his mighty power. Put on the full armor of God, so that you can take your stand against*

> *the devil's schemes. For our struggle is not against flesh and blood, but against the rulers, against the authorities, against the powers of this dark world and against the spiritual forces of evil in the heavenly realms. Therefore put on the full armor of God, so that when the day of evil comes, you may be able to stand your ground, and after you have done everything to stand. Stand firm then, with the belt of truth buckled around your waist, with the breastplate of righteousness in place, and with your feet fitted with the readiness that comes from the gospel of peace. In addition to all this, take up the shield of faith, with which you can extinguish all the flaming arrows of the evil one. Take the helmet of salvation and the sword of the Spirt, which is the word of God."*

Having reached the climax of his letter, Paul brings his message home. He takes on the air of a commanding general sending troops into battle. What he says is reminiscent of the Lord's three-fold charge to Joshua, "Be strong and very courageous, because you will lead . . . Be strong and very courageous. Be careful to obey . . . Be strong and courageous. Do not be afraid; do not be discouraged, for the Lord your God will be with you wherever you go" (Josh 1:6–9).

## Images of Discipleship

When Paul wrote this letter, he was in prison and guarded around the clock by Roman soldiers. It is hardly surprising that he chose the armor of God to bring his message home. The apostle Paul used some vivid metaphors to shape our understanding of Christian living. His *thorn in the flesh* teaches us that Christ's grace is sufficient for us no matter what and God's power is made perfect in weakness. He used a simple *clay pot* to symbolize his ministry and highlight the fact that it was not his appearance or his eloquence or his popularity that mattered. Everything in his life and ministry depended on the power and authority of Christ. Paradoxically, Paul was just as comfortable using a fully armed Roman centurion as an object lesson for believers as he was a clay pot and a thorn in the flesh. He saw no contradiction between images of weakness and images of strength. But what is surprising is how he used the metaphor to contrast the weapons of the world with the weapons of righteousness. His description in Ephesians is consistent with what he said to the believers at Corinth. "For though we live in the world, we do not wage war as the world does. The weapons we fight with are not the weapons of the world. On the contrary, they have divine power to demolish strongholds" (2 Cor 10:3-4).

David's battle with Goliath is consistent with Paul's collage of images. Against what appears to be impossible odds, David confronts the Philistine Goliath: "You come against me with sword and spear and javelin, but I come against you in the name of the Lord Almighty . . . All those gathered here will know that it is not by sword or spear that the Lord saves; for the battle is the Lord's . . ." (1 Sam 17:45-47). If we think we are more vulnerable clothed in truth, righteousness, peace, faith, salvation, and the Word of God, we should think again.

Paul makes an abrupt transition from peaceful homes and positive working relationships to confronting spiritual conflict and resisting the devil's schemes. We need to pay attention to the fact that the clothing he has in mind for "mutual submission" is different from the armor he insists on for fighting a war against demonic insurgency. On the home front, God's chosen people, holy and dearly loved, must clothe themselves with "compassion, kindness, humility, gentleness and patience" (Col 3:12), but on the battle line, God's soldiers must "put on the full armor of God, so that [they] can take [their] stand against the devil's schemes" (6:10-11). Of course believers need both wardrobes all the time—continuously and simultaneously. Paul envisions the convergence of submission and strength.

## Full Armor

Taking a stand against the "devil's schemes" implies that we are up against a combination of tactical shrewdness and ingenious deception. This is hand-to-hand combat. The command to be strong in the Lord is not a wish but an order. Paul's imperative is not something we need to debate, it is something we must determine to do. We can drift into sin but we cannot drift into righteousness. We need to make a determination to be strong or we never will be strong.

Clothing often defines the roles we play. A uniform, for example, creates a set of expectations. Put it on and you are expected to conform to those expectations. You are on duty. Certain things are required of you. You act in a prescribed way, in the way that you have been trained to act. "All the armor language is a way to talk about identification with God and his purposes."[2]

---

2. Snodgrass, *Ephesians*, 339.

God's power is available to us, but not everyone can put on this armor. Only those in Christ can buckle up the belt of truth and wear the helmet of salvation. Those who have been issued this armor understand how to use it. They are certified to wear it. S.W.A.T. team officers have to undergo training and testing before they are qualified to receive and use their specialized equipment. Pilots wear their wings with pride because they have earned them through rigorous training and certification. Many remember Mark Twain's famous adage, "Clothes make the man," but few remember his next line, "Naked people have little or no influence on society." Out-of-uniform Christians are of little kingdom value. We need to intentionally prepare for spiritual combat. We have a responsibility to put on the full armor of God and a responsibility to help others put on their armor.

What we "put off" and "put on" is important (Eph 4:22—5:1; Col 3:12). This "putting on" requires an intentional discipline on our part ("jocking up" as the Navy SEALS say). Now is the time to put on the full armor of God ("so that when the day of evil comes, you may be able to stand your ground") and now is the time to determine that you will never give up no matter what ("after you have done everything, to stand"). Paul offers a "no excuse" strategy for spiritual preparedness. He challenges us to make the most of every opportunity, "because the days are evil," and he commands us to put on the full armor of God, "so that when the day of evil comes," we may be able to stand our ground, having done everything to stand. Paul expects his readers "to realize that they are already in evil days (5:16), but that these will culminate in a climactic evil day, when resistance will be especially necessary" (6:13).[3]

The nature of the struggle is supernatural. "Attempts to rank spiritual forces is groundless and fanciful speculation. All four of the expressions in 6:12 point to the same reality; the fourth is perhaps the most descriptive and helpful—the spiritual forces of evil."[4] This truth is not designed to scare us but to inform us and motivate us to be prepared. New Testament scholar Gordon Fee offers a wise perspective on this challenge:

> The tendencies are toward one extreme or the other, to deny the existence of such beings as "the mythology of another day," or to recognize and then to attribute to them a prominence all out of proportion to that which Paul here affords them. As in most such matters, Paul's position lies in the "radical middle": to take

---

3. Lincoln, *Ephesians*, 446.
4. Snodgrass, *Ephesians*, 340.

## The Strength of Christ

them with dead seriousness, but also to recognize that they are a tethered foe, restrained by Christ's victory over them in the cross and resurrection (Col 2:15; Eph 2:6–7). . . . The thrust of this passage is not for us to become enamored with them, but to withstand them through the armor provided by Christ in the gospel and through the weapons of the Spirit."[5]

To recognize "the devil's schemes" is to see the world from God's perspective. The forces of evil behind man's inhumanity to man defy human explanation. There is a demonic source and energy behind atrocities and catastrophes. Human culpability plus demonic activity magnifies and compounds evil beyond human calculation. I am speaking here of such evils as genocide, the sex-slave industry, the brainwashed child warriors of Uganda, witchcraft and animism, and the ideological captivity of the West. There is a demonic twist to nature-alone scientism and the nihilistic dismissal of salvation history. The war on terrorism reminds us that we are in the war to end all wars, because this war will not end until Christ comes again. Jesus underscored the power behind the power when he spoke to Pilate. "You would have no power over me if it were not given to you from above. Therefore the one who handed me over to you is guilty of a greater sin" (John 19:11). Knowing the enemy behind our enemies helps us to respond to others the way Jesus did.

Paul may have drawn his metaphor of the divine warrior from the Roman centurion standing outside his prison cell, but his description of the fully prepared Christian soldier comes right out of the prophet Isaiah. The coming Messiah is belted with righteousness with a sash of faithfulness wrapped around his waist (Isa 11:5). He "put on righteousness as his breastplate, and the helmet of salvation on his head" (Isa 59:17). And those who spread the good news of his coming are greeted with song, "How beautiful on the mountains are the feet of those who bring good news, who proclaim peace, who bring good tidings, who proclaim salvation . . ." (Isa 52:7). To put on the full armor of God is to identify with God and his salvation.

The elements of the armor: truth, righteousness, peace, faith, salvation, and the Holy Spirit are completely consistent with the terms of engagement. There is no indication of a Christian *jihad* or *holy war*. Paul's use of the military metaphor cannot be used to justify physical violence. This is the armor that Jesus wore before Pilate and that Stephen put on before the Sanhedrin. Paul was dressed in this armor as he defended the

---

5. Fee, *God's Empowering Presence*, 726.

gospel before Jewish and Roman authorities. This is the armor that we are commanded to put on. We are under orders to stand our ground for Christ and his kingdom.

Each element of the armor represents both a gift from God and an act of obedience to God. The armor combines the gifts of the Spirit with the fruit of the Spirit. We have to put it on, but God provides it. We are working out what God has worked in (Phil 2:12–13).

The belt of truth refers to both "speaking the truth in love" (4:15) and speaking "truthfully to your neighbor" (4:25). Truth is the "the truth that is in Jesus" (4:21) and living truthfully (5:9). Truth in doctrine; truth in praxis. This is the liberating truth found in Jesus' teaching (John 8:31–32) and the truthfulness found in the imitation of Christ. As we said earlier, the simple truth will do more for the cause of Christ than complex arguments for the nature of truth. For those who have given up on truth in principle, truthful people are the only way they may come to understand the truth.

The breastplate of righteousness is the imputed righteousness that comes from Christ and is received by faith (Rom 5:17) and it is the life of righteousness and sanctification lived out by faith. We put off the old self and put on the new self, "created to be like God in true righteousness and holiness" (Eph 4:22, 24). Children of the light live a life consisting of "all goodness, righteousness and truth" (Eph 5:9). As we have seen, Paul's description of righteousness is deeply personal as well as profoundly social. Spirituality and ethics go hand-in-hand. True righteousness unites our eternal righteousness in Christ with the Jesus way of visible righteousness put forth in the Sermon on the Mount.

The boots of gospel peace stand for stability and security in Christ as well as the readiness to move forward with the good news of Christ (Isa 52:7). We are equipped to stand firm and move out quickly. We are at peace with God and ambassadors of his peace. Christ himself "is our peace" (Eph 2:14), even as we are called to "make every effort to keep the unity of the Spirit through the bond of peace" (Eph 4:3). Eighteenth-century British parliamentarian and Christian activist William Wilberforce modeled the comprehensive nature of Christian peacemaking. Not only did he fight for slaves, but he was an advocate for the poor and an apologist for Christian truth and character. In addition, he was an evangelist. Eric Metaxas describes Wilberforce's efforts to share the gospel of peace,

> Everywhere he went, and with everyone he met, he tried, as best he could, to bring the conversation around to the question of

eternity. Wilberforce would prepare lists of his friends' names and next to the entries make notes on how he might best encourage them in their faith, if they had faith, and toward a faith if they still had none. He would list subjects he could bring up with each friend that might launch them into a conversation about spiritual issues. He even called these subjects and questions "launchers" and was always looking for opportunities to introduce them.[6]

The shield of faith represents the fullness of faith, primarily the faithfulness of God, but also "faith in the Lord Jesus" (Eph 1:15), and the faith of Jesus. There is no greater defense than the faith of God: "For it is by grace you have been saved, through faith" (Eph 2:8). God's faithfulness makes faith in Jesus possible and inspires the faith of Jesus in us. "If we are faithless," wrote Paul to Timothy, "he remains faithful, for he cannot disown himself" (1 Tim 2:13).

The helmet of salvation symbolizes salvation received and salvation anticipated. We are protected now and for eternity. In Isaiah, God himself is said to wear the helmet of salvation (Isa 59:17), therefore we identify with and come under God's saving protection. If the Lord is our light and our salvation—whom shall we fear (Ps 27:1)?

The sword of the Spirit, "which is the word of God," literally refers to the short sword used in hand-to-hand combat and figuratively it refers to sharing the gospel *personally* through the power of the Holy Spirit. The believer is armed with the Word of God, which is alive and active. "Sharper than any double-edged sword, it penetrates even to dividing soul and spirit, joints and marrow; it judges the thoughts and attitudes of the heart" (Heb 4:12).

Each element emphasizes both God's saving work and our response to God's saving work. Paul's fully armed soldier in Christ's army takes the dual imperative seriously. This soldier is both self-disciplined and filled with the Spirit (Eph 5:15, 18).

## Stand Your Ground

The apostle Paul saw no contradiction between submitting to one another out of reverence for Christ and putting on the full armor of God. Jesus' metaphor of the easy yoke and Paul's metaphor of the armor of God are compatible. Clothing ourselves with compassion, kindness, humility,

6. Metaxas, *Amazing Grace*, 167.

gentleness, and patience is consistent with equipping ourselves with truth, righteousness, peace, faith, salvation, and the word of God.

Paul has in mind two kinds of weakness, one to be overcome and one to be accepted. Paul expected victory over the old sinful nature. He anticipated the practical reality of the new creation in Christ.

> Living according to the flesh belongs to our existence *before* and *outside* of Christ; it is totally incompatible with life "according to the Spirit." Paul, therefore, contrary to popular—and much scholarly—opinion, does not view life in the Spirit as a constant struggle between the flesh and the Spirit, in which the flesh generally has the upper hand. . . . Nowhere does Paul describe life in the Spirit as one of constant struggle with the flesh. . . . His point, rather, is the sufficiency of the Spirit as we live in our present "already but not yet" existence. . . . The Spirit is sufficient and stands over against the flesh in every way.[7]

The weakness that belongs to the old sinful nature must be overcome, but the weakness that belongs to living for Christ in a sin-twisted world must be embraced. There is a difference between living in the flesh and living according to the flesh. "Paul saw no contradiction, but actually a confirmation, for the converting power of the Gospel to correspond to the obvious weakness of the messenger. God's greater glory rests on the manifestation of his grace and power through the weakness of the human vessel, precisely so that there will never be any confusion as to the source."[8] The apostle "assumed the closest correlation between the Spirit's power and present weaknesses."[9] Paul wanted to know both the power of the resurrection and the fellowship of his sufferings. He wanted to take after his crucified Lord.

In Hitler's Germany leading up to and during the war, Christendom was divided between the German Christian movement, which was pro-Nazi, and the Confessing Church, known for its courageous resistance to the Führer and the Third Reich. German Christians were known for being anti-Jew, anti-doctrine, and strong supporters of a "manly" church. They emptied the apostle's armor metaphor of all biblical meaning and filled it with Nazi propaganda. In an effort to appease their Nazi and neopagan critics who charged the church with weakness, humility, and defeatism, they proclaimed that they were the "storm troopers of the church." They

---

7. Fee, *God's Empowering Presence*, 817.
8. Ibid., 824.
9. Ibid., 825.

didn't want a church for old ladies. They wanted a soldier's church with manly qualities. German Christians claimed that their militant, nationalistic church inspired bravery, hardness, and heroism. The German nature demanded a "fighting Christ," not a cowardly Christ who assumed the guilt of others. As one leading German Christian said, "We can naturally have nothing to do with a little lamb kind of Christianity."[10]

The Confessing Church saw through this blasphemy. They called the German Christian anti-Jew, anti-doctrine, manly church for what it was—heresy. They risked their lives to stand up to Hitler. German Christians and their "manly" church capitulated to the horrors of Nazism, while Confessing Church leaders Martin Niemoller, Dietrich Bonhoeffer, Karl Barth, and many others risked their lives to defend the faith. The "manly" church was the weak church, a tool in the hand of Hitler, used for his demonic advantage. But the Confessing Church was the strong church, faithful to the Lord Jesus Christ and marked by the cross. They put on the full armor of God and "took their stand against the devil's schemes."

In his sermon "Thy Kingdom Come," Bonhoeffer warned, "An escapist church can be certain that it will immediately win over all the weaklings, all those who are only too glad to be lied to and deceived, all the starry-eye dreamers, all the unborn sons of the earth."[11]

Bonhoeffer did not mean that the church should not care for the weak. "What church would be so merciless, so inhuman, as not to deal compassionately with this weakness of suffering people and thereby save souls for the kingdom of heaven? . . . Should the weakling remain without help? Would that be in the spirit of Jesus Christ? No, the weak should receive help. We do in fact receive help, from Christ. However, Christ does not will or intend this weakness; instead, he makes us strong. He does not lead us in a religious flight from this world to other worlds beyond; rather, he gives us back to the earth as its loyal children."[12]

The church that entertains the admirers of Jesus and caters to their felt needs inevitably attracts a host of self-absorbed weaklings who have no intention of changing their egocentric ways. They use their many weaknesses to bully the church into paying attention to them. They are narcissistic, hungry for attention, eager to have their opinion heard and totally absorbed in their own story. What better place to try to satisfy their insatiable needs than the church, where they feel people are supposed to

---

10. Bergen, *Twisted Cross*, 74.
11. Huntemann, *The Other Bonhoeffer*, 101.
12. Bonhoeffer, *A Testament To Freedom*, 89.

pay attention to them. Such weaklings have withdrawn from the world and retreated to the church. They have done this without confronting their sin or turning to Christ for transformation. Frequently they have left a trail of relational destruction in their path, but they have no intention of setting things right. When they attempt to serve others they are usually more trouble than they're worth, because they serve according to their whim and preference, always expecting to receive high praise for their efforts. Christ did not call his followers to this kind of weakness. This is the sin-nursing, blame-casting weakness that he came to overcome.

No one can read the Bible honestly and come up with the notion that it's okay for the people of God to be slothful, complacent, fearful, permissive, and indulgent. This is definitely not the cross-bearing weakness that teaches obedience, but the worldly weakness that results from disobedience. This is the weakness that Christ overcomes when he strengthens believers through his Spirit in their inner being (Eph 3:16). This is the fear and timidity that is dispelled when we truly remember that God addresses us as his children, "Be strong and courageous. Do not be terrified; do not be discouraged, for the Lord your God will be with you wherever you go" (Josh 1:9). This is the sadness that is driven out when we let the joy of the Lord be our strength (Neh 8:10). This is the apathy and complacency that is routed when we determine to "be strong in the Lord and in his mighty power" (Eph 6:10).

# 15

## *The Spirit of Christ*

> *"And pray in the Spirit on all occasions with all kinds of prayers and requests. With this in mind, be alert and always keep on praying for all the Lord's people."*
>
> Ephesians 6:18

John Bunyan wrote *The Pilgrim's Progress* from an English jail. He was imprisoned for preaching the gospel, and like the apostle Paul, he used his jail time to meditate on the Christian life. Bunyan developed an allegory depicting the journey of salvation through the experience of his pilgrim named Christian. When Christian journeys through the Valley of the Shadow of Death, he finds himself walking along the edge of Hell. There is no one there to fight, but the dangers are very real. Since his sword is of no use, he takes up another weapon called "All-Prayer." Undoubtedly John Bunyan had in mind the resources described in Ephesians.[1] "All-Prayer" describes the four "alls" Paul used to frame his imperative to pray: on *all* occasions, with *all* kinds of prayers, in *all* readiness, for *all* the Lord's people.

---

1. Bunyan, *Pilgrim's Progress*, 57.

## Pray in the Spirit

(6:18–20) *"And pray in the Spirit on all occasions with all kinds of prayers and requests. With this in mind, be alert and always keep on praying for all the Lord's people. Pray also for me, that whenever I speak, words may be given me so that I will fearlessly make known the mystery of the gospel, for which I am an ambassador in chains. Pray that I may declare it fearlessly, as I should."*

To pray in the Spirit is to pray within the fellowship and wisdom of the triune God. In each section of Ephesians, Paul is careful to center his spiritual direction in the community of the Father, Son, and Holy Spirit. He begins his letter with, "Grace and peace to you from God our Father and the Lord Jesus Christ," and ends the opening benediction with the guarantee of the Holy Spirit. "When you believed, you were marked in [Christ] with a seal, the promised Holy Spirit, who is a deposit guaranteeing our inheritance until the redemption of those who are God's possession—to the praise of his glory" (Eph 1:13–14). Now at the end, he begins the final section with a command, "Pray in the Spirit . . ." followed by a closing benediction: "Peace to the brothers and sisters, and love with faith from God the Father and the Lord Jesus Christ. Grace to all who love our Lord Jesus Christ with an undying love" (Eph 6:18, 23–24). Both the opening and concluding sections are framed by the triune God, with the members of the Trinity named in reverse order.

"God our Father and the Lord Jesus Christ. . . . [opening benediction] . . . marked by the Spirit."

"Pray in the Spirit. . . . [final farewell] . . . love with faith from God the Father and the Lord Jesus Christ."

Paul's Ephesians prayers are an example of what it means to pray in the Spirit.

"I keep asking that the God of our Lord Jesus Christ, the glorious Father, may give you the Spirit of wisdom and revelation, so that you might know him better" (Eph 1:17).

"I pray that out of his glorious riches he may strengthen you with power through his Spirit in your inner being, so that Christ may dwell in your hearts through faith" (Eph 3:16).

To pray in the Spirit means that we are invited into the family dialogue of the triune God.

## The Spirit of Christ

"The Spirit you received brought about your adoption to sonship. And by him we cry, 'Abba, Father.' The Spirit himself testifies with our spirit that we are God's children" (Rom 8:15–16; see Gal 4:6; Jude 20).

The Spirit not only brings us into this intimate family conversation, but represents our deepest thoughts and feelings, the concerns that we cannot even put into words.

"The Spirit helps us in our weakness. We do not know what we ought to pray for, but the Spirit himself intercedes for us through wordless groans. And he who searches our hearts knows the mind of the Spirit, because the Spirit intercedes for God's people in accordance with the will of God" (Rom 8:26–27).

The purpose of prayer is intimacy with God. I once heard a pastor use the word *intercourse* to describe his relationship with God. We were discussing the tendency among pastors to yield to sexual temptation. There were twelve of us analyzing the pitfalls and preventive measures involved in this complex problem when John, a pastor from Louisiana in his forties, began to speak. His voice and manner conveyed a quiet passion. Earlier his comments had been about football, hunting, and golf, but now he was speaking from the heart about reverence for God, his devotion to Jesus and his life in the Spirt. John was expressing thoughts long held and deeply felt. He had everyone's attention and the usual banter ceased.

John spoke of his own need and desire to love Christ more. "Worship," he said, "is communion with Christ. Prayer is intercourse with God." We may blush, because this word is used for sex, and even then, the word *intercourse* is rarely used today. But John insisted on *intercourse*'s primary meaning, that is communication between people. He used the word with special reference to our communion with God in the deepest and most personal way possible. "When there's not a true intercourse with God," John continued, "love for my wife suffers. But when my worship of God is real and my love for Jesus is what it ought to be, I'm more in love with my wife and my children. Intercourse with Jesus is the key to intimacy with my wife." By that time, everyone was ready for the subject to change, and get back to something safe like football or lunch, but John in a beautiful, almost lyrical way, had revealed his heart for God and his love for his wife.

## Prayer and Strength

The call to be strengthened is a call to prayer. The imperative to "*stand firm,*" previously linked to putting on the full armor of God, is also linked to "praying" and "keeping alert." Judging from Paul's letter, he was into body language. We are *seated* with Christ in the heavenly realms (Eph 2:6). We are exhorted to *walk* in a manner worthy of the calling we have received in Christ (Eph 4:1). We are to "walk in the way of love" and, if Paul's own body language is any indication, we are to *kneel* in prayer. "I kneel before the Father, from whom every family in heaven and on earth derives its name" (Eph 3:14).

Prayer is not a form of self-expression available to us to download our complaints and frustrations. Prayer is a spiritual discipline that leads us and everything about us into the presence of God. If the history of the people of God is an indication, our lament will be pretty raw at times.

Jesus taught that there are good reasons to be suspicious of piety. People pray cut-flower prayers in pious self-consciousness, seeking to impress others with their spirituality. Jesus said, "Don't be like the hypocrites, for they love to pray . . . to be seen by others" (Matt 6:5). People pray manipulative prayers, maneuvering to get what they want from God. People pray gossipy prayers. Under the pretense of prayer they spread rumors and innuendo about others. Jesus said, "Don't keep on babbling like pagans, for they think they will be heard because of their many words" (Matt 6:7).

If we are not careful we may enable weak believers to remain weak, because we do worship, prayer, and ministry *for them*. Do we empower or pacify? Is it too easy to make weak believers feel religious without being righteous, and self-satisfied without becoming sanctified? These are the concerns that a caring, conscientious body of believers must face. Prayer in the Spirit removes the spectator mentality toward spiritual growth. The apostle expected all believers to enter into this life of prayer in the Spirit, but his admonition is filled with grace. There is no hint of guilt. He imposes no new spiritual legalism that artificially measures outward compliance.

## All-Prayer

Pray on *all* occasions with *all* kinds of prayers, in *all* alertness, for *all* the Lord's people. There we have it, stated as succinctly as possible, a beautiful mission statement on prayer. Paul's spiritual direction reminds us of what he has said elsewhere in his letters. To the church at Philippi, he said, "I thank my God every time I remember you. In all my prayers for all of you, I always pray with joy because of your partnership in the gospel . . ." (Phil 1:3–5). Paul leaves us with the distinct impression that he saw prayer primarily as a way of life, rather than an activity limited to quiet times and liturgical prayers. "Life is characterized as one uninterrupted address and response to God, a cry for help from the depth, an expression of memory and hope based on God's great deeds, an attempt to do justice to the fact that only from Him, with Him, and for Him can man exist from day to day and pass through the final tribulation."[2]

## All Occasions

Prayer is to be as constant and as necessary as breathing. "Rejoice in the Lord always. I will say it again: Rejoice! Let your gentleness be evident to all. The Lord is near. Do not be anxious about anything, but in every situation, by prayer and petition, with thanksgiving, present your requests to God. And the peace of God, which transcends all understanding, will guard your hearts and your minds in Christ Jesus" (Phil 4:6–7). To the saints at Thessalonica, he wrote, "Rejoice always, pray continually, give thanks in all circumstances; for this is God's will for you in Christ Jesus. Do not put out the Spirit's fire" (1 Thess 5:16–19).

Many of us are trying to live impossible schedules and often the first thing to go is prayer. As one friend shared with me, "My time with God amounts to me saying, 'Okay God, this is the only time I have for you right now. So, if you are going to speak, please do it quickly and clearly so that I can move onto the next task on my 'to do' list.' " He went on to explain that this was not his intention, but the result of a "go, go, go" schedule that left no space or time for coming into the presence of God.

We need to recover the rhythm of work and prayer. Prayer sanctifies the daily schedule and protects us from turning our work into an idol. Work keeps our prayers from becoming empty and sanctimonious. Throughout the day we pray for our work and work on our prayers. We refuse to think that we can accomplish good things "without actually relying on God for wisdom and power . . . for only God can accomplish what has transcendent value and eternal significance."[3]

## All Kinds of Prayers

To pray "all kinds of prayers and requests" is meant to encompass everything about our lives and the lives of others. Nothing is excluded from the

2. Barth, *Ephesians*, 806.
3. Sittser, *Water from a Deep Well*, 115.

sanctifying presence and provision of the triune God. Nothing is too small or too big. This is not an invitation to be self-preoccupied. It is, rather, an exhortation to bring everything under the Lordship of Christ. There are no un-prayed-for compartments in one's life, no closets of hidden sins and selfish preoccupations that exclude the praying imagination.

The Psalms show us the scope of prayer. They guide us in the fullness of prayer. To spend anytime in the Psalms is to learn that prayer ranges from pulsating praise to heart-throbbing lament. The Psalms give voice to our confession. They articulate the cry of our moral pain. We may be in the habit of feeling our way into worship instead of worshiping our way into feelings. We may depend upon our feelings to move and inspire us, but feelings are unreliable guides. Feelings are fickle and flighty, easily shaken and shifty. This is where the Psalms are especially helpful, because the Psalms are dependable guides; our feelings are not. The Psalms lead us in prayer. They provide the solid ground we need to stand on for worship. We are coached in confidence and nurtured in poise—our feelings get in shape.

## *Always Alert*

To be *always* prayerfully alert recalls Jesus in the Garden of Gethsemane, when he challenged the disciples to stay alert and keep watch. Yet in that hour of crisis they couldn't even keep their eyes open. In the final days of his earthly ministry, Jesus stressed the need to be watchful: "Be always on the watch, and pray that you may be able to escape all that is about to happen, and that you may be able to stand before the Son of Man" (Luke 21:36). Paul exhorted believers, "Be on your guard; stand firm in the faith; be courageous; be strong. Do everything in love" (1 Cor 16:13). To the Colossians he wrote, "Devote yourself to prayer, being watchful and thankful. And pray for us, too, that God may open a door for our message . . ." (Col 4:2–3).

The apostles do not appear to have felt the need for planning and devising church growth strategies as much as praying and waiting upon the Lord. One wonders if their expectation of the imminent return of Christ dissuaded them from goal setting and vision-casting for the future. Peter wrote, "Humble yourselves, therefore, under God's mighty hand, that he may lift you up in due time. Cast all your anxiety on him because he cares for you. Be alert and of sober mind. Your enemy the devil prowls around like a roaring lion looking for someone to devour" (1 Pet 5:6–8).

## All the Lord's People

To be in prayer "for all the Lord's people" is consistent with the thrust of Paul's message throughout the letter. We pray to the Lord who will bring unity to all things in heaven and on earth in Christ (Eph 1:10). We pray to the Savior who joins together those who were first to put their hope in Christ with those who have now received the word of truth, the gospel of salvation (Eph 1:12–13). We pray to the one who has broken down the wall of hostility between Jews and Gentiles (Eph 2:14). We kneel before the Father from whom every family in heaven and earth derives its name (Eph 3:14). And in mutual submission to one another out of reverence for Christ we pray for each other regardless of our gender, generational, racial, social, or economic differences.

About fifteen years ago Eric Young decided to start a prayer list with the hope that this would remind him to pray for the people he had promised to pray for and to prompt him to pray more regularly. It was good to know that I was on that list. Beyond including family and friends, he added the likes of the Muslim carpet merchant he met in Bangalore, the bartender in Toronto who didn't care that he had given up alcohol for Lent, and "Sam the Surfer" who was working hard to stay off drugs in San Francisco. He never expected to see these random souls again, but for some reason God prompted Eric to pray for them and not to forget them, so on to the list they went.

Last month Eric received a call from a man who works at the prep school he long ago attended. Eric didn't catch his name. He was calling to inquire about the MBA program at Georgetown University, where Eric works. In the process of the conversation, Eric happened to mention his past career at Accenture. The caller casually commented, "I once knew an Eric Young at Accenture. He spoke to us at the Fellowship of Christian Athletes where I was a college intern for a summer." Eric's mind began to race. "What did you say your name was?" he asked. The caller answered, "Rob Wright."

"Rob Wright?!" Eric exclaimed, "I've been praying for you for years. I remember that you sat at the end of the table. You were into music and were living with your grandmother, where you weren't keeping your room particularly neat." Eric dug the prayer list out of his pocket and there he was under his Monday intentions, "FCA, Robbie Wright." Since then Eric and Rob have met for dinner. Eric learned that God has been working in Rob's life over the years. Rob, now a husband and father, had embraced his faith in dramatic ways. Eric never expected to run across Rob again, but he was led to pray for him, and to keep praying for him.

Paul's call for prayer reminds me of Miss Van Dyck. When I first met her, she was in her nineties, bedridden, and in a nursing home in Buffalo, New York. She had devoted her life to proclaiming the gospel in China. I was sixteen. At the suggestion of my pastor, I visited Miss Van Dyck. I went to encourage an elderly Christian woman. It didn't take me long to realize who was ministering to whom. Her body was weak but her spirit was strong. Miss Van Dyck was a person of prayer. I went to her thinking how miserable it must be to be so weak that you could not get out of bed. But I always left impressed by the power of God. Prayer seemed to transform her small room into a vast mission field. She was not defined by the limitations of her body but by the vitality and power of her praying imagination. She meant nothing impressive by this and expected no attention.

Gantumur Badrakh is a Beeson Divinity School student from Mongolia. He wears a different cap to class everyday. His caps represent different nations from all over the world. So far he has nine nation caps. Each day, prompted by his cap, he prays throughout the day for that nation and the church that lives for Christ in that country.

## *Always Fearless*

The fifth "all" pertains to praying for Paul himself, that he would make known the mystery of the gospel with all boldness. Having prayed for the saints at Ephesus, he now requests prayer for himself. But he does not ask them to pray for his release from prison or for his health or for his failing eyesight. I imagine the prison food was not all that good, but he does not ask them to pray for better food. Nor does he request prayer for discouragement or anxiety. His only request is that he would be able to freely, boldly, and fearlessly make known the gospel. That is not to suggest that these other matters were unimportant, but it is to say that Paul's passion to proclaim the gospel boldly was uppermost in his mind and heart.

Paul calls himself the least of the saints (Eph 3:8), unfit to be called an apostle (1 Cor 15:9) and the foremost of sinners (1 Tim 1:15). Twice in the letter he refers to himself as a prisoner of the Lord (Eph 3:1; 4:1). Paul's self-designation indicates neither low self-esteem nor inferiority. It is his way of expressing genuine humility and gratitude for the grace of Christ that rescued even him. Paul never took his own salvation for granted and he lived to proclaim the gospel boldly to others.

## The Spirit of Christ

Paul was an ambassador in chains. He used metaphors to paint a picture. His images of surrender, such as the thorn in the flesh and jars of clay, captured the ethos of his discipleship. "To talk of an ambassador in chains is to employ an oxymoron. Normally an ambassador had diplomatic immunity and could not be imprisoned by those to whom he was sent, but prison chains now become the insignia for representing the gospel, the mark of the suffering apostle."[4] Writing to Timothy, Paul expressed his philosophy of ministry: "This is my gospel, for which I am suffering even to the point of being chained like a criminal. But God's word is not chained" (2 Tim 2:9).

The image of an ambassador in chains underscores the difference between worldly weakness and the weakness of the cross; the weakness that ought to be overcome and the weakness that needed to be embraced. The apostle Paul describes his attitude toward the latter. "I will boast all the more gladly about my weaknesses, so that Christ's power may rest on me. That is why, for Christ's sake, I delight in weaknesses, in insults, in hardships, in persecutions, in difficulties. For when I am weak, then I am strong" (2 Cor 12:9–10). Those who cling to worldly weakness use grace as an excuse, but those who embrace the weakness of the cross depend upon grace as an empowerment to obey God's will. "Since the 'chains' are no obstacle to his mission, God need not be entreated to unloose them. Paul is so totally preoccupied with his missionary ministry that he has no time for self-pity. He asks for special intercession only because his task cannot be fulfilled unless he lives from grace to grace."[5]

Paul's prayer request for boldness and freedom as an ambassador in chains is consistent with Luke's concluding description of Paul in the Book of Acts: "He proclaimed the kingdom of God and taught about the Lord Jesus Christ—with all boldness and without hindrance!" (Acts 28:31). Luke's final word, "unhindered," is especially significant, because it is the same word used in Ephesians and is translated "boldly" (ESV) and "fearlessly" (TNIV) (παρρησιάσωμαι). If there ever was a word that summed up Paul's whole philosophy of ministry it is this word. Paul is chained to a Roman soldier and a victim of judicial foot-dragging. He is vulnerable to state-sponsored persecution and opposed by a hard-hearted, stiff-necked Jewish resistance, but none of these count as hindrances! Instead of bemoaning his situation he is praying for boldness. This one word should cause us to rethink what helps and hurts the advance of the gospel.

4. Lincoln, *Ephesians*, 454.
5. Barth, *Ephesians*, 807.

## Trusted Tychicus

(6:21–24) *"Tychicus, the dear brother and faithful servant in the Lord, will tell you everything, so that you also may know how I am and what I am doing. I am sending him to you for this very purpose, that you may know how we are, and that he may encourage you.*

*Peace to the brothers and sisters, and love with faith from the God the Father and the Lord Jesus Christ. Grace to all who love our Lord Jesus Christ with an undying love."*

We end on a note of friendship. Paul introduces his trusted friend and confidant Tychicus (Acts 20:4; Col 4:7; 2 Tim 4:12). He describes him as his dear brother and faithful servant in the Lord. What is truly remarkable about Tychicus is that Paul trusts him to give an accurate report on everything. This is not easily done. People who can accurately represent someone else's attitudes and actions are hard to find. Since Paul had not used the letter to talk about himself, either to describe how he was feeling or what he had been doing, he was dependent on Tychicus to fill in the personal details, share his heart, and articulate his outlook. No one could accuse Paul of using spiritual direction as a venue for self-expression. He left other people's perception of his reputation, emotional state, and course of action up to Tychicus.

The apostle's refusal to make the letter about himself may be one reason why we do not feel intimidated by him. He left his story in the hands of another, confident that his friend and colleague would report thoughtfully and honestly. Tychicus must have known Paul's mind and heart, understood his actions, and harbored no secret competitive desires. He was a capable, competent, loyal, and articulate representative, who conveyed Paul's life and mission to people who may never have met the apostle. Paul was never the hero of his own story, painting a picture that left others feeling inferior and second-rate. For his part, he was always Christ-focused.

Healthy congregations follow the Tychicus model and entrust their reputations to one another. We could all use a friend like Tychicus, but the more important question is whether we are a friend like Tychicus. If we had been with Paul, listened to his preaching, observed his actions, and experienced his passion for Christ, would we have been willing and able to do what Tychicus did? Could Paul have sent us in his place, knowing that his mind and heart, feelings and actions, would be thoughtfully conveyed and accurately represented? May we be a friend like Tychicus.

## The Explicit Christ

Paul's Christ Letter is free of cliché and ambiguity. His Christ-explicitness is personal and penetrating. Nothing rote. He insists on using the name of Christ boldly and often, but he can never be accused of jargon and god-talk. Paul's final word brackets his trinitarian emphasis on prayer, highlights peace, love, faith, and grace, and repeats twice for emphasis the Lord Jesus Christ. It sounds like two benedictions in one. Either one of which says it all. The first, "Peace to the brothers and sisters, and love with faith from God the Father and the Lord Jesus Christ," stresses God's peace and love with faith for us.

The second, "Grace to all who love our Lord Jesus Christ with an undying love," stresses our love for God, an incorruptible love, an everlasting love, an undying love. There is enough ambiguity in the Greek text to lead scholars to debate the meaning of the sentence. Is the Lord loving us with an incorruptible, everlasting, and undying love or are we loving the Lord with an incorruptible, everlasting, undying love? The former is the gift of grace that we don't deserve but we know to be true, and the latter is the goal of grace that we pray is true. What a great note to finish on! May the Lord Jesus Christ be praised.

# Bibliography

Allen, Roland. *Missionary Methods: St. Paul's or Ours?* Grand Rapids: Eerdmans, 1962.
Ahlquist, Dale. *Common Sense 101: Lessons from G. K. Chesterton.* San Francisco: Ignatius, 2006.
Augsburger, David. *Dissident Discipleship.* Grand Rapids: Brazos, 2006.
Augustine. "On Christian Doctrine." *Nicene and Post-Nicene Fathers*, vol. 2, Book 4:6. Translated by J. F. Shaw. Edited by Philip Schaff. Peabody, MA: Hendrickson, 1995.
Barna, George. *Revolution.* Carol Stream, IL: Tyndale, 2005.
Barth, Markus. *Ephesians: The Anchor Bible*, vol. 34. New York: Doubleday, 1974.
Bergen, Doris L. *Twisted Cross: The German Christian Movement in The Third Reich.* Chapel Hill: The University of North Carolina Press, 1996.
Bloesch, Donald G. *Essentials of Evangelical Theology*, vol. 1. San Francisco: Harper & Row, 1978.
Bloom, Allan. *The Closing of the American Mind.* New York: Simon and Schuster, 1987.
Bonhoeffer, Dietrich. *A Testament To Freedom.* Edited by Geffrey Kelly and Burton Nelson. San Francisco: HarperCollins, 1995.
———. *Life Together.* San Francisco: HarperCollins, 1954.
———. *The Cost of Discipleship.* New York: Macmillan, 1970.
Brand, Paul and Philip Yancey. *Pain: The Gift Nobody Wants.* New York: HarperCollins, 1993.
Brooks, David. "Social Animal." *The New Yorker* (January 17, 2011).
———. "The 'Freedom' Agenda." *The New York Times* (September 20, 2010).
Brown, Jr. H. Jackson. *Life's Little Instruction Book.* Nashville: Rutledge Hill, 1991.
Bruner, Frederick Dale. *The Churchbook: Matthew,* vol. 1–2. Grand Rapids: Eerdmans, 2004.
Bunyan, John. *Pilgrim's Progress.* New York: Penguin Classic, 2009.
Calvin, John. *Institutes of the Christian Religion,* vol. 1–2. Translated by Henry Beveridge. Grand Rapids: Eerdmans, 1981.
Chambers, Oswald. *So Send I You.* London: Marshall, Morgan and Scott, 1930.
Chesterton, G. K. *Orthodoxy.* New York: Image, 1959.
Chrysostom, John. "Homilies on Ephesians." *Nicene and Post-Nicene Fathers*, vol. 13. Translated by Gross Alexander. Edited by Philip Schaff. Peabody, MA: Hendrickson, 1995.
Clark, Chap. *Hurt: Inside the World of Today's Teenagers.* Grand Rapids: Baker Academic, 2004.
Cohick, Lynn H. *Ephesians.* Eugene, OR: Cascade, 2010.
Douglas, J. D. editor. "The Lausanne Covenant." *Let the Earth Hear His Voice: International Congress on Evangelization, Lausanne, Switzerland.* Minneapolis: World Wide Publications, 1975.

## Bibliography

Dubay, Thomas. *The Evidential Power of Beauty: Science and Theology Meet*. San Francisco: Ignatius, 1999.

Fee, Gordon D. *God's Empowering Presence: The Holy Spirit in the Letters of Paul*. Peabody, MA: Hendrickson, 1994.

———. "On Getting the Spirit Back Into Spirituality." *Life in the Spirit: Spiritual Formation in Theological Perspective*. Edited by Jeffrey P. Greenman and George Kalantzis. Downers Grove, IL: InterVarsity, 2010.

———. *The First Epistle to the Corinthians*. Grand Rapids: Eerdmans, 1987.

Forbes, Cheryl. *The Religion of Power*. Grand Rapids: Zondervan, 1983.

Gagnon, Robert A. J. "The Bible and Homosexual Practice: Theology, Analogies, and Genes." *Theology Matters: A Publication of Presbyterians for Faith, Family and Ministry*, vol. 7 (November/December 2001): 1–13.

Gilbreath, Edward. *Reconciliation Blues: A Black Evangelical's Inside View of White Christianity*. Downers Grove, IL: InterVarsity, 2006.

Goetz, David. *Death by Suburb*. San Francisco: HarperCollins, 2006.

Hatch, Nathan. "Purging the Poisoned Well Within." *Christianity Today* (March 3, 1979) 15–16.

Hoehner, Harold W. *Ephesians: An Exegetical Commentary*. Grand Rapids: Baker, 2002.

Houston, James M. *Joyful Exiles*. Downers Grove, IL: InterVarsity, 2006.

Huntemann, Georg. *The Other Bonhoeffer*. Grand Rapids: Baker, 1993.

Huxley, Aldous. *Brave New World*. London: Granada, 1981.

Kierkegaard, Søren. *Fear and Trembling* and *The Sickness Unto Death*. Translated by Walter Lowrie. Princeton: Princeton University Press, 1974.

———. *The Present Age* and *Of the Difference Between a Genius and an Apostle*. Translated by Alexander Dru. New York: Harper Torchbooks, 1962.

Lewis, C. S. *Miracles*. London: Fontana, 1978.

———. *Surprised By Joy*. London: Fontana, 1972.

———. *The Four Loves*. New York: Harcourt Brace, 1960.

———. *The Problem of Pain*. New York: MacMillan, 1962.

———. *The Screwtape Letters*. San Francisco: HarperOne, 2001.

Lincoln, Andrew T. *Ephesians: Word Biblical Commentary*. Dallas: Word, 1990.

Longenecker, Richard N. *Galatians: Word Biblical Commentary*. Dallas: Word, 1990.

Metaxas, Eric. *Amazing Grace: William Wilberforce and the Heroic Campaign to End Slavery*. New York: HarperCollins, 2007.

McEwan, Ian. *Saturday*. New York: Knopf, 2006.

McKinstry, Carolyn Maul, with Denise George. *While the World Watched*. Carol Stream, IL: Tyndale, 2011.

Mouw, Richard. "The Life of Bondage in the Light of Grace." *Christianity Today* (December 9, 1988) 41–42.

Muggeridge, Malcolm, quoted in Philip Yancey. "Sin." *Christianity Today* (March 6, 1987) 33.

Newbigin, Leslie. *The Gospel in a Pluralistic Society*. Grand Rapids: Eerdmans, 1989.

Palmer, Parker. *A Place Called Community*. Wallingford, PA: Pendle Hill, 1977.

Perkins, John. *A Quiet Revolution*. Waco, TX: Word, 1976.

Peterson, Eugene H. *Christ Plays In Ten Thousand Places: A Conversation on Spiritual Theology*. Grand Rapids: Eerdmans, 2005.

———. *Growing Up With Your Teenager*. Old Tappan, NJ: Revell, 1987.

———. *Reversed Thunder: The Revelation of John & the Praying Imagination*. San Francisco: Harper & Row, 1988.
———. *The Message*. Colorado Springs: NavPress, 1993.
Schaeffer, Edith. *What Is a Family?* Old Tappan, NJ: Revell, 1975.
Schaeffer, Francis A. *How Should We Then Live?* Old Tappan, NJ: Revell, 1976.
Seaver, George. *David Livingstone: His Life and Letters*. New York: Harper & Brothers, 1957.
Sittser, Gerald L. *A Grace Disguised*. Grand Rapids: Zondervan, 1996.
———. *Water from a Deep Well*. Downers Grove, IL: InterVarsity, 2007.
Smith, Timothy. *The Danger of Raising Nice Kids*. Downers Grove, IL: InterVarsity, 2006.
Snodgrass, Klyne. *Ephesians: The NIV Application Commentary*. Grand Rapids: Zondervan, 1996.
Steiner, George. *After Babel*. New York: Oxford University Press, 1998.
Stevens, Paul. "Breaking the Gender Impasse." *Christianity Today* (January 13, 1992) 31.
Stockett, Kathryn. *The Help*. New York: Putnam, 2009.
Stott, John R. W. *God's New Society: The Message of Ephesians*. Downers Grove, IL: InterVarsity, 1979.
Sullivan, Andrew. "When Not Seeing Is Believing." *Time* (October 6, 2006) 59.
Sumner, Sarah. "Bridging the Ephesian 5 Divide." *Christianity Today* (November, 2005) 61.
Swartley, Willard M. *Slavery, Sabbath, War and Women: Case Studies in Biblical Interpretation*. Scottdale, PA: Herald, 1983.
Thielman, Frank. *Ephesians: Baker Exegetical Commentary*. Grand Rapids: Baker, 2010.
Thiselton, Anthony C. *The First Epistle to the Corinthians: The New International Greek Testament Commentary*. Grand Rapids: Eerdmans, 2000.
Volf, Miroslav. *Exclusion and Embrace*. Nashville: Abingdon, 1996.
Wangerin, Walter. *As For Me And My House: Crafting Your Marriage to Last*. Nashville: Thomas Nelson, 1987.
Wells, David F. *No Place For Truth*. Grand Rapids: Eerdmans, 1993.
Wesley, John. "Letter on Preaching Christ, Dec. 20, 1751." *The Works of the Rev. John Wesley*, vol. XI: 486. London: Wesleyan-Methodist Book Room.
Westermann, W. L. *The Slave Systems of Greek and Roman Antiquity*. 3rd ed. Philadelphia: American Philosophical Society, 1984.
Willimon, William. "Working on Our Grammar." *Modern Reformation* (January/February 2001) 30–31.

www.ingramcontent.com/pod-product-compliance
Lightning Source LLC
Chambersburg PA
CBHW031814220426
43662CB00007B/640